JAVASCRIPT FOR KIDS

Autumn McConda

JAVASCRIPT
FOR KIDS

A PLAYFUL INTRODUCTION
TO PROGRAMMING

BY NICK MORGAN

**no starch
press**

San Francisco

Printed in USA

First printing

18 17 16 15 14   1 2 3 4 5 6 7 8 9

ISBN-10: 1-59327-408-4
ISBN-13: 978-1-59327-408-5

Publisher: William Pollock
Production Editor: Riley Hoffman
Cover Illustration: Tina Salameh
Illustrator: Miran Lipovača
Developmental Editors: William Pollock and Seph Kramer
Technical Reviewer: Angus Croll
Copyeditor: Rachel Monaghan
Compositor: Riley Hoffman
Proofreader: Paula L. Fleming

For information on distribution, translations, or bulk sales, please contact No Starch Press, Inc. directly:
No Starch Press, Inc.
245 8th Street, San Francisco, CA 94103
phone: 415.863.9900; info@nostarch.com
www.nostarch.com

Library of Congress Control Number: 2014953113

To Philly
(and Pancake)

ABOUT THE AUTHOR

Nick Morgan is a frontend engineer at Twitter. He loves all programming languages but has a particular soft spot for JavaScript. Nick lives in San Francisco (the foggy part) with his fiancée and their fluffy dog, Pancake. He blogs at *skilldrick.co.uk*.

ABOUT THE ILLUSTRATOR

Miran Lipovača is the author of *Learn You a Haskell for Great Good!*. He enjoys boxing, playing bass guitar, and, of course, drawing. He has a fascination with dancing skeletons and the number 71, and when he walks through automatic doors he pretends that he's actually opening them with his mind.

ABOUT THE TECHNICAL REVIEWER

Angus Croll is the author of *If Hemingway Wrote JavaScript*, and he is obsessed with JavaScript and literature in equal measure. He works on Twitter's UI framework team, where he co-authored the Flight framework. He writes the influential *JavaScript, JavaScript* blog and speaks at conferences worldwide. He tweets at @angustweets.

BRIEF CONTENTS

Acknowledgments xxi

Introduction xxiii

PART I: FUNDAMENTALS

Chapter 1: What Is JavaScript? 3

Chapter 2: Data Types and Variables 13

Chapter 3: Arrays 39

Chapter 4: Objects 63

Chapter 5: The Basics of HTML 77

Chapter 6: Conditionals and Loops 89

Chapter 7: Creating a Hangman Game 105

Chapter 8: Functions 123

PART II: ADVANCED JAVASCRIPT

Chapter 9: The DOM and jQuery 143

Chapter 10: Interactive Programming 155

Chapter 11: Find the Buried Treasure! 167

Chapter 12: Object-Oriented Programming 181

PART III: CANVAS

Chapter 13: The canvas Element 199

Chapter 14: Making Things Move on the Canvas 217

Chapter 15: Controlling Animations with the Keyboard 235

Chapter 16: Making a Snake Game: Part 1 251

Chapter 17: Making a Snake Game: Part 2 267

Afterword: Where to Go from Here 293

Glossary 299

Index 305

CONTENTS IN DETAIL

ACKNOWLEDGMENTS   XXI

INTRODUCTION   XXIII

Who Should Read This Book?...xxiv
How to Read This Book..xxiv
What's in This Book? xxv
Have Fun! xxvi

PART I: FUNDAMENTALS

1
WHAT IS JAVASCRIPT?   3

Meet JavaScript 4
Why Learn JavaScript? 6
Writing Some JavaScript 7
The Structure of a JavaScript Program.................................. 8
    Syntax 10
    Comments 10
What You Learned 11

2
DATA TYPES AND VARIABLES   13

Numbers and Operators..15
Variables 17
    Naming Variables 19
    Creating New Variables Using Math.............................19
    Incrementing and Decrementing 21
    += (plus-equals) and −= (minus-equals).......................22
Strings 23
    Joining Strings 25
    Finding the Length of a String................................25
    Getting a Single Character from a String 26
    Cutting Up Strings 27
    Changing Strings to All Capital or All Lowercase Letters 28
Booleans...30
    Logical Operators 30
    Comparing Numbers with Booleans 33

undefined and null 37
What You Learned 38

3
ARRAYS   39

Why Should You Care About Arrays? 40
Creating an Array. 41
Accessing an Array's Elements 42
Setting or Changing Elements in an Array. 43
Mixing Data Types in an Array 45
Working with Arrays 46
    Finding the Length of an Array 46
    Adding Elements to an Array. 47
    Removing Elements from an Array 48
    Adding Arrays 50
    Finding the Index of an Element in an Array 52
    Turning an Array into a String 53
Useful Things to Do with Arrays. 54
    Finding Your Way Home 54
    Decision Maker 56
    Creating a Random Insult Generator 59
What You Learned 60
Programming Challenges. 61
    #1: New Insults 61
    #2: More Sophisticated Insults. 61
    #3: Use + or join?. 61
    #4: Joining Numbers. 61

4
OBJECTS   63

Creating Objects 64
    Keys Without Quotes 65
Accessing Values in Objects. 66
Adding Values to Objects 67
    Adding Keys with Dot Notation 68
Combining Arrays and Objects 69
    An Array of Friends 69
Exploring Objects in the Console. 71
Useful Things to Do with Objects 72
    Keeping Track of Owed Money. 72
    Storing Information About Your Movies 74
What You Learned 75

Programming Challenges 76
    #1: Scorekeeper 76
    #2: Digging into Objects and Arrays 76

5
THE BASICS OF HTML   77

Text Editors 78
Our First HTML Document 79
Tags and Elements 80
    Heading Elements 80
    The p Element 81
    Whitespace in HTML and Block-Level Elements 81
    Inline Elements 82
A Full HTML Document 83
HTML Hierarchy 84
Adding Links to Your HTML 85
    Link Attributes 86
    Title Attributes 87
What You Learned 88

6
CONDITIONALS AND LOOPS   89

Embedding JavaScript in HTML 90
Conditionals 91
    if Statements 91
    if...else Statements 93
    Chaining if...else Statements 94
Loops 96
    while Loops 97
    for Loops 99
What You Learned 102
Programming Challenges 103
    #1: Awesome Animals 103
    #2: Random String Generator 103
    #3: h4ck3r sp34k 104

7
CREATING A HANGMAN GAME   105

Interacting with a Player 106
    Creating a Prompt 106
    Using confirm to Ask a Yes or No Question 108
    Using Alerts to Give a Player Information 109
    Why Use alert Instead of console.log? 109

Designing Your Game. 110
    Using Pseudocode to Design the Game 110
    Tracking the State of the Word 111
    Designing the Game Loop. 112
Coding the Game. 113
    Choosing a Random Word. 113
    Creating the Answer Array 114
    Coding the Game Loop 114
    Ending the Game 118
The Game Code. 118
What You Learned 120
Programming Challenges. 121
    #1: More Words 121
    #2: Capital Letters 121
    #3: Limiting Guesses. 121
    #4: Fixing a Bug 121

8
FUNCTIONS   123

The Basic Anatomy of a Function 124
Creating a Simple Function 124
Calling a Function 125
Passing Arguments into Functions 126
    Printing Cat Faces! 127
    Passing Multiple Arguments to a Function. 128
Returning Values from Functions 129
Using Function Calls as Values. 131
Using Functions to Simplify Code 132
    A Function to Pick a Random Word. 132
    A Random Insult Generator 133
    Making the Random Insult Generator into a Function 134
Leaving a Function Early with return. 135
Using return Multiple Times Instead of if...else Statements. 136
What You Learned 138
Programming Challenges. 138
    #1: Doing Arithmetic with Functions. 138
    #2: Are These Arrays the Same? 138
    #3: Hangman, Using Functions 139

PART II: ADVANCED JAVASCRIPT

9
THE DOM AND JQUERY
143

Selecting DOM Elements 144
    Using id to Identify Elements 145
    Selecting an Element Using getElementById 145
    Replacing the Heading Text Using the DOM 146
Using jQuery to Work with the DOM Tree 148
    Loading jQuery on Your HTML Page 148
    Replacing the Heading Text Using jQuery 148
Creating New Elements with jQuery 150
Animating Elements with jQuery 151
Chaining jQuery Animations 152
What You Learned 153
Programming Challenges 154
    #1: Listing Your Friends with jQuery
        (And Making Them Smell!) 154
    #2: Making a Heading Flash 154
    #3: Delaying Animations 154
    #4: Using fadeTo 154

10
INTERACTIVE PROGRAMMING
155

Delaying Code with setTimeout 156
Canceling a Timeout 157
Calling Code Multiple Times with setInterval 158
Animating Elements with setInterval 159
Responding to User Actions 162
    Responding to Clicks 162
    The mousemove Event 164
What You Learned 165
Programming Challenges 165
    #1: Follow the Clicks 165
    #2: Create Your Own Animation 165
    #3: Cancel an Animation with a Click 166
    #4: Make a "Click the Header" Game! 166

11
FIND THE BURIED TREASURE!   167

Designing the Game 168
Creating the Web Page with HTML 169
Picking a Random Treasure Location 170
     Picking Random Numbers 170
     Setting the Treasure Coordinates 171
The Click Handler. 171
     Counting Clicks. 172
     Calculating the Distance Between the Click and the Treasure . . . 172
     Using the Pythagorean Theorem 173
     Telling the Player How Close They Are. 175
     Checking If the Player Won 176
Putting It All Together 176
What You Learned 178
Programming Challenges. 179
     #1: Increasing the Playing Area. 179
     #2: Adding More Messages. 179
     #3: Adding a Click Limit. 179
     #4: Displaying the Number of Remaining Clicks 179

12
OBJECT-ORIENTED PROGRAMMING   181

A Simple Object. 182
Adding Methods to Objects. 182
     Using the this Keyword 183
     Sharing a Method Between Multiple Objects 183
Creating Objects Using Constructors 185
     Anatomy of the Constructor 185
     Creating a Car Constructor 186
Drawing the Cars 188
Testing the drawCar Function. 189
Customizing Objects with Prototypes 190
     Adding a draw Method to the Car Prototype. 191
     Adding a moveRight Method 192
     Adding the Left, Up, and Down move Methods. 193
What You Learned 195
Programming Challenges. 195
     #1: Drawing in the Car Constructor. 195
     #2: Adding a speed Property. 196
     #3: Racing Cars 196

PART III: CANVAS

13
THE CANVAS ELEMENT 199

Creating a Basic Canvas 200
Drawing on the Canvas 200
    Selecting and Saving the canvas Element. 201
    Getting the Drawing Context 201
    Drawing a Square 201
    Drawing Multiple Squares 202
Changing the Drawing Color 203
Drawing Rectangle Outlines 205
Drawing Lines or Paths 206
Filling Paths 207
Drawing Arcs and Circles. 209
    Drawing a Quarter Circle or an Arc. 210
    Drawing a Half Circle 211
    Drawing a Full Circle 211
Drawing Lots of Circles with a Function. 212
What You Learned 214
Programming Challenges. 214
    #1: A Snowman-Drawing Function 214
    #2: Drawing an Array of Points 215
    #3: Painting with Your Mouse 215
    #4: Drawing the Man in Hangman 215

14
MAKING THINGS MOVE ON THE CANVAS 217

Moving Across the Page 218
    Clearing the Canvas 219
    Drawing the Rectangle 219
    Changing the Position. 219
    Viewing the Animation in the Browser 219
Animating the Size of a Square 220
A Random Bee. 221
    A New circle Function. 222
    Drawing the Bee 222
    Updating the Bee's Location. 224
    Animating Our Buzzing Bee. 225
Bouncing a Ball! 227
    The Ball Constructor. 227
    Drawing the Ball. 228

Moving the Ball. 229
Bouncing the Ball 229
Animating the Ball 231
What You Learned 232
Programming Challenges. 233
#1: Bouncing the Ball Around a Larger Canvas 233
#2: Randomizing this.xSpeed and this.ySpeed 233
#3: Animating More Balls. 234
#4: Making the Balls Colorful. 234

15
CONTROLLING ANIMATIONS WITH THE KEYBOARD   235

Keyboard Events. 236
Setting Up the HTML File 236
Adding the keydown Event Handler 237
Using an Object to Convert Keycodes into Names 238
Moving a Ball with the Keyboard 239
Setting Up the Canvas 240
Defining the circle Function. 240
Creating the Ball Constructor 240
Defining the move Method 241
Defining the draw Method 242
Creating a setDirection Method. 243
Reacting to the Keyboard 244
Animating the Ball 245
Putting It All Together. 246
Running the Code 248
What You Learned 249
Programming Challenges. 249
#1: Bouncing Off the Walls 249
#2: Controlling the Speed 249
#3: Flexible Controls 249

16
MAKING A SNAKE GAME: PART 1   251

The Game Play 252
The Structure of the Game. 253
Using setInterval to Animate the Game 254
Creating the Game Objects. 254
Setting Up Keyboard Control 255
Game Setup. 255
Creating the HTML 255
Defining the canvas, ctx, width, and height Variables. 256

Dividing the Canvas into Blocks 256
Defining the score Variable 258
Drawing the Border 258
Displaying the Score. 260
Setting the Text Baseline 261
Setting the Size and Font 262
Writing the drawScore Function 263
Ending the Game 264
What You Learned 265
Programming Challenges. 266
#1: Putting It Together 266
#2: Animating the Score 266
#3: Adding Text to Hangman 266

17
MAKING A SNAKE GAME: PART 2   267
Building the Block Constructor 268
Adding the drawSquare Method 269
Adding the drawCircle Method 270
Adding the equal Method 272
Creating the Snake. 273
Writing the Snake Constructor 273
Drawing the Snake 274
Moving the Snake 275
Adding the move Method 275
Adding the checkCollision Method. 279
Setting the Snake's Direction with the Keyboard. 281
Adding the keydown Event Handler 281
Adding the setDirection Method 282
Creating the Apple 283
Writing the Apple Constructor. 283
Drawing the Apple 283
Moving the Apple 284
Putting It All Together 285
What You Learned 291
Programming Challenges. 291
#1: Making the Game Bigger 291
#2: Coloring the Snake 291
#3: Making the Game Speed Up as You Play 292
#4: Fixing the apple.move Method. 292

AFTERWORD
WHERE TO GO FROM HERE   **293**

More JavaScript 294
Web Programming 294
    HTML 294
    CSS. 295
    Server-Side Code with Node.js 295
Graphical Programming. 295
    canvas 295
    SVG Using Raphaël 296
3D Programming. 296
Programming Robots 296
Audio Programming 297
Game Programming 297
Sharing Your Code Using JSFiddle. 297

GLOSSARY   **299**

INDEX   **305**

ACKNOWLEDGMENTS

So many thanks to my wonderful fiancée, Philly, for her encouragement and support during the past 18 months. I truly couldn't have done it without her. And thanks to Pancake, our dog, for graciously allowing me to use him in my code examples.

Thanks to Angus, without whom I wouldn't be here, in San Francisco, writing this book. Angus referred me to Twitter back in 2011, and then in 2013 suggested to Bill Pollock that I might be interested in writing this book you're holding. And to top it all, he agreed to be the technical reviewer, catching a great number of JavaScript faux pas.

Thanks to Bill Pollock, Seph Kramer, Riley Hoffman, Tyler Ortman, and everyone else at No Starch Press, who patiently guided me through the process of writing this book. Special thanks to Bill and Seph for massaging my writing into its current form.

Thanks to the young reviewers River Bradley, Damien Champ, and Alex Chu, who had some great feedback on the early PDFs.

Finally, thanks to Miran Lipovača. I've been a fan of Miran for years—his book *Learn You a Haskell for Great Good* is one of my favorite programming books, and his illustrations for it are amazing. Finding out he'd be illustrating my book was like a dream come true. His pictures for this book are better than I could have imagined, and I'm humbled to have had the chance to work with him.

INTRODUCTION

Welcome to *JavaScript for Kids*! In this book, you'll learn to program with JavaScript, the language of the Web. But more than that, you'll become a programmer—someone who not only *uses* computers but also *controls* them. Once you learn to program, you can bend computers to your will and make them do whatever you want!

JavaScript is a great programming language to learn because it's used everywhere. Web browsers like Chrome, Firefox, and Internet Explorer all use JavaScript. With the power of JavaScript, web programmers can transform web pages from simple documents into full-blown interactive applications and games.

But you're not limited to building web pages. JavaScript can run on web servers to create whole websites and can even be used to control robots and other hardware!

WHO SHOULD READ THIS BOOK?

This book is for anyone who wants to learn JavaScript or to start programming for the first time. The book is designed to be kid friendly, but it can serve as a first programming book for beginners of all ages.

With this book, you'll build up your knowledge of JavaScript gradually, starting with JavaScript's simple data types, before moving onto complex types, control structures, and functions. After that you'll learn how to write code that reacts when the user moves the mouse or presses a key on the keyboard. Finally, you'll learn about the canvas element, which lets you use JavaScript to draw and animate anything you can imagine!

Along the way, you'll create a few games to stretch your programming skills and put what you've learned to good use.

HOW TO READ THIS BOOK

First off, read it in order! That might sound like a silly thing to say, but lots of people want to jump straight into the fun stuff, like making games. But each chapter is meant to build on what was covered in earlier chapters, so if you begin at the beginning, you'll have an easier time when you get to the games.

Programming languages are like spoken languages: you have to learn the grammar and the vocabulary, and this takes time. The only way to improve is by writing (and reading) a lot of code. As you write more and more JavaScript, you'll find certain parts of the language become second nature, and eventually you'll become a fluent writer of JavaScript.

As you read, I encourage you to type out and test the code examples throughout the book. If you don't fully understand what's going on, try making small changes to see what effect they have. If the changes don't have the effect you expected, see if you can find out why.

Above all, work through the "Try It Out" and "Programming Challenges" sections. Typing out the code that appears in the book is a good first step, but you'll understand programming at a deeper level when you start writing your own code. If you find a challenge interesting, then keep at it! Come up with your own challenges to build even more onto the programs you've written.

You'll find sample solutions to the programming challenges (as well as the code files for the games and other examples) at *http:// nostarch.com/javascriptforkids/*. Try looking at the solutions after you've solved a challenge, so you can compare your approach to mine. Or, if you're stuck, you can check the solution for hints. But remember that these are just *sample* solutions. There are many, many different ways to accomplish the same goal in JavaScript, so don't worry if you end up with a completely different solution from mine!

If you come across a word and you don't know what it means, check the glossary at the back of the book. The glossary contains definitions for many of the programming terms you'll encounter in this book.

WHAT'S IN THIS BOOK?

Chapter 1 gives you a quick introduction to JavaScript and gets you started writing JavaScript in Google Chrome.

Chapter 2 introduces variables and the basic data types used by JavaScript: numbers, strings, and Booleans.

Chapter 3 is all about arrays, which are used to hold lists of other pieces of data.

Chapter 4 is about objects, which contain pairs of keys and values.

Chapter 5 is an introduction to HTML, the language used to create web pages.

Chapter 6 shows you how to gain more control over your code using if statements, for loops, and other control structures.

Chapter 7 puts together everything you've learned so far to create a simple Hangman word-guessing game.

Chapter 8 shows you how to write your own functions so you can group together and reuse blocks of code.

Chapter 9 introduces jQuery, a tool that makes it easy to control web pages using JavaScript.

Chapter 10 shows you how to use timeouts, intervals, and event handlers to make your code more interactive.

Chapter 11 uses functions, jQuery, and event handlers to create a game called "Find the Buried Treasure!"

Chapter 12 teaches a style of programming called *object-oriented programming*.

Chapter 13 introduces the canvas element, which allows you to draw graphics on a web page with JavaScript.

Chapter 14 builds on the animation techniques you learned in Chapter 10 so you can create animations with canvas, and **Chapter 15** shows you how to control those canvas animations with the keyboard.

In **Chapters 16 and 17**, you'll program a complete Snake game, using everything you learned in the previous 15 chapters!

The **Afterword** gives you some ideas for how to learn even more about programming.

The **Glossary** contains definitions for many of the new words you'll encounter.

HAVE FUN!

One last thing to remember: Have fun! Programming can be a playful and creative activity, just like drawing or playing a game (in fact, you'll be drawing and playing games with JavaScript a lot in this book). Once you get the hang of how to write code, the only limit is your imagination. Welcome to the amazing world of computer programming—I hope you have a blast!

PART I

FUNDAMENTALS

1

WHAT IS JAVASCRIPT?

Computers are incredibly powerful machines, capable of performing amazing feats like playing competitive chess, serving thousands of web pages, or making millions of complex calculations in less than a few seconds. But deep down, computers are actually pretty dumb. Computers can *only* do exactly what we humans tell them to do. We tell computers how to behave using computer programs, which are just sets of instructions for the computers to follow. Without programs, computers can't do anything at all!

MEET JAVASCRIPT

Even worse, computers can't understand English or any other spoken language. Computer programs are written in a *programming language* like JavaScript. You might not have heard of JavaScript before, but you've certainly used it. The JavaScript programming language is used to write programs that run in web pages. JavaScript can control how a web page looks or make the page respond when a viewer clicks a button or moves the mouse.

Sites like Gmail, Facebook, and Twitter use JavaScript to make it easier to send email, post comments, or browse websites. For example, when you're on Twitter reading tweets from @nostarch and you see more tweets at the bottom of the page as you scroll down, that's JavaScript in action.

You only have to visit a couple of websites to see why JavaScript is so exciting.

- JavaScript lets you play music and create amazing visual effects. For example, you can fly through an interactive music video created by HelloEnjoy for Ellie Goulding's song "Lights" (*http://lights.helloenjoy.com/*), as shown in Figure 1-1.

- JavaScript lets you build tools for others to make their own art. Patatap (*http://www.patatap.com/*) is a kind of virtual "drum machine" that creates all kinds of cool noises—and cool animations to go along with them—as shown in Figure 1-2.

Figure 1-1: You control the flashing cursor in HelloEnjoy's "Lights" music video.

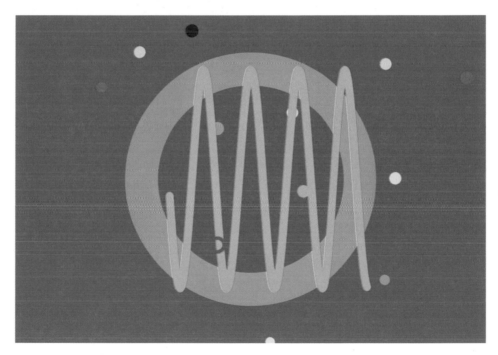

Figure 1-2: When you visit Patatap, try pressing a bunch of keys to make different noises!

- JavaScript lets you play fun games. *CubeSlam* (*https://www.cubeslam.com/*) is a 3D re-creation of the classic game Pong, which looks a little like air hockey. You can play against one of your friends or a computer-generated bear, as shown in Figure 1-3.

Figure 1-3: The CubeSlam game is programmed entirely in JavaScript!

WHY LEARN JAVASCRIPT?

JavaScript isn't the only programming language out there—in fact, there are literally hundreds of programming languages. But there are many reasons to learn JavaScript. For one, it's a lot easier (and more fun) to learn than many other programming languages. But perhaps best of all, in order to write and run JavaScript programs, all you need is a web browser like Internet Explorer, Mozilla Firefox, or Google Chrome. Every web browser comes with a JavaScript *interpreter* that understands how to read JavaScript programs.

Once you've written a JavaScript program, you can send people a link to it, and they can run it in a web browser on their computer, too! (See "Sharing Your Code Using JSFiddle" on page 297.)

WRITING SOME JAVASCRIPT

Let's write a bit of simple JavaScript in Google Chrome (*http://www.google.com/chrome/*). Install Chrome on your computer (if it's not already installed), and then open it and type `about:blank` in the address bar. Now press ENTER and you'll see a blank page, like the one in Figure 1-4.

We'll begin by coding in Chrome's JavaScript console, which is a secret way programmers can test out short JavaScript programs. On Microsoft Windows or Linux, hold down the CTRL and SHIFT keys and press J. On Mac OS, hold down the COMMAND and OPTION keys and press J.

If you've done everything correctly, you should see a blank web page and, beneath that, a blinking cursor (|) next to a right angle bracket (>), as shown in Figure 1-4. That's where you'll write JavaScript!

NOTE   *The Chrome console will color your code text; for example, the text you input will be blue, and output will be colored based on its type. In this book, we'll use similar colors for our code text wherever we're using the console.*

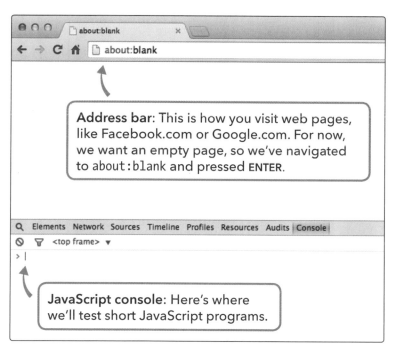

Figure 1-4: Google Chrome's JavaScript console

When you enter code at the cursor and press ENTER, JavaScript should run, or *execute*, your code and display the result (if any) on the next line. For example, type this into the console:

```
3 + 4;
```

Now press ENTER. JavaScript should output the answer (7) to this simple bit of addition on the following line:

```
3 + 4;
7
```

Well, that's easy enough. But isn't JavaScript more than a glorified calculator? Let's try something else.

THE STRUCTURE OF A JAVASCRIPT PROGRAM

Let's create something a bit sillier—a JavaScript program to print a series of cat faces that look like this:

```
=^.^=
```

Unlike our addition program, this JavaScript program will take up multiple lines. To type the program into the console, you'll have to add new lines by pressing SHIFT-ENTER at the end of each line. (If you just press ENTER, Chrome will try to execute what you've written, and the program won't work as expected. I warned you that computers were dumb!)

Type this into your browser console:

```javascript
// Draw as many cats as you want!
var drawCats = function (howManyTimes) {
  for (var i = 0; i < howManyTimes; i++) {
    console.log(i + " =^.^=");
  }
};

drawCats(10); // You can put any number here instead of 10.
```

At the very end, press ENTER instead of SHIFT-ENTER. When you do that, you should see the following output:

```
0 =^.^=
1 =^.^=
2 =^.^=
3 =^.^=
4 =^.^=
5 =^.^=
6 =^.^=
7 =^.^=
8 =^.^=
9 =^.^=
```

If you made any typos, your output might look very different or you might get an error. That's what I mean when I say computers are dumb—even a simple piece of code must be perfect for a computer to understand what you want it to do!

I won't go through exactly how this code *works* for now (we'll return to this program in Chapter 8), but let's look at some of the features of this program and of JavaScript programs in general.

SYNTAX

Our program includes lots of symbols, including parentheses (), semicolons ;, curly brackets {}, plus signs +, and a few words that might seem mysterious at first (like var and console.log). These are all part of JavaScript's *syntax*—that is, JavaScript's rules for how to combine symbols and words to create working programs.

When you're learning a new programming language, one of the trickiest parts is getting used to the rules for how to write different kinds of instructions to the computer. When you're first starting out, it's easy to forget when to include parentheses, or to mix up the order in which you need to include certain values. But as you practice, you'll start to get the hang of it.

In this book, we'll go slow and steady, introducing new syntax little by little so that you can build increasingly powerful programs.

COMMENTS

The first line in our cats program is this:

```
// Draw as many cats as you want!
```

This is called a *comment*. Programmers use comments to make it easier for other programmers to read and understand their code. The computer ignores comments completely. Comments in JavaScript start with two forward slashes (//). Everything following the slashes (on the same line) is ignored by the JavaScript interpreter, so the comments don't have any effect on how a program is executed—they are just there to provide a description.

In the code in this book, you'll see comments that describe what's happening in the code. As you write your own code, add your own comments. Then when you look at your code later, your comments will remind you how the code works and what's happening in each step.

There's another code comment on the last line of our program. Remember, everything after that // isn't run by the computer!

```
drawCats(10); // You can put any number here instead of 10.
```

Code comments can be on their own line, or they can come after your code. If you put the // at the front, like this:

```
// drawCats(10);
```

. . . nothing will happen! Chrome sees the whole line as a comment, even if it's JavaScript.

Once you start reading JavaScript code out in the wild world, you'll also see comments that look like this:

```
/*
Draw as many cats
as you want!
*/
```

This is a different style of commenting, which is typically used for comments that are longer than one line. But it does the same thing: everything between the /* and the */ is a comment that the computer won't run.

WHAT YOU LEARNED

In this chapter, you learned a bit about what JavaScript is and what it can be used for. You also learned how to run JavaScript using the Google Chrome browser and tried out a sample program. All of the code examples in this book, unless I say otherwise, can (and should!) be used in Chrome's JavaScript console. Don't just read the code—try typing things out! It's the only way to learn to program.

In the next chapter, you'll start learning the fundamentals of JavaScript, beginning with the three basic types of information you can work with: numbers, strings, and Booleans.

2

DATA TYPES AND VARIABLES

Programming is all about manipulating data, but what *is* data? *Data* is information that we store in our computer programs. For example, your name is a piece of data, and so is your age. The color of your hair, how many siblings you have, where you live, whether you're male or female—these things are all data.

In JavaScript, there are three basic types of data: numbers, strings, and Booleans. Numbers are used for representing, well, numbers! For example, your age can be represented as a number, and so can your height. Numbers in JavaScript look like this:

```
5;
```

Strings are used to represent text. Your name can be represented as a string in JavaScript, as can your email address. Strings look like this:

```
"Hi, I'm a string";
```

Booleans are values that can be true or false. For example, a Boolean value about you would be whether you wear glasses. Another could be whether you like broccoli. A Boolean looks like this:

```
true;
```

There are different ways to work with each data type. For example, you can multiply two numbers, but you can't multiply two strings. With a string, you can ask for the first five characters. With Booleans, you can check to see whether two values are both true. The following code example illustrates each of these possible operations.

```
99 * 123;
12177
"This is a long string".slice(0, 4);
"This"
true && false;
false
```

All data in JavaScript is just a combination of these types of data. In this chapter, we'll look at each type in turn and learn different ways to work with each type.

NOTE   *You may have noticed that all of these commands end with a semicolon (;). Semicolons mark the end of a particular JavaScript command or instruction (also called a* statement*), sort of like the period at the end of a sentence.*

NUMBERS AND OPERATORS

JavaScript lets you perform basic mathematical operations like addition, subtraction, multiplication, and division. To make these calculations, we use the symbols +, -, *, and /, which are called *operators*.

You can use the JavaScript console just like a calculator. We've already seen one example, adding together 3 and 4. Let's try something harder. What's 12,345 plus 56,789?

```
12345 + 56789;
69134
```

That's not so easy to work out in your head, but JavaScript calculated it in no time.

You can add multiple numbers with multiple plus signs:

```
22 + 33 + 44;
99
```

JavaScript can also do subtraction . . .

```
1000 - 17;
983
```

and multiplication, using an asterisk . . .

```
123 * 456;
56088
```

and division, using a forward slash . . .

```
12345 / 250;
49.38
```

You can also combine these simple operations to make something more complex, like this:

```
1234 + 57 * 3 - 31 / 4;
1397.25
```

Here it gets a bit tricky, because the result of this calculation (the answer) will depend on the order that JavaScript does each operation. In math, the rule is that multiplication and division always take place before addition and subtraction, and JavaScript follows this rule as well.

Figure 2-1 shows the order JavaScript would follow. First, JavaScript multiplies 57 * 3 and gets 171 (shown in red). Then it divides 31 / 4 to get 7.75 (shown in blue). Next it adds 1234 + 171 to get 1405 (shown in green). Finally it subtracts 1405 - 7.75 to get 1397.25, which is the final result.

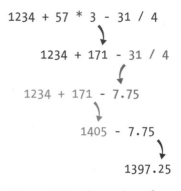

```
1234 + 57 * 3 - 31 / 4

   1234 + 171 - 31 / 4

   1234 + 171 - 7.75

        1405 - 7.75

             1397.25
```

Figure 2-1: The order of operations: multiplication, division, addition, subtraction

What if you wanted to do the addition and the subtraction first, before doing the multiplication and division? For example, say you have 1 brother and 3 sisters and 8 candies, and you want to split the candies equally among your 4 siblings? (You've already taken your share!) You would have to divide 8 by your number of siblings.

Here's an attempt:

```
8 / 1 + 3;
11
```

That can't be right! You can't give each sibling 11 candies when you've only got 8! The problem is that JavaScript does division before addition, so it divides 8 by 1 (which equals 8) and then adds 3 to that, giving you 11. To fix this and make JavaScript do the addition first, we can use *parentheses*:

```
8 / (1 + 3);
2
```

That's more like it! Two candies to each of your siblings. The parentheses force JavaScript to add 1 and 3 *before* dividing 8 by 4.

VARIABLES

JavaScript lets you give names to values using *variables*. You can think of a variable as a box that you can fit one thing in. If you put something else in it, the first thing goes away.

To create a new variable, use the keyword var, followed by the name of the variable. A *keyword* is a word that has special meaning in JavaScript. In this case, when we type var, JavaScript knows that we are about to enter the name of a new variable. For example, here's how you'd make a new variable called nick:

```
var nick;
undefined
```

We've created a new variable called nick. The console spits out undefined in response. But this isn't an error! That's just what JavaScript does whenever a command doesn't return a value. What's a return value? Well, for example, when you typed 12345 + 56789;, the console returned the value 69134. Creating a variable in JavaScript doesn't return a value, so the interpreter prints undefined.

To give the variable a value, use the equal sign:

```
var age = 12;
undefined
```

Setting a value is called *assignment* (we are assigning the value 12 to the variable age). Again, undefined is printed, because we're creating another new variable. (In the rest of my examples, I won't show the output when it's undefined.)

The variable age is now in our interpreter and set to the value 12. That means that if you type age on its own, the interpreter will show you its value:

```
age;
12
```

Cool! The value of the variable isn't set in stone, though (they're called *variables* because they can *vary*), and if you want to update it, just use = again:

```
age = 13;
13
```

This time I didn't use the var keyword, because the variable age already exists. You need to use var only when you want to *create* a variable, not when you want to change the value of a variable. Notice also, because we're not creating a new variable, the value 13 is returned from the assignment and printed on the next line.

This slightly more complex example solves the candies problem from earlier, without parentheses:

```
var numberOfSiblings = 1 + 3;
var numberOfCandies = 8;
numberOfCandies / numberOfSiblings;
2
```

First we create a variable called numberOfSiblings and assign it the value of 1 + 3 (which JavaScript works out to be 4). Then we create the variable numberOfCandies and assign 8 to it. Finally, we write numberOfCandies / numberOfSiblings. Because numberOfCandies is 8 and numberOfSiblings is 4, JavaScript works out 8 / 4 and gives us 2.

NAMING VARIABLES

Be careful with your variable names, because it's easy to misspell them. Even if you just get the capitalization wrong, the JavaScript interpreter won't know what you mean! For example, if you accidentally used a lowercase *c* in `numberOfCandies`, you'd get an error:

```
numberOfcandies / numberOfSiblings;
ReferenceError: numberOfcandies is not defined
```

Unfortunately, JavaScript will only do exactly what you ask it to do. If you misspell a variable name, JavaScript has no idea what you mean, and it will display an error message.

Another tricky thing about variable names in JavaScript is that they can't contain spaces, which means they can be difficult to read. I could have named my variable `numberofcandies` with no capital letters, which makes it even harder to read because it's not clear where the words end. Is this variable "numb erof can dies" or "numberofcan dies"? Without the capital letters, it's hard to tell.

One common way to get around this is to start each word with a capital letter as in `NumberOfCandies`. (This convention is called *camel case* because it supposedly looks like the humps on a camel.)

The standard practice is to have variables start with a lowercase letter, so it's common to capitalize each word except for the first one, like this: `numberOfCandies`. (I'll follow this version of the camel case convention throughout this book, but you're free to do whatever you want!)

CREATING NEW VARIABLES USING MATH

You can create new variables by doing some math on older ones. For example, you can use variables to find out how many seconds there are in a year—and how many seconds old you are! Let's start by finding the number of seconds in an hour.

SECONDS IN AN HOUR

First we create two new variables called secondsInAMinute and minutesInAnHour and make them both 60 (because, as we know, there are 60 seconds in a minute and 60 minutes in an hour). Then we create a variable called secondsInAnHour and set its value to the result of multiplying secondsInAMinute and minutesInAnHour. At ❶, we enter secondsInAnHour, which is like saying, "Tell me the value of secondsInAnHour right now!" JavaScript then gives you the answer: it's 3600.

```
   var secondsInAMinute = 60;
   var minutesInAnHour = 60;
   var secondsInAnHour = secondsInAMinute * minutesInAnHour;
❶  secondsInAnHour;
   3600
```

SECONDS IN A DAY

Now we create a variable called hoursInADay and set it to 24. Next we create the variable secondsInADay and set it equal to secondsInAnHour multiplied by hoursInADay. When we ask for the value secondsInADay at ❶, we get 86400, which is the number of seconds in a day.

```
   var hoursInADay = 24;
   var secondsInADay = secondsInAnHour * hoursInADay;
❶  secondsInADay;
   86400
```

SECONDS IN A YEAR

Finally, we create the variables daysInAYear and secondsInAYear. The daysInAYear variable is assigned the value 365, and the variable secondsInAYear is assigned the value of secondsInADay multiplied by daysInAYear. Finally, we ask for the value of secondsInAYear, which is 31536000 (more than 31 million)!

```
   var daysInAYear = 365;
   var secondsInAYear = secondsInADay * daysInAYear;
   secondsInAYear;
   31536000
```

AGE IN SECONDS

Now that you know the number of seconds in a year, you can easily figure out how old you are in seconds (to the nearest year). For example, as I'm writing this, I'm 29:

```
var age = 29;
age * secondsInAYear;
914544000
```

To figure out your age in seconds, enter the same code, but change the value in age to *your* age. Or just leave out the age variable altogether and use a number for your age, like this:

```
29 * secondsInAYear;
914544000
```

I'm more than 900 million seconds old! How many seconds old are you?

INCREMENTING AND DECREMENTING

As a programmer, you'll often need to increase or decrease the value of a variable containing a number by 1. For example, you might have a variable that counts the number of high-fives you received today. Each time someone high-fives you, you'd want to increase that variable by 1.

Increasing by 1 is called *incrementing*, and decreasing by 1 is called *decrementing*. You increment and decrement using the operators ++ and --.

```
var highFives = 0;
++highFives;
1
++highFives;
2
--highFives;
1
```

When we use the ++ operator, the value of highFives goes up by 1, and when we use the -- operator, it goes down by 1. You can also put these operators *after* the variable. This does the same thing, but the value that gets returned is the value *before* the increment or decrement.

```
highFives = 0;
highFives++;
0
highFives++;
1
highFives;
2
```

In this example, we set `highFives` to 0 again. When we call `highFives++`, the variable is incremented, but the value that gets printed is the value *before* the increment happened. You can see at the end (after two increments) that if we ask for the value of `highFives`, we get 2.

+= (PLUS-EQUALS) AND -= (MINUS-EQUALS)

To increase the value of a variable by a certain amount, you could use this code:

```
var x = 10;
x = x + 5;
x;
15
```

Here, we start out with a variable called x, set to 10. Then, we assign x + 5 to x. Because x was 10, x + 5 will be 15. What we're doing here is using the old value of x to work out a new value for x. Therefore, x = x + 5 really means "add 5 to x."

JavaScript gives you an easier way of increasing or decreasing a variable by a certain amount, with the += and -= operators. For example, if we have a variable x, then x += 5 is the same as saying x = x + 5. The -= operator works in the same way, so x -= 9 would be the same as x = x - 9 ("subtract 9 from x"). Here's an example using both of these operators to keep track of a score in a video game:

```
var score = 10;
score += 7;
17
score -= 3;
14
```

In this example, we start with a score of 10 by assigning the value 10 to the variable score. Then we beat a monster, which increases score by 7 using the += operator. (score += 7 is the same as score = score + 7.) Before we beat the monster, score was 10, and 10 + 7 is 17, so this operation sets score to 17.

After our victory over the monster, we crash into a meteor and score is reduced by 3. Again, score -= 3 is the same as score = score - 3. Because score is 17 at this point, score - 3 is 14, and that value gets reassigned to score.

TRY IT OUT!

There are some other operators that are similar to += and -=. For example, there are *= and /=. What do you think these do? Give them a try:

```
var balloons = 100;
balloons *= 2;
???
```

What does balloons *= 2 do? Now try this:

```
var balloons = 100;
balloons /= 4;
???
```

What does balloons /= 4 do?

STRINGS

So far, we've just been working with numbers. Now let's look at another type of data: *strings*. Strings in JavaScript (as in most programming languages) are just sequences of characters, which can include letters, numbers, punctuation, and spaces. We put strings between quotes so JavaScript knows where they start and end. For example, here's a classic:

```
"Hello world!";
"Hello world!"
```

To enter a string, just type a double quotation mark (") followed by the text you want in the string, and then close the string with another double quote. You can also use single quotes ('), but to keep things simple, we'll just be using double quotes in this book.

You can save strings into variables, just like numbers:

```
var myAwesomeString = "Something REALLY awesome!!!";
```

There's also nothing stopping you from assigning a string to a variable that previously contained a number:

```
var myThing = 5;
myThing = "this is a string";
"this is a string"
```

What if you put a number between quotes? Is that a string or a number? In JavaScript, a string is a string (even if it happens to have some characters that are numbers). For example:

```
var numberNine = 9;
var stringNine = "9";
```

numberNine is a number, and stringNine is a string. To see how these are different, let's try adding them together:

```
numberNine + numberNine;
18
stringNine + stringNine;
"99"
```

When we add the number values 9 and 9, we get 18. But when we use the + operator on "9" and "9", the strings are simply joined together to form "99".

JOINING STRINGS

As you just saw, you can use the + operator with strings, but the result is very different from using the + operator with numbers. When you use + to join two strings, you make a new string with the second string attached to the end of the first string, like this:

```
var greeting = "Hello";
var myName = "Nick";
greeting + myName;
"HelloNick"
```

Here, we create two variables (greeting and myName) and assign each a string value ("Hello" and "Nick", respectively). When we add these two variables together, the strings are combined to make a new string, "HelloNick".

That doesn't look right, though—there should be a space between Hello and Nick. But JavaScript won't put a space there unless we specifically tell it to by adding a space in one of the original strings:

```
❶ var greeting = "Hello ";
var myName = "Nick";
greeting + myName;
"Hello Nick"
```

The extra space inside the quotes at ❶ puts a space in the final string as well.

You can do a lot more with strings other than just adding them together. Here are some examples.

FINDING THE LENGTH OF A STRING

To get the length of a string, just add .length to the end of it.

```
"Supercalifragilisticexpialidocious".length;
34
```

You can add .length to the end of the actual string or to a variable that contains a string:

```
var java = "Java";
java.length;
4
```

```
var script = "Script";
script.length;
6
var javascript = java + script;
javascript.length;
10
```

Here we assign the string "Java" to the variable java and the string "Script" to the variable script. Then we add .length to the end of each variable to determine the length of each string, as well as the length of the combined strings.

Notice that I said you can add .length to "the actual string *or to a variable* that contains a string." This illustrates something very important about variables: anywhere you can use a number or a string, you can also use a variable containing a number or a string.

GETTING A SINGLE CHARACTER FROM A STRING

Sometimes you want to get a single character from a string. For example, you might have a secret code where the message is made up of the second character of each word in a list of words. You'd need to be able to get just the second characters and join them all together to create a new word.

To get a character from a particular position in a string, use square brackets, [ ]. Just take the string, or the variable containing the string, and put the number of the character you want in a pair of square brackets at the end. For example, to get the first character of myName, use myName[0], like this:

```
var myName = "Nick";
myName[0];
"N"
myName[1];
"i"
myName[2];
"c"
```

Notice that to get the first character of the string, we use 0 rather than 1. That's because JavaScript (like many other programming languages) starts counting at zero. That means when you want the first character of a string, you use 0; when you want the second one, you use 1; and so on.

Let's try out our secret code, where we hide a message in some words' second characters. Here's how to find the secret message in a sequence of words:

```
var codeWord1 = "are";
var codeWord2 = "tubas";
var codeWord3 = "unsafe";
var codeWord4 = "?!";
codeWord1[1] + codeWord2[1] + codeWord3[1] + codeWord4[1];
"run!"
```

Again, notice that to get the second character of each string, we use 1.

CUTTING UP STRINGS

To "cut off" a piece of a big string, you can use slice. For example, you might want to grab the first bit of a long movie review to show as a teaser on your website. To use slice, put a period after a string (or a variable containing a string), followed by the word slice and opening and closing parentheses. Inside the parentheses, enter the start and end positions of the slice of the string you want, separated by a comma. Figure 2-2 shows how to use slice.

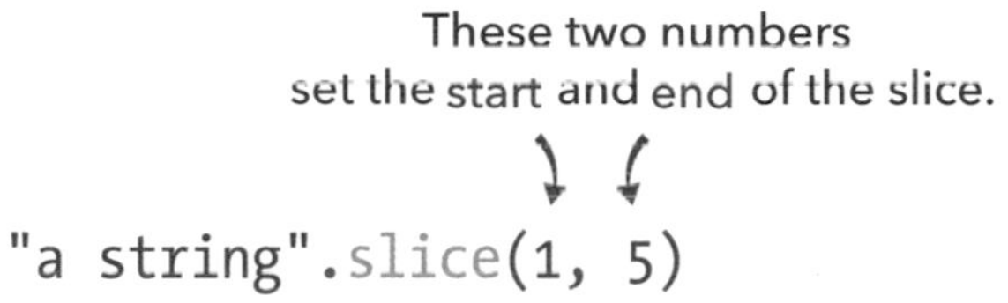

These two numbers
set the start and end of the slice.

❭ ❬

```
"a string".slice(1, 5)
```

Figure 2-2: How to use *slice* to get characters from a string

For example:

```
var longString = "My long string is long";
longString.slice(3, 14);
"long string"
```

The first number in parentheses is the number of the character that begins the slice, and the second number is the number of the character *after* the last character in the slice. Figure 2-3 shows which characters this retrieves, with the start value (3) and stop value (14) highlighted in blue.

```
M  y        l  o  n  g        s  t  r  i  n  g      i  s        l  o  n  g
0  1   2    3  4  5  6   7   8   9 10 11 12 13   14 15 16 17 18 19 20 21
```

Figure 2-3: In the example above, slice grabs the characters shown in the gray box.

Here we basically tell JavaScript, "Pull a slice out of this longer string starting at the character at place 3 and keep going until you hit place 14."

If you include only one number in the parentheses after slice, the string that it slices will start from that number and continue all the way to the end of the string, like this:

```
var longString = "My long string is long";
longString.slice(3);
"long string is long"
```

CHANGING STRINGS TO ALL CAPITAL OR ALL LOWERCASE LETTERS

If you have some text that you just want to shout, try using toUpperCase to turn it all into capital letters.

```
"Hello there, how are you doing?".toUpperCase();
"HELLO THERE, HOW ARE YOU DOING?"
```

When you use .toUpperCase() on a string, it makes a new string where all the letters are turned into uppercase.

You can go the other way around, too:

```
"hELlo THERE, hOW ARE yOu doINg?".toLowerCase();
"hello there, how are you doing?"
```

As the name suggests, .toLowerCase() makes all of the characters lowercase. But shouldn't sentences always start with a capital letter? How can we take a string and make the first letter uppercase but turn the rest into lowercase?

See if you can figure out how to turn "hELlo THERE, hOW ARE yOu doINg?" into "Hello there, how are you doing?" using the tools you just learned. If you get stuck, review the sections on getting a single character and using slice. *Once you're done, come back and have a look at how I did it.*

Here's one approach:

```
❶ var sillyString = "hELlo THERE, hOW ARE yOu doINg?";
❷ var lowerString = sillyString.toLowerCase();
❸ var firstCharacter = lowerString[0];
❹ var firstCharacterUpper = firstCharacter.toUpperCase();
❺ var restOfString = lowerString.slice(1);
❻ firstCharacterUpper + restOfString;
  "Hello there, how are you doing?"
```

Let's go through this line by line. At ❶, we create a new variable called sillyString and save the string we want to modify to that variable. At ❷, we get the lowercase version of sillyString ("hello there how are you doing?") with .toLowerCase() and save that in a new variable called lowerString.

At ❸, we use [0] to get the first character of lowerString ("h") and save it in firstCharacter (0 is used to grab the first character). Then, at ❹, we create an uppercase version of firstCharacter ("H") and call that firstCharacterUpper.

At ❺, we use slice to get all the characters in lowerString, starting from the second character ("ello there how are you doing?") and save that in restOfString. Finally, at ❻, we add firstCharacterUpper ("H") to restOfString to get "Hello there, how are you doing?".

Because values and variables can be substituted for each other, we could turn lines ❷ through ❻ into just one line, like this:

```
var sillyString = "hELlo THERE, hOW ARE yOu doINg?";
sillyString[0].toUpperCase() + sillyString.slice(1).toLowerCase();
"Hello there, how are you doing?"
```

It can be confusing to follow along with code written this way, though, so it's a good idea to use variables for each step of a complicated task like this—at least until you get more comfortable reading this kind of complex code.

BOOLEANS

Now for Booleans. A *Boolean* value is simply a value that's either true or false. For example, here's a simple Boolean expression.

```
var javascriptIsCool = true;
javascriptIsCool;
true
```

In this example, we created a new variable called `javascriptIsCool` and assigned the Boolean value true to it. On the second line, we get the value of `javascriptIsCool`, which, of course, is true!

LOGICAL OPERATORS

Just as you can combine numbers with mathematical operators (+, -, *, /, and so on), you can combine Boolean values with Boolean operators. When you combine Boolean values with Boolean operators, the result will always be another Boolean value (either true or false).

The three main Boolean operators in JavaScript are &&, ||, and !. They may look a bit weird, but with a little practice, they're not hard to use. Let's try them out.

&& (AND)

&& means "and." When reading aloud, people call it "and," "and-and," or "ampersand-ampersand." (*Ampersand* is the name of the character &.) Use the && operator with two Boolean values to see if they're *both* true.

For example, before you go to school, you want to make sure that you've had a shower *and* you have your backpack. If both are true, you can go to school, but if one or both are false, you can't leave yet.

```
var hadShower = true;
var hasBackpack = false;
hadShower && hasBackpack;
false
```

Here we set the variable hadShower to true and the variable hasBackpack to false. When we enter hadShower && hasBackpack, we are basically asking JavaScript, "Are both of these values true?" Since they aren't both true (you don't have your backpack), JavaScript returns false (you're not ready for school).

Let's try this again, with both values set to true:

```
var hadShower = true;
var hasBackpack = true;
hadShower && hasBackpack;
true
```

Now JavaScript tells us that hadShower && hasBackpack is true. You're ready for school!

|| (OR)

The Boolean operator || means "or." It can be pronounced "or," or even "or-or," but some people call it "pipes," because programmers call the | character a *pipe*. You can use this operator with two Boolean values to find out whether *either* one is true.

For example, say you're still getting ready to go to school and you need to take a piece of fruit for lunch, but it doesn't matter whether you take an apple or an orange or both. You can use JavaScript to see whether you have at least one, like this:

```
var hasApple = true;
var hasOrange = false;
```

```
hasApple || hasOrange;
true
```

hasApple || hasOrange will be true if either hasApple or hasOrange
is true, or if both are true. But if *both* are false, the result will be
false (you don't have any fruit).

! (NOT)

! just means "not." You can call it "not," but lots of people call it
"bang." (An exclamation point is sometimes called a *bang*.) Use it
to turn false into true or true into false. This is useful for working
with values that are opposites. For example:

```
var isWeekend = true;
var needToShowerToday = !isWeekend;
needToShowerToday;
false
```

In this example, we set the variable isWeekend to true. Then
we set the variable needToShowerToday to !isWeekend. The bang
converts the value to its opposite—so if isWeekend is true, then
!isWeekend is *not* true (it's false). So when we ask for the value of
needToShowerToday, we get false (you don't need to shower today,
because it's the weekend).

Because needToShowerToday is false, !needToShowerToday will
be true:

```
needToShowerToday;
false
!needToShowerToday;
true
```

In other words, it's *true* that you do *not* need to shower today.

COMBINING LOGICAL OPERATORS

Operators get interesting when you start combining them. For
example, say you should go to school if it's *not* the weekend *and*
you've showered *and* you have an apple *or* you have an orange. We
could check whether all of this is true with JavaScript, like this:

```
var isWeekend = false;
var hadShower = true;
var hasApple = false;
```

```
var hasOrange = true;
var shouldGoToSchool = !isWeekend && hadShower && (hasApple || hasOrange);
shouldGoToSchool;
true
```

In this case, it's not the weekend, you have showered, and you don't have an apple but you do have an orange—so you should go to school.

`hasApple || hasOrange` is in parentheses because we want to make sure JavaScript works out that bit first. Just as JavaScript calculates * before + with numbers, it also calculates && before || in logical statements.

COMPARING NUMBERS WITH BOOLEANS

Boolean values can be used to answer questions about numbers that have a simple yes or no answer. For example, imagine you're running a theme park and one of the rides has a height restriction: riders must be at least 60 inches tall, or they might fall out! When someone wants to go on the ride and tells you their height, you need to know if it's greater than this height restriction.

GREATER THAN

We can use the greater-than operator (>) to see if one number is greater than another. For example, to see if the rider's height (65 inches) is greater than the height restriction (60 inches), we could set the variable height equal to 65 and the variable heightRestriction equal to 60, and then use > to compare the two:

```
var height = 65;
var heightRestriction = 60;
height > heightRestriction;
true
```

With `height > heightRestriction`, we're asking JavaScript to tell us whether the first value is greater than the second. In this case, the rider is tall enough!

What if a rider were exactly 60 inches tall, though?

```
var height = 60;
var heightRestriction = 60;
height > heightRestriction;
false
```

Oh no! The rider isn't tall enough! But if the height restriction is 60, then shouldn't people who are exactly 60 inches be allowed in? We need to fix that. Luckily, JavaScript has another operator, >=, which means "greater than or equal to":

```
var height = 60;
var heightRestriction = 60;
height >= heightRestriction;
true
```

Good, that's better—60 *is* greater than or equal to 60.

LESS THAN

The opposite of the greater-than operator (>) is the less-than operator (<). This operator might come in handy if a ride were designed only for small children. For example, say the rider's height is 60 inches, but riders must be no more than 48 inches tall:

```
var height = 60;
var heightRestriction = 48;
height < heightRestriction;
false
```

We want to know if the rider's height is *less* than the restriction, so we use <. Because 60 is not less than 48, we get false (someone whose height is 60 inches is too tall for this ride).

And, as you may have guessed, we can also use the operator <=, which means "less than or equal to":

```
var height = 48;
var heightRestriction = 48;
height <= heightRestriction;
true
```

Someone who is 48 inches tall is still allowed to go on the ride.

EQUAL TO

To find out if two numbers are exactly the same, use the triple equal sign (===), which means "equal to." But be careful not to confuse === with a single equal sign (=), because === means "are these two numbers equal?" and = means "save the value on the right in the variable on the left." In other words, === asks a question, while = assigns a value to a variable.

When you use =, a variable name has to be on the left and the value you want to save to that variable must be on the right. On the other hand, === is just used for comparing two values to see if they're the same, so it doesn't matter which value is on which side.

For example, say you're running a competition with your friends Chico, Harpo, and Groucho to see who can guess your secret number, which is 5. You make it easy on your friends by saying that the number is between 1 and 9, and they start to guess. First you set mySecretNumber equal to 5. Your first friend, Chico, guesses that it's 3 (chicoGuess). Let's see what happens next:

```
var mySecretNumber = 5;
var chicoGuess = 3;
mySecretNumber === chicoGuess;
false
var harpoGuess - 7;
mySecretNumber === harpoGuess;
false
var grouchoGuess = 5;
mySecretNumber === grouchoGuess;
true
```

The variable mySecretNumber stores your secret number. The variables chicoGuess, harpoGuess, and grouchoGuess represent your friends' guesses, and we use === to see whether each guess is the same as your secret number. Your third friend, Groucho, wins by guessing 5.

When you compare two numbers with ===, you get true only when both numbers are the same. Because grouchoGuess is 5 and mySecretNumber is 5, mySecretNumber === grouchoGuess returns true. The other guesses didn't match mySecretNumber, so they returned false.

You can also use === to compare two strings or two Booleans. If you use === to compare two different types—for example, a string and a number—it will always return false.

DOUBLE EQUALS

Now to confuse things a bit: there's another JavaScript operator (double equals, or ==) that means "equal-ish." Use this to see whether two values are the same, even if one is a string and the other is a number. All values have some kind of type. So the number 5 is different from the string "5", even though they basically look like the same thing. If you use === to compare the number 5 and the string "5", JavaScript will tell you they're not equal. But if you use == to compare them, it will tell you they're the same:

```
var stringNumber = "5";
var actualNumber = 5;
stringNumber === actualNumber;
false
stringNumber == actualNumber;
true
```

At this point, you might be thinking to yourself, "Hmm, it seems much easier to use double equals than triple equals!" You have to be very careful, though, because double equals can be very confusing. For example, do you think 0 is equal to false? What about the string "false"? When you use double equals, 0 is equal to false, but the string "false" is not:

```
0 == false;
true
"false" == false;
false
```

This is because when JavaScript tries to compare two values with double equals, it first tries to make them the same type. In this case, it converts the Boolean into a number. If you convert Booleans to numbers, false becomes 0, and true becomes 1. So when you type 0 == false, you get true!

Because of this weirdness, it's probably safest to just stick with === for now.

You've been asked by the local movie theater managers to implement some JavaScript for a new automated system they're building. They want to be able to work out whether someone is allowed into a PG-13 movie or not.

The rules are, if someone is 13 or over, they're allowed in. If they're not over 13, but they are accompanied by an adult, they're also allowed in. Otherwise, they can't see the movie.

```
var age = 12;
var accompanied = true;
???
```

Finish this example using the age and accompanied variables to work out whether this 12-year-old is allowed to see the movie. Try changing the values (for example, set age to 13 and accompanied to false) and see if your code still works out the right answer.

UNDEFINED AND NULL

Finally, we have two values that don't fit any particular mold. They're called undefined and null. They're both used to mean "nothing," but in slightly different ways.

undefined is the value JavaScript uses when it doesn't have a value for something. For example, when you create a new variable, if you don't set its value to anything using the = operator, its value will be set to undefined:

```
var myVariable;
myVariable;
undefined
```

The null value is usually used when you want to deliberately say "This is empty."

```
var myNullVariable = null;
myNullVariable;
null
```

At this point, you won't be using undefined or null very often. You'll see undefined if you create a variable and don't set its value, because undefined is what JavaScript will always give you when it doesn't have a value. It's not very common to set something to undefined; if you feel the need to set a variable to "nothing," you should use null instead.

null is used only when you actually want to say something's not there, which is very occasionally helpful. For example, say you're using a variable to track what your favorite vegetable is. If you hate all vegetables and don't have a favorite, you might set the favorite vegetable variable to null.

Setting the variable to null would make it obvious to anyone reading the code that you don't have a favorite vegetable. If it were undefined, however, someone might just think you hadn't gotten around to setting a value yet.

WHAT YOU LEARNED

Now you know all the basic data types in JavaScript—numbers, strings, and Booleans—as well as the special values null and undefined. Numbers are used for math-type things, strings are used for text, and Booleans are used for yes or no questions. The values null and undefined are there to give us a way to talk about things that don't exist.

In the next two chapters, we'll look at arrays and objects, which are both ways of joining basic types to create more complex collections of values.

3

ARRAYS

So far we've learned about numbers and strings, which are types of data that you can store and use in your programs. But numbers and strings are kind of boring. There's not a lot that you can do with a string on its own. JavaScript lets you create and group together data in more interesting ways with *arrays*. An array is just a list of other JavaScript data values.

For example, if your friend asked you what your three favorite dinosaurs were, you could create an array with the names of those dinosaurs, in order:

```
var myTopThreeDinosaurs = ["T-Rex", "Velociraptor", "Stegosaurus"];
```

So instead of giving your friend three separate strings, you can just use the single array myTopThreeDinosaurs.

WHY SHOULD YOU CARE ABOUT ARRAYS?

Let's look at dinosaurs again. Say you want to use a program to keep track of the many kinds of dinosaurs you know about. You could create a variable for each dinosaur, like this:

```
var dinosaur1 = "T-Rex";
var dinosaur2 = "Velociraptor";
var dinosaur3 = "Stegosaurus";
var dinosaur4 = "Triceratops";
var dinosaur5 = "Brachiosaurus";
var dinosaur6 = "Pteranodon";
var dinosaur7 = "Apatosaurus";
var dinosaur8 = "Diplodocus";
var dinosaur9 = "Compsognathus";
```

This list is pretty awkward to use, though, because you have nine different variables when you could have just one. Imagine if you were keeping track of 1000 dinosaurs! You'd need to create 1000 separate variables, which would be almost impossible to work with.

It's like if you had a shopping list, but every item was on a different piece of paper. You'd have one piece of paper that said "eggs," another piece that said "bread," and another piece that said "oranges." Most people would write the full list of things they want to buy on a single piece of paper. Wouldn't it be much easier if you could group all nine dinosaurs together in just one place?

You can, and that's where arrays come in.

CREATING AN ARRAY

To create an array, you just use square brackets, []. In fact, an empty array is simply a pair of square brackets, like this:

```
[];
[]
```

But who cares about an empty array? Let's fill it with our dinosaurs!

To create an array with values in it, enter the values, separated by commas, between the square brackets. We can call the individual values in an array *items* or *elements*. In this example, our elements will be strings (the names of our favorite dinosaurs), so we'll write them with quote marks. We'll store the array in a variable called dinosaurs:

```
var dinosaurs = ["T-Rex", "Velociraptor", "Stegosaurus", ↵
"Triceratops", "Brachiosaurus", "Pteranodon", "Apatosaurus", ↵
"Diplodocus", "Compsognathus"];
```

NOTE *Because this is a book and the page is only so wide, we can't actually fit the whole array on one line. The ↵ is to show where we've put the code onto an extra line because the page is too narrow. When you type this into your computer, you can type it all on one line.*

Long lists can be hard to read on one line, but luckily that's not the only way to format (or lay out) an array. You can also format an array with an opening square bracket on one line, the list of items in the array each on a new line, and a closing square bracket, like this:

```
var dinosaurs = [
  "T-Rex",
  "Velociraptor",
  "Stegosaurus",
  "Triceratops",
  "Brachiosaurus",
  "Pteranodon",
  "Apatosaurus",
  "Diplodocus",
  "Compsognathus"
];
```

If you want to type this into your browser console, you'll need to hold down the SHIFT key when you press the ENTER key for each new line. Otherwise the JavaScript interpreter will think you're trying to execute the current, incomplete, line. While we're working in the interpreter, it's easier to write arrays on one line.

Whether you choose to format the items in an array on one line or on separate lines, it's all the same to JavaScript. However many line breaks you use, JavaScript just sees an array—in this example, an array containing nine strings.

ACCESSING AN ARRAY'S ELEMENTS

When it's time to access elements in an array, you use square brackets with the *index* of the element you want, as you can see in the following example:

```
dinosaurs[0];
"T-Rex"
dinosaurs[3];
"Triceratops"
```

An *index* is the number that corresponds to (or matches) the spot in the array where a value is stored. Just as with strings, the first element in an array is at index 0, the second is at index 1, the third at index 2, and so on. That's why asking for index 0 from the dinosaurs array returns "T-Rex" (which is first in the list), and index 3 returns "Triceratops" (which is fourth in the list).

It's useful to be able to access individual elements from an array. For example, if you just wanted to show someone your absolute favorite dinosaur, you wouldn't need the whole dinosaurs array. Instead you would just want the first element:

```
dinosaurs[0];
"T-Rex"
```

SETTING OR CHANGING ELEMENTS IN AN ARRAY

You can use indexes in square brackets to set, change, or even add elements to an array. For example, to replace the first element in the dinosaurs array ("T-Rex") with "Tyrannosaurus Rex", you could do this:

```
dinosaurs[0] = "Tyrannosaurus Rex";
```

After you've done that, the dinosaurs array would look like this:

```
["Tyrannosaurus Rex", "Velociraptor", "Stegosaurus", "Triceratops",
"Brachiosaurus", "Pteranodon", "Apatosaurus", "Diplodocus",
"Compsognathus"]
```

You can also use square brackets with indexes to add new elements to an array. For example, here's how you could create the dinosaurs array by setting each element individually with square brackets:

```
var dinosaurs = [];
dinosaurs[0] = "T-Rex";
dinosaurs[1] = "Velociraptor";
dinosaurs[2] = "Stegosaurus";
dinosaurs[3] = "Triceratops";
dinosaurs[4] = "Brachiosaurus";
dinosaurs[5] = "Pteranodon";
dinosaurs[6] = "Apatosaurus";
dinosaurs[7] = "Diplodocus";
dinosaurs[8] = "Compsognathus";

dinosaurs;
["T-Rex", "Velociraptor", "Stegosaurus", "Triceratops",
"Brachiosaurus", "Pteranodon", "Apatosaurus", "Diplodocus",
"Compsognathus"]
```

First we create an empty array with var dinosaurs = []. Then, with each following line we add a value to the list with a series of dinosaurs[] entries, from index 0 to index 8. Once we finish the list, we can view the array (by typing dinosaurs;). We see that JavaScript has stored all the names ordered according to the indexes.

You can actually add an element at any index you want. For example, to add a new (made-up) dinosaur at index 33, you could write the following:

```
dinosaurs[33] = "Philosoraptor";

dinosaurs;
["T-Rex", "Velociraptor", "Stegosaurus", "Triceratops",
"Brachiosaurus", "Pteranodon", "Apatosaurus", "Diplodocus",
"Compsognathus", undefined × 24 "Philosoraptor"]
```

The elements between indexes 8 and 33 will be undefined. When you output the array, Chrome helpfully tells you how many elements were undefined, rather than listing them all individually.

MIXING DATA TYPES IN AN ARRAY

Array elements don't all have to be the same type. For example, the next array contains a number (3), a string ("dinosaurs"), an array (["triceratops", "stegosaurus", 3627.5]), and another number (10):

```
var dinosaursAndNumbers = [3, "dinosaurs", ["triceratops", ↵
"stegosaurus", 3627.5], 10];
```

To access an individual element in this array's inner array, you would just use a second set of square brackets. For example, while dinosaursAndNumbers[2]; returns the entire inner array, dinosaursAndNumbers[2][0]; returns only the first element of that inner array, which is "triceratops".

```
dinosaursAndNumbers[2];
["triceratops", "stegosaurus", 3627.5]
dinosaursAndNumbers[2][0];
"triceratops"
```

When we type dinosaursAndNumbers[2][0];, we tell JavaScript to look at index 2 of the array dinosaursAndNumbers, which contains the array ["triceratops", "stegosaurus", 3627.5], and to return the value at index 0 of that second array. Index 0 is the first value of the second array, which is "triceratops". Figure 3-1 shows the index positions for this array.

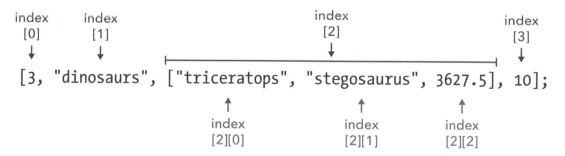

Figure 3-1: The index positions of the main array are labeled in red, and the indexes of the inner array are labeled in blue.

WORKING WITH ARRAYS

Properties and *methods* help you work with arrays. Properties generally tell you something about the array, and methods usually do something to change the array or return a new array. Let's have a look.

FINDING THE LENGTH OF AN ARRAY

Sometimes it's useful to know how many elements there are in an array. For example, if you kept adding dinosaurs to your dinosaurs array, you might forget how many dinosaurs you have.

The length property of an array tells you how many elements there are in the array. To find the length of an array, just add .length to the end of its name. Let's try it out. First we'll make a new array with three elements:

```
var maniacs = ["Yakko", "Wakko", "Dot"];
maniacs[0];
"Yakko"
maniacs[1];
"Wakko"
maniacs[2];
"Dot"
```

To find the length of the array, add .length to maniacs:

```
maniacs.length;
3
```

JavaScript tells us that there are 3 elements in the array, and we already know they have the index positions 0, 1, and 2. This gives us a useful piece of information: the last index in an array is always the same number as the length of the array minus 1. This means that there is an easy way to access the last element in an array, however long that array is:

```
maniacs[maniacs.length - 1];
"Dot"
```

Here, we're asking JavaScript for an element from our array. But instead of entering an index number in the square brackets, we use a little bit of math: the length of the array minus 1. JavaScript finds `maniacs.length`, gets 3, and then subtracts 1 to get 2. Then it returns the element from index 2—the last maniac in the array, `"Dot"`.

ADDING ELEMENTS TO AN ARRAY

To add an element to the end of an array, you can use the `push` method. Add `.push` to the array name, followed by the element you want to add inside parentheses, like this:

```
var animals = [];
animals.push("Cat");
1
animals.push("Dog");
2
animals.push("Llama");
3
animals;
["Cat", "Dog", "Llama"]
animals.length;
3
```

Here we create an empty array with `var animals = [];`, and then use the `push` method to add `"Cat"` to the array. Then, we use `push` again to add on `"Dog"` and then `"Llama"`. When we display `animals;`, we see that `"Cat"`, `"Dog"`, and `"Llama"` were added to the array, in the same order we entered them.

The act of running a method in computer-speak is known as *calling* the method. When you call the `push` method, two things happen. First, the element in parentheses is added to the array. Second, the new length of the array is returned. That's why you see those numbers printed out every time you call `push`.

To add an element to the beginning of an array, you can use
.unshift(*element*), like this:

```
  animals;
  ["Cat", "Dog", "Llama"]
❶ animals[0];
  "Cat"
  animals.unshift("Monkey");
  4
  animals;
  ["Monkey", "Cat", "Dog", "Llama"]
  animals.unshift("Polar Bear");
  5
  animals;
  ["Polar Bear", "Monkey", "Cat", "Dog", "Llama"]
  animals[0];
  "Polar Bear"
❷ animals[2];
  "Cat"
```

Here we started with the
array that we've been using,
["Cat", "Dog", "Llama"]. Then,
as we add the elements "Monkey"
and "Polar Bear" to the beginning of the array with unshift,
the old values get pushed along
by one index each time. So
"Cat", which was originally at
index 0 ❶, is now at index 2 ❷.

Again, unshift returns the
new length of the array each
time it is called, just like push.

REMOVING ELEMENTS FROM AN ARRAY

To remove the last element from an array, you can pop it off by
adding .pop() to the end of the array name. The pop method can be
particularly handy because it does two things: it removes the last
element, *and* it returns that last element as a value. For example,
let's start with our animals array, ["Polar Bear", "Monkey", "Cat",
"Dog", "Llama"]. Then we'll create a new variable called lastAnimal
and save the last animal into it by calling animals.pop().

```
animals;
["Polar Bear", "Monkey", "Cat", "Dog", "Llama"]
❶ var lastAnimal = animals.pop();
lastAnimal;
"Llama"
animals;
["Polar Bear", "Monkey", "Cat", "Dog"]
❷ animals.pop();
"Dog"
animals;
["Polar Bear", "Monkey", "Cat"]
❸ animals.unshift(lastAnimal);
4
animals;
["Llama", "Polar Bear", "Monkey", "Cat"]
```

When we call `animals.pop()` at ❶, the last item in the `animals` array, `"Llama"`, is returned and saved in the variable `lastAnimal`. `"Llama"` is also removed from the array, which leaves us with four animals. When we call `animals.pop()` again at ❷, `"Dog"` is removed from the array and returned, leaving only three animals in the array.

When we used `animal.pop()` on `"Dog"`, we didn't save it into a variable, so that value isn't saved anywhere anymore. The `"Llama"`, on the other hand, was saved to the variable `lastAnimal`, so we can use it again whenever we need it. At ❸, we use `unshift(lastAnimal)` to add `"Llama"` back onto the front of the array. This gives us a final array of `["Llama", "Polar Bear", "Monkey", "Cat"]`.

Pushing and popping are a useful pair because sometimes you care about only the end of an array. You can push a new item onto the array and then pop it off when you're ready to use it. We'll look at some ways to use pushing and popping later in this chapter.

To remove and return the first element of an array, use
`.shift()`:

```
animals;
["Llama", "Polar Bear", "Monkey", "Cat"]
var firstAnimal = animals.shift();
firstAnimal;
"Llama"
animals;
["Polar Bear", "Monkey", "Cat"]
```

animals.shift() does the same thing as animals.pop(), but
the element comes off the beginning instead. At the start of
this example, animals is ["Llama", "Polar Bear", "Monkey", "Cat"].
When we call .shift() on the array, the first element, "Llama", is
returned and saved in firstAnimal. Because .shift() removes the
first element as well as returning it, at the end animals is just
["Polar Bear", "Monkey", "Cat"].

You can use unshift and shift to add and remove items from
the beginning of an array just as you'd use push and pop to add and
remove items from the end of an array.

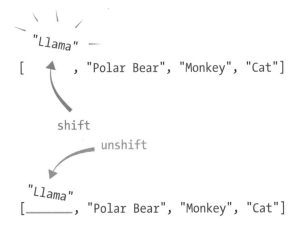

ADDING ARRAYS

To add two arrays together to make a new, single array, you can
use *firstArray*.concat(*otherArray*). The term concat is short for
concatenate, a fancy computer science word for joining two values
together. The concat method will combine both arrays into a new
array, with the values from *firstArray* added in front of those from
otherArray.

For example, say we have a list of some furry animals and another list of some scaly animals, and we want to combine them. If we put all of our furry animals in an array called furryAnimals and all of our scaly animals in an array called scalyAnimals, entering furryAnimals.concat(scalyAnimals) will create a new array that has the values from the first array at the beginning and the values from the second array at the end.

```
var furryAnimals = ["Alpaca", "Ring-tailed Lemur", "Yeti"];
var scalyAnimals = ["Boa Constrictor", "Godzilla"];
var furryAndScalyAnimals = furryAnimals.concat(scalyAnimals);
furryAndScalyAnimals;
["Alpaca", "Ring-tailed Lemur", "Yeti", "Boa Constrictor", "Godzilla"]
furryAnimals;
["Alpaca", "Ring-tailed Lemur", "Yeti"]
scalyAnimals;
["Boa Constrictor", "Godzilla"]
```

Even though *firstArray*.concat(*otherArray*) returns an array containing all the elements from *firstArray* and *secondArray*, neither of the original arrays is changed. When we look at furryAnimals and scalyAnimals, they're the same as when we created them.

JOINING MULTIPLE ARRAYS

You can use concat to join more than two arrays together. Just put the extra arrays inside the parentheses, separated by commas:

```
var furryAnimals = ["Alpaca", "Ring-tailed Lemur", "Yeti"];
var scalyAnimals = ["Boa Constrictor", "Godzilla"];
var featheredAnimals = ["Macaw", "Dodo"];
var allAnimals = furryAnimals.concat(scalyAnimals, featheredAnimals);
allAnimals;
["Alpaca", "Ring-tailed Lemur", "Yeti", "Boa Constrictor", "Godzilla",
"Macaw", "Dodo"]
```

Here the values from featheredAnimals get added to the very end of the new array, since they are listed last in the parentheses after the concat method.

concat is useful when you have multiple arrays that you want to combine into one. For example, say you have a list of your favorite books, and your friend also has a list of favorite books, and you want to go see if the books are available to buy all at once at the bookstore. It would be easier if you had only one list of books. All you'd have to do is concat your list with your friend's, and voilà! One list of books.

FINDING THE INDEX OF AN ELEMENT IN AN ARRAY

To find the index of an element in an array, use .indexOf(*element*). Here we define the array colors and then ask for the index positions of "blue" and "green" with colors.indexOf("blue") and colors.indexOf("green"). Because the index of "blue" in the array is 2, colors.indexOf("blue") returns 2. The index of "green" in the array is 1, so colors.indexOf("green") returns 1.

```
var colors = ["red", "green", "blue"];
colors.indexOf("blue");
2
colors.indexOf("green");
1
```

indexOf is like the reverse of using square brackets to get a value at a particular index; colors[2] is "blue", so colors .indexOf("blue") is 2:

```
colors[2];
"blue"
colors.indexOf("blue");
2
```

Even though "blue" appears third in the array, its index position is 2 because we always start counting from 0. And the same goes for "green", of course, at index 1.

If the element whose position you ask for is not in the array, JavaScript returns -1.

```
colors.indexOf("purple");
-1
```

This is JavaScript's way of saying "That doesn't exist here," while still returning a number.

If the element appears more than once in the array, the indexOf method will return the first index of that element in the array.

```
var insects = ["Bee", "Ant", "Bee", "Bee", "Ant"];
insects.indexOf("Bee");
0
```

TURNING AN ARRAY INTO A STRING

You can use .join() to join all the elements in an array together into one big string.

```
var boringAnimals = ["Monkey", "Cat", "Fish", "Lizard"];
boringAnimals.join();
"Monkey,Cat,Fish,Lizard"
```

When you call the join method on an array, it returns a string containing all the elements, separated by commas. But what if you don't want to use commas as the separator?

You can use .join(*separator*) to do the same thing, but with your own chosen separator between each value. The separator is whatever string you put inside the parentheses. For example, we can use three different separators: a hyphen with spaces on either side, an asterisk, and the word *sees* with spaces on either side. Notice that you need quote marks around the separator, because the separator is a string.

```
var boringAnimals = ["Monkey", "Cat", "Fish", "Lizard"];
boringAnimals.join(" - ");
"Monkey - Cat - Fish - Lizard"
boringAnimals.join("*")
"Monkey*Cat*Fish*Lizard"
boringAnimals.join(" sees ")
"Monkey sees Cat sees Fish sees Lizard"
```

This is useful if you have an array that you want to turn into a string. Say you have lots of middle names and you've got them stored in an array, along with your first and last name. You might be asked to give your full name as a string. Using join, with a single space as the separator, will join all your names together into a single string:

```
var myNames = ["Nicholas", "Andrew", "Maxwell", "Morgan"];
myNames.join(" ");
"Nicholas Andrew Maxwell Morgan"
```

If you didn't have join, you'd have to do something like this, which would be really annoying to type out:

```
myNames[0] + " " + myNames[1] + " " + myNames[2] + " " + myNames[3];
"Nicholas Andrew Maxwell Morgan"
```

Also, this code would work only if you had exactly two middle names. If you had one or three middle names, you'd have to change the code. With join, you don't have to change anything—it prints out a string with all of the elements of the array, no matter how long the array is.

If the values in the array aren't strings, JavaScript will convert them to strings before joining them together:

```
var ages = [11, 14, 79];
ages.join(" ");
"11 14 79"
```

USEFUL THINGS TO DO WITH ARRAYS

Now you know lots of different ways to create arrays and play around with them. But what can you actually do with all these properties and methods? In this section, we'll write a few short programs that show off some useful things to do with arrays.

FINDING YOUR WAY HOME

Picture this: your friend has come over to your house. Now she wants to show you her house. The only problem is that you've never been to her house before, and later you'll have to find your way back home on your own.

Luckily, you have a clever idea to help you with your problem: on the way to your friend's house, you'll keep a list of all the landmarks you see. On the way back, you'll go through the list in reverse and check items off the end of the list every time you pass a landmark so you know where to go next.

BUILDING THE ARRAY WITH PUSH

Let's write some code that would do exactly that. We start off by creating an empty array. The array starts off empty because you don't know what landmarks you'll see until you actually start walking to your friend's house. Then, for each landmark on the way to your friend's house, we'll push a description of that landmark onto the end of the array. Then, when it's time to go home, we'll pop each landmark off the array.

```
var landmarks = [];
landmarks.push("My house");
landmarks.push("Front path");
landmarks.push("Flickering streetlamp");
landmarks.push("Leaky fire hydrant");
landmarks.push("Fire station");
landmarks.push("Cat rescue center");
landmarks.push("My old school");
landmarks.push("My friend's house");
```

Here we create an empty array named landmarks and then use push to store all the landmarks you pass on the way to your friend's house.

GOING IN REVERSE WITH POP

Once you arrive at your friend's house, you can inspect your array of landmarks. Sure enough, the first item is "My house", followed by "Front path", and so on through the end of the array, with the final item "My friend's house". When it's time to go home, all you need to do is pop off the items one by one, and you'll know where to go next.

```
landmarks.pop();
"My friend's house"
landmarks.pop();
"My old school"
landmarks.pop();
"Cat rescue center"
landmarks.pop();
"Fire station"
landmarks.pop();
"Leaky fire hydrant"
```

```
landmarks.pop();
"Flickering streetlamp"
landmarks.pop();
"Front path"
landmarks.pop();
"My house"
```

Phew, you made it home!

Did you notice how the first landmark you put in the array was also the last one you got out of it? And the last landmark you put in the array was the first one that came out? You might have thought that you'd always want the first item you put in to be the first item you get out, but you can see that it's sometimes helpful to go back through an array in reverse.

It's actually very common to use a process like this in larger programs, which is why JavaScript makes pushing and popping so easy.

NOTE *This technique is known as a* stack *in computer-speak. Think of it like a stack of pancakes. Every time you cook a new pancake, it goes on top (like push), and every time you eat one, it comes off the top (like pop). Popping a stack is like going back in time: the last item you pop is the first one you pushed. It's the same with pancakes: the last pancake you eat is the first one that was cooked. In programming jargon, this is also called* Last In, First Out (LIFO). *The alternative to LIFO is* First In, First Out (FIFO). *This is also known as a* queue, *because it acts like a queue (or line) of people. The first person to join the queue is the first person to be served.*

DECISION MAKER

We can use arrays in JavaScript to build a program to make decisions for us (like a Magic 8-Ball). First, though, we need to find out how to get random numbers.

USING MATH.RANDOM()

We can produce random numbers using a special method called Math.random(), which returns a random number between 0 and 1 each time it's called. Here's an example:

```
Math.random();
0.8945409457664937
Math.random();
0.3697543195448816
Math.random();
0.48314980138093233
```

It's important to note that Math.random() always returns a number *less than* 1 and will never return 1 itself.

If you want a bigger number, just multiply the result of calling Math.random(). For example, if you wanted numbers between 0 and 10, you would multiply Math.random() by 10:

```
Math.random() * 10;
7.648027329705656
Math.random() * 10;
9.7565904534421861
Math.random() * 10;
0.21483442978933454
```

ROUNDING DOWN WITH MATH.FLOOR()

We can't use these numbers as array indexes, though, because indexes have to be whole numbers with nothing after the decimal point. To fix that, we need another method called Math.floor(). This takes a number and rounds it down to the whole number below it (basically getting rid of everything after the decimal point).

```
Math.floor(3.7463463);
3
Math.floor(9.9999);
9
Math.floor(0.793423451963426);
0
```

We can combine these two techniques to create a random index. All we need to do is multiply Math.random() by the length of the array and then call `Math.floor()` on that value. For example, if the length of the array were 4, we would do this:

```
Math.floor(Math.random() * 4);
2 // could be 0, 1, 2, or 3
```

Every time you call the code above, it returns a random number from 0 to 3 (including 0 and 3). Because `Math.random()` always returns a value less than 1, `Math.random() * 4` will never return 4 or anything higher than 4.

Now, if we use that random number as an index, we can select a random element from an array:

```
var randomWords = ["Explosion", "Cave", "Princess", "Pen"];
var randomIndex = Math.floor(Math.random() * 4);
randomWords[randomIndex];
"Cave"
```

Here we use `Math.floor(Math.random() * 4);` to pick a random number from 0 to 3. Once that random number is saved to the variable `randomIndex`, we use it as an index to ask for a string from the array `randomWords`.

In fact, we could shorten this by doing away with the `randomIndex` variable altogether and just say:

```
randomWords[Math.floor(Math.random() * 4)];
"Princess"
```

THE COMPLETE DECISION MAKER

Now let's create our array of phrases, and we can use this code to pick a random one. This is our decision maker! I'm using comments here to show some questions you might want to ask your computer.

```
var phrases = [
  "That sounds good",
  "Yes, you should definitely do that",
  "I'm not sure that's a great idea",
  "Maybe not today?",
  "Computer says no."
];
```

```
// Should I have another milkshake?
phrases[Math.floor(Math.random() * 5)];
"I'm not sure that's a great idea"
// Should I do my homework?
phrases[Math.floor(Math.random() * 5)];
"Maybe not today?"
```

Here we created an array called phrases that stores different pieces of advice. Now, every time we have a question, we can ask for a random value from the phrases array, and it will help us make a decision!

Notice that because our array of decisions has five items, we multiply Math.random() by 5. This will always return one of five index positions: 0, 1, 2, 3, or 4.

CREATING A RANDOM INSULT GENERATOR

We can extend the decision maker example to create a program that generates a random insult every time you run it!

```
var randomBodyParts = ["Face", "Nose", "Hair"];
var randomAdjectives = ["Smelly", "Boring", "Stupid"];
var randomWords = ["Fly", "Marmot", "Stick", "Monkey", "Rat"];

// Pick a random body part from the randomBodyParts array:
❶ var randomBodyPart = randomBodyParts[Math.floor(Math.random() * 3)];
// Pick a random adjective from the randomAdjectives array:
❷ var randomAdjective = randomAdjectives[Math.floor(Math.random() * 3)];
// Pick a random word from the randomWords array:
❸ var randomWord = randomWords[Math.floor(Math.random() * 5)];
// Join all the random strings into a sentence:
var randomInsult = "Your " + randomBodyPart + " is like a " + ↵
randomAdjective + " " + randomWord + "!!!";
randomInsult;
"Your Nose is like a Stupid Marmot!!!"
```

Here we have three arrays, and in lines ❶, ❷, and ❸, we use three indexes to pull a random word from each array. Then, we combine them all in the variable randomInsult to create a complete insult. At ❶ and ❷ we're multiplying by 3 because randomAdjectives and randomBodyParts both contain three elements. Likewise, we're multiplying by 5 at ❸ because randomWords is

five elements long. Notice that we add a string with a single space between `randomAdjective` and `randomWord`. Try running this code a few times—you should get a different random insult each time!

TRY IT OUT!

If you wanted to be really clever, you could replace line ❸ with this:

```
var randomWord = randomWords[Math.floor(Math.random() * ↵
randomWords.length)];
```

We know that we always need to multiply `Math.random()` by the length of the array, so using `randomWords.length` means we don't have to change our code if the length of the array changes.

Here's another way to build up our random insult:

```
var randomInsult = ["Your", randomBodyPart, "is", "like", "a", ↵
randomAdjective, randomWord + "!!!"].join(" ");
"Your Hair is like a Smelly Fly!!!"
```

In this example, each word of the sentence is a separate string in an array, which we join with the space character. There's only one place where we *don't* want a space, which is in between `randomWord` and `"!!!"`. In this case, we use the + operator to join those two strings without the space.

WHAT YOU LEARNED

As you've seen, JavaScript arrays are a way to store a list of values. Now you know how to create and work with arrays, and you have many ways of accessing their elements.

Arrays are one of the ways JavaScript gives you to bring multiple values together into one place. In the next chapter, we'll look at objects, which are another way of storing multiple values as a single unit. Objects use *string keys* to access the elements, rather than number indexes.

PROGRAMMING CHALLENGES

Try out these challenges to practice the skills you learned in this chapter.

#1: NEW INSULTS

Make your own random insult generator with your own set of words.

#2: MORE SOPHISTICATED INSULTS

Extend the random insult generator so it generates insults like "Your [body part] is more [adjective] than a [animal]'s [animal body part]." (Hint: You'll need to create another array.)

#3: USE + OR JOIN?

Make two versions of your random insult generator: one that uses the + operator to create the string, and one that creates an array and joins it with " ". Which do you prefer, and why?

#4: JOINING NUMBERS

How could you turn the array [3, 2, 1] into the string "3 is bigger than 2 is bigger than 1" using the join method?

4

OBJECTS

Objects in JavaScript are very similar to arrays, but objects use strings instead of numbers to access the different elements. The strings are called *keys* or *properties*, and the elements they point to are called *values*. Together these pieces of information are called *key-value pairs*. While arrays are mostly used to represent lists of multiple things, objects are often used to represent single things with multiple characteristics, or *attributes*. For example, in Chapter 3 we made several arrays that listed different animal names. But what if we wanted to store different pieces of information about one animal?

CREATING OBJECTS

We could store lots of information about a single animal by creating a JavaScript object. Here's an object that stores information about a three-legged cat named Harmony.

```
var cat = {
  "legs": 3,
  "name": "Harmony",
  "color": "Tortoiseshell"
};
```

Here we create a variable called cat and assign an object to it with three key-value pairs. To create an object, we use curly brackets, {}, instead of the straight brackets we used to make arrays. In between the curly brackets, we enter key-value pairs. The curly brackets and everything in between them are called an *object literal*. An object literal is a way of creating an object by writing out the entire object at once.

NOTE   *We've also seen array literals (for example, ["a", "b", "c"]), number literals (for example, 37), string literals (for example, "moose"), and Boolean literals (true and false). Literal just means that the whole value is written out at once, not built up in multiple steps.*

For example, if you wanted to make an array with the numbers 1 through 3 in it, you could use the array literal [1, 2, 3]. Or you could create an empty array and then use the push method to add 1, 2, and 3 to the array. You don't always know at first what's going to be in your array or object, which is why you can't always use literals to build arrays and objects.

Figure 4-1 shows the basic syntax for creating an object.

When you create an object, the key goes before the colon (:), and the value goes after. The colon acts a bit like an equal sign—the values on the right get assigned to the names on the left, just like when you create variables. In between each key-value pair, you have to put a comma. In our example, the commas are at the ends of the lines—but notice that you don't need a comma after the last key-value pair (color: "Tortoiseshell"). Because it's the last key-value pair, the closing curly bracket comes next, instead of a comma.

```
{ "key1": 99 }
```

The key, which is always a string

The value, which can be of any type

Figure 4-1: The general syntax for creating an object

KEYS WITHOUT QUOTES

In our first object, we put each key in quotation marks, but you don't necessarily need quotes around the keys—this is a valid cat object literal as well:

```
var cat = {
  legs: 3,
  name: "Harmony",
  color: "Tortoiseshell"
};
```

JavaScript knows that the keys will always be strings, which is why you can leave out the quotes. If you don't put quotes around the keys, the unquoted keys have to follow the same rules as variable names: spaces aren't allowed in an unquoted key, for example. If you put the key in quotes, then spaces are allowed:

```
var cat = {
  legs: 3,
  "full name": "Harmony Philomena Snuggly-Pants Morgan",
  color: "Tortoiseshell"
};
```

Note that, while a key is always a string (with or without quotes), the value for that key can be any kind of value, or even a variable containing a value.

You can also put the whole object on one line, but it can be harder to read like that:

```
var cat = { legs: 3, name: "Harmony", color: "Tortoiseshell" };
```

ACCESSING VALUES IN OBJECTS

You can access values in objects using square brackets, just like with arrays. The only difference is that instead of the index (a number), you use the key (a string).

```
cat["name"];
"Harmony"
```

Just as the quotes around keys are optional when you create an object literal, the quotes are also optional when you are accessing keys in objects. If you're not going to use quotes, however, the code looks a bit different:

```
cat.name;
"Harmony"
```

This style is called *dot notation*. Instead of typing the key name in quotes inside square brackets after the object name, we just use a period, followed by the key, without any quotes. As with unquoted keys in object literals, this will work only if the key doesn't contain any special characters, such as spaces.

Instead of looking up a value by typing its key, say you wanted to get a list of all the keys in an object. JavaScript gives you an easy way to do that, using `Object.keys()`:

```
var dog = { name: "Pancake", age: 6, color: "white", bark: "Yip yap ↵
yip!" };
var cat = { name: "Harmony", age: 8, color: "tortoiseshell" };
Object.keys(dog);
["name", "age", "color", "bark"]
Object.keys(cat);
["name", "age", "color"]
```

`Object.keys(anyObject)` returns an array containing all the keys of *anyObject*.

ADDING VALUES TO OBJECTS

An empty object is just like an empty array, but it uses curly brackets, { }, instead of square brackets:

```
var object = {};
```

You can add items to an object just as you'd add items to an array, but you use strings instead of numbers:

```
var cat = {};
cat["legs"] = 3;
cat["name"] = "Harmony";
cat["color"] = "Tortoiseshell";
cat;
{ color: "Tortoiseshell", legs: 3, name: "Harmony" }
```

Here, we started with an empty object named cat. Then we added three key-value pairs, one by one. Then, we type cat;, and the browser shows the contents of the object. Different browsers may output objects differently, though. For example, Chrome (at the time I'm writing this) outputs the cat object like this:

```
Object {legs: 3, name: "Harmony", color: "Tortoiseshell"}
```

While Chrome prints out the keys in that order (legs, name, color), other browsers may print them out differently. This is because JavaScript doesn't store objects with their keys in any particular order.

Arrays obviously have a certain order: index 0 is before index 1, and index 3 is after index 2. But with objects, there's no obvious way to order each item. Should color go before legs or after? There's no "correct" answer to this question, so objects simply store keys without assigning them any particular order, and as a result different browsers will print the keys in different orders. For this reason, you should never write a program that relies on object keys being in a precise order.

ADDING KEYS WITH DOT NOTATION

You can also use dot notation when adding new keys. Let's try the previous example, where we started with an empty object and added keys to it, but this time we'll use dot notation:

```
var cat = {};
cat.legs = 3;
cat.name = "Harmony";
cat.color = "Tortoiseshell";
```

If you ask for a property that JavaScript doesn't know about, it returns the special value undefined. undefined just means "There's nothing here!" For example:

```
var dog = {
  name: "Pancake",
  legs: 4,
  isAwesome: true
};
dog.isBrown;
undefined
```

Here we define three properties for dog: name, legs, and isAwesome. We didn't define isBrown, so dog.isBrown returns undefined.

COMBINING ARRAYS AND OBJECTS

So far, we've looked only at arrays and objects that contain simple types like numbers and strings. But there's nothing stopping you from using another array or object as a value in an array or object.

For example, an array of dinosaur objects might look like this:

```
var dinosaurs = [
  { name: "Tyrannosaurus Rex", period: "Late Cretaceous" },
  { name: "Stegosaurus", period: "Late Jurassic" },
  { name: "Plateosaurus", period: "Triassic" }
];
```

To get all the information about the first dinosaur, you can use the same technique we used before, entering the index in square brackets:

```
dinosaurs[0];
{ name: "Tyrannosaurus Rex", period: "Late Cretaceous" }
```

If you want to get only the name of the first dinosaur, you can just add the object key in square brackets after the array index:

```
dinosaurs[0]["name"];
"Tyrannosaurus Rex"
```

Or, you can use dot notation, like this:

```
dinosaurs[1].period;
"Late Jurassic"
```

NOTE   *You can use dot notation only with objects, not with arrays.*

AN ARRAY OF FRIENDS

Let's look at a more complex example now. We'll create an array of friend objects, where each object also contains an array. First, we'll make the objects, and then we can put them all into an array.

```
var anna = { name: "Anna", age: 11, luckyNumbers: [2, 4, 8, 16] };
var dave = { name: "Dave", age: 5, luckyNumbers: [3, 9, 40] };
var kate = { name: "Kate", age: 9, luckyNumbers: [1, 2, 3] };
```

First, we make three objects and save them into variables called anna, dave, and kate. Each object has three keys: name, age, and luckyNumbers. Each name key has a string value assigned to it, each age key has a single number value assigned to it, and each luckyNumbers key has an array assigned to it, containing a few different numbers.

Next we'll make an array of our friends:

```
var friends = [anna, dave, kate];
```

Now we have an array saved to the variable friends with three elements: anna, dave, and kate (which each refer to objects). You can retrieve one of these objects using its index in the array:

```
friends[1];
{ name: "Dave", age: 5, luckyNumbers: Array[3] }
```

This retrieves the second object in the array, dave (at index 1). Chrome prints out Array[3] for the luckyNumbers array, which is just its way of saying, "This is a three-element array." (You can use Chrome to see what's in that array; see "Exploring Objects in the Console" on page 71.) We can also retrieve a value within an object by entering the index of the object in square brackets followed by the key we want:

```
friends[2].name
"Kate"
```

This code asks for the element at index 2, which is the variable named kate, and then asks for the property in that object under the key "name", which is "Kate". We could even retrieve a value from an array that's inside one of the objects inside the friends array, like so:

```
friends[0].luckyNumbers[1];
4
```

Figure 4-2 shows each index. friends[0] is the element at index 0 in the friends array, which is the object anna. friends[0].luckyNumbers is the array [2, 4, 8, 16] from the object called anna. Finally, friends[0].luckyNumbers[1] is index 1 in that array, which is the number value 4.

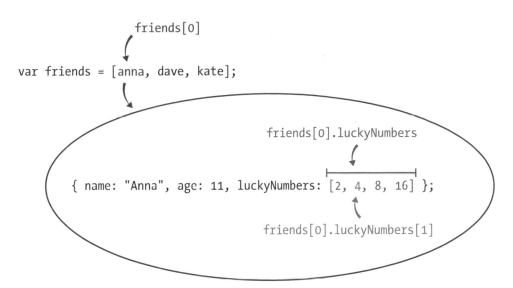

Figure 4-2: Accessing nested values

EXPLORING OBJECTS IN THE CONSOLE

Chrome will let you dig into objects that you print out in the console. For example, if you type . . .

```
friends[1];
```

Chrome will display the output shown in Figure 4-3.

```
friends[1];
▶ Object {name: "Dave", age: 5, LuckyNumbers: Array[3]}
```

Figure 4-3: How an object is displayed in the Chrome interpreter

The triangle on the left means that this object can be expanded. Click the object to expand it, and you'll see what's shown in Figure 4-4.

```
friends[1];
▼ Object {name: "Dave", age: 5, LuckyNumbers: Array[3]} ⓘ
    age: 5
  ▶ luckyNumbers: Array[3]
    name: "Dave"
  ▶ __proto__: Object
```

Figure 4-4: Expanding the object

You can expand luckyNumbers, too, by clicking it (see Figure 4-5).

```
friends[1];
▼ Object {name: "Dave", age: 5, LuckyNumbers: Array[3]} ⓘ
    age: 5
  ▼ luckyNumbers: Array[3]
      0: 3
      1: 9
      2: 40
      length: 3
    ▶ __proto__: Array[0]
    name: "Dave"
  ▶ __proto__: Object
```

Figure 4-5: Expanding an array within the object

Don't worry about those __proto__ properties—they have to do with the object's *prototype*. We'll look at prototypes later, in Chapter 12. Also, you'll notice that the interpreter shows the value of the array's length property.

You can also view the entire friends array and expand each element in the array, as shown in Figure 4-6.

```
friends
[▼ Object ⓘ            , ▼ Object ⓘ            , ▼ Object ⓘ                      ]
    age: 11                 age: 5                  age: 9
  ▶ luckyNumbers: Array[4]   ▶ luckyNumbers: Array[3]   ▶ luckyNumbers: Array[3]
    name: "Anna"            name: "Dave"            name: "Kate"
  ▶ __proto__: Object      ▶ __proto__: Object      ▶ __proto__: Object
```

Figure 4-6: All three objects from the friends array, as shown in the Chrome interpreter

USEFUL THINGS TO DO WITH OBJECTS

Now that you know a few different ways to create objects and add properties to them, let's put what we've learned to use by trying out some simple programs.

KEEPING TRACK OF OWED MONEY

Let's say you've decided to start a bank. You lend your friends money, and you want to have a way to keep track of how much money each of them owes you.

You can use an object as a way of linking a string and a value together. In this case, the string would be your friend's name, and the value would be the amount of money he or she owes you. Let's have a look.

```
❶ var owedMoney = {};
❷ owedMoney["Jimmy"] = 5;
❸ owedMoney["Anna"] = 7;
❹ owedMoney["Jimmy"];
  5
❺ owedMoney["Jinen"];
  undefined
```

At ❶, we create a new empty object called owedMoney. At ❷, we assign the value 5 to the key "Jimmy". We do the same thing at ❸, assigning the value 7 to the key "Anna". At ❹, we ask for the value associated with the key "Jimmy", which is 5. Then at ❺, we ask for the value associated with the key "Jinen", which is undefined because we didn't set it.

Now let's imagine that Jimmy borrows some more money (say, $3). We can update our object and add 3 to the amount Jimmy owes with the plus-equals operator (+=) that you saw in Chapter 2.

```
owedMoney["Jimmy"] += 3;
owedMoney["Jimmy"];
8
```

This is like saying owedMoney["Jimmy"] = owedMoney["Jimmy"] + 3. We can also look at the entire object to see how much money each friend owes us:

```
owedMoney;
{ Jimmy: 8, Anna: 7 }
```

STORING INFORMATION ABOUT YOUR MOVIES

Let's say you have a large collection of movies on DVD and Blu-ray. Wouldn't it be great to have the information about those movies on your computer so you can find out about each movie easily?

You can create an object to store information about your movies, where every key is a movie title, and every value is another object containing information about the movie. Values in objects can be objects themselves!

```
var movies = {
  "Finding Nemo": {
    releaseDate: 2003,
    duration: 100,
    actors: ["Albert Brooks", "Ellen DeGeneres", "Alexander Gould"],
    format: "DVD"
  },
  "Star Wars: Episode VI - Return of the Jedi": {
    releaseDate: 1983,
    duration: 134,
    actors: ["Mark Hamill", "Harrison Ford", "Carrie Fisher"],
    format: "DVD"
  },
  "Harry Potter and the Goblet of Fire": {
    releaseDate: 2005,
    duration: 157,
    actors: ["Daniel Radcliffe", "Emma Watson", "Rupert Grint"],
    format: "Blu-ray"
  }
};
```

You might have noticed that I used quotes for the movie titles (the keys in the outer object) but not for the keys in the inner objects. That's because the movie titles need to have spaces—otherwise, I'd have to type each title like `StarWarsEpisodeVIReturnOfTheJedi`, and that's just silly! I didn't need quotes for the keys in the inner objects, so I left them off. It can make code look a bit cleaner when there aren't unnecessary punctuation marks in it.

Now, when you want information about a movie, it's easy to find:

```
var findingNemo = movies["Finding Nemo"];
findingNemo.duration;
100
findingNemo.format;
"DVD"
```

Here we save the movie information about *Finding Nemo* into a variable called `findingNemo`. We can then look at the properties of this object (like `duration` and `format`) to find out about the movie.

You can also easily add new movies to your collection:

```
var cars = {
  releaseDate: 2006,
  duration: 117,
  actors: ["Owen Wilson", "Bonnie Hunt", "Paul Newman"],
  format: "Blu-ray"
};
movies["Cars"] = cars;
```

Here we create a new object of movie information about *Cars*. We then insert this into the `movies` object, under the key `"Cars"`.

Now that you're building up your collection, you might want to find an easy way to list the names of all your movies. That's where `Object.keys` comes in:

```
Object.keys(movies);
["Finding Nemo", "Star Wars: Episode VI - Return of the Jedi", "Harry
Potter and the Goblet of Fire", "Cars"]
```

WHAT YOU LEARNED

Now you've seen how objects work in JavaScript. They're a lot like arrays, because you can use them to hold lots of pieces of information together in one unit. One major difference is that you use strings to access elements in an object and you use numbers to access elements in an array. For this reason, arrays are ordered, while objects are not.

We'll be doing a lot more with objects in later chapters, once we've learned about more of JavaScript's features. In the next chapter, we'll look at *conditionals* and *loops*, which are both ways of adding structure to our programs to make them more powerful.

PROGRAMMING CHALLENGES

Try out these challenges to practice working with objects.

#1: SCOREKEEPER

Imagine you're playing a game with some friends and you want to keep track of the score. Create an object called scores. The keys will be the names of your friends, and the values will be the scores (which will all start at 0). As the players earn points, you must increase their scores. How would you increase a player's score in the scores object?

#2: DIGGING INTO OBJECTS AND ARRAYS

Say you had the following object:

```
var myCrazyObject = {
  "name": "A ridiculous object",
  "some array": [7, 9, { purpose: "confusion", number: 123 }, 3.3],
  "random animal": "Banana Shark"
};
```

How would you get the number 123 out of this object using one line of JavaScript? Try it out in the console to see if you're right.

5

THE BASICS OF HTML

The browser-based JavaScript console that we've been using so far is great for trying out small snippets of code, but in order to create actual programs, we'll need something a bit more flexible, like a web page with some JavaScript in it. In this chapter, we'll learn how to create a basic HTML web page.

HTML (HyperText Markup Language) is the language used to make web pages. The word *HyperText* refers to text that is connected by *hyperlinks*, the links on a web page. A *markup language* is used to annotate documents so that they're not just plaintext. The markup tells software (like a web browser) how to display the text and what to do with it.

In this chapter, I'll show you how to write HTML documents in a *text editor*, a simple program designed for writing plaintext files without the formatting you find in word processors like Microsoft Word. Word-processed documents contain *formatted* text (with different fonts, type colors, font sizes, etc.), and word processors are designed to make it easy to change the formatting of the text. Word processors usually allow you to insert images and graphics as well.

Plaintext files contain just text, without any information about the font, color, size, and so on. You can't put an image in a text file unless you make it out of text—like this cat, for example.

```
 /\_/\
=(  °w°  )=
 )   (  //
(__ __)//
```

TEXT EDITORS

We'll write our HTML in the *cross-platform* (compatible with Windows, Mac OS, and Linux) Sublime Text editor. You can download and use Sublime Text for free, but after a while you'll be asked to pay for a license. If you don't like that idea, I've listed some completely free alternatives below. My instructions in this chapter are geared toward Sublime Text, but since text editors are relatively simple, the instructions should work pretty much the same for any editor.

- Gedit is a cross-platform text editor from the GNOME project (*https://wiki.gnome.org/Apps/Gedit/*).
- For Microsoft Windows, Notepad++ (*http://notepad-plus-plus .org/*) is another good alternative.
- On Mac OS, TextWrangler (*http://www.barebones.com/ products/textwrangler/*) is a good option.

To install Sublime Text, visit *http://www.sublimetext.com/*. Installation instructions differ for each operating system, but you should find them pretty clear. If you run into any problems, try the Support section at the Sublime Text home page.

OUR FIRST HTML DOCUMENT

Once you've installed Sublime Text, start the program and create a new file with **File ▸ New File**. Next, choose **File ▸ Save** to save your new, blank file; name it *page.html* and save it to your desktop.

Now it's time to write some HTML. Enter the following text into your *page.html* file:

```
<h1>Hello world!</h1>
<p>My first web page.</p>
```

Save your updated version of *page.html* with **File ▸ Save**. Now let's see what that page would look like in a web browser. Open Chrome, choose **File ▸ Open File**, and select *page.html* from your desktop. You should see something like Figure 5-1.

Figure 5-1: Your first HTML page in Chrome

You've just created your first HTML document! Although you're viewing it in your web browser, it's not actually on the Internet. Chrome is opening your page locally and just reading your markup tags to figure out what to do with its text.

TAGS AND ELEMENTS

HTML documents are made up of *elements*. An element starts with a *start tag* and ends with an *end tag*. For example, in our document so far we have two elements: h1 and p. The h1 element starts with the start tag <h1> and ends with the end tag </h1>. The p element starts with the start tag <p> and ends with the end tag </p>. Anything between the opening and closing tags is the *content* of the element.

Start tags consist of the element name surrounded by angle brackets: < and >. End tags are the same, but they have a forward slash (/) before the element name.

HEADING ELEMENTS

Each element has a special meaning and use. For example, the h1 element means "This is a top-level heading." The content you put in between the opening and closing <h1> tags is displayed by the browser on its own line, in a large, bold font.

There are six levels of heading elements in HTML: h1, h2, h3, h4, h5, and h6. They look like this:

```
<h1>First-level heading</h1>
<h2>Second-level heading</h2>
<h3>Third-level heading</h3>
<h4>Fourth-level heading</h4>
<h5>Fifth-level heading</h5>
<h6>Sixth-level heading</h6>
```

Figure 5-2 shows how the headings look on a web page.

Figure 5-2: The different heading elements

THE P ELEMENT

The p element is used to define separate paragraphs of text. Any text you put between <p> tags will display in a separate paragraph, with some space above and below the paragraph. Let's try creating multiple p elements. Add this new line to your *page.html* document (the old lines are shown in gray):

```
<h1>Hello world!</h1>
<p>My first web page.</p>
<p>Let's add another paragraph.</p>
```

Figure 5-3 shows the web page with the new paragraph.

Figure 5-3: The same page but with an extra paragraph

Notice that the paragraphs appear on different lines and are separated by a bit of space. This is all because of the <p> tags.

WHITESPACE IN HTML AND BLOCK-LEVEL ELEMENTS

What would our page look like without the tags? Let's take a look:

```
Hello world!
My first web page.
Let's add another paragraph.
```

Figure 5-4 shows our page without any tags.

Figure 5-4: The same page but with no HTML tags

Oh no! Not only have we lost the formatting, but everything's on one long line! The reason is that in HTML, all *whitespace* is collapsed into a single space. Whitespace means any character that results in blank space on the page—for example, the space character, the tab character, and the newline character (the character that is inserted when you press ENTER or RETURN). Any blank lines you insert between two pieces of text in an HTML document will get collapsed into a single space.

The p and h1 elements are called *block-level* elements because they display their content in a separate block, starting on a new line, and with any following content on a new line.

INLINE ELEMENTS

Let's add two more elements to our document, em and strong:

```
<h1>Hello world!</h1>
<p>My <em>first</em> <strong>web page</strong>.</p>
<p>Let's add another <strong><em>paragraph</em></strong>.</p>
```

Figure 5-5 shows what the page looks like with the new tags.

Figure 5-5: The em and strong elements

The em element makes its content italic. The strong element makes its content bold. The em and strong elements are both *inline* elements, which means that they don't put their content onto a new line, as block-level elements do.

To make content bold *and* italic, put it inside both tags. Notice in the previous example that the bold italic text has the tags in this order: `<strong><em>paragraph</em></strong>`. It's important to properly *nest* elements. Nesting means that if an element is inside another element, its opening and closing tags should both be inside the parent element. For example, this is not allowed:

```
<strong><em>paragraph</strong></em>
```

In this case, the closing `</strong>` tag comes before the closing `</em>` tag. Browsers generally won't tell you when you've made a mistake like this, but getting nesting wrong can cause your pages to break in strange ways.

A FULL HTML DOCUMENT

What we've looked at so far is really just a snippet of HTML. A full HTML document requires some extra elements. Let's take a look at an example of a complete HTML document and what each part means. Update your *page.html* file with these new elements:

```
<!DOCTYPE html>
<html>
<head>
    <title>My first proper HTML page</title>
</head>

<body>
    <h1>Hello world!</h1>
    <p>My <em>first</em> <strong>web page</strong>.</p>
    <p>Let's add another <strong><em>paragraph</em></strong>.</p>
</body>
</html>
```

NOTE *Sublime Text should automatically indent certain lines for you, as shown in this example. It's actually identifying lines based on their tags (like `<html>`, `<h1>`, and so on) and indenting them according to their nesting. Sublime Text doesn't indent the `<head>` and `<body>` tags, though some editors do.*

Figure 5-6 shows the complete HTML document.

Figure 5-6: The complete HTML document

Let's take a walk through the elements in our *page.html* file. The `<!DOCTYPE html>` tag is just a declaration. It simply says, "This is an HTML document." Next comes the opening `<html>` tag (the closing `</html>` tag is at the very end). All HTML documents must have an `html` element as their outermost element.

There are two elements inside the `html` element: `head` and `body`. The `head` element contains certain information about your HTML document, such as the `title` element, which contains the document's title. For example, notice that in Figure 5-6, the title in the browser tab—"My first proper HTML page"—matches what we entered in the `title` element. The `title` element is contained inside the `head` element, which is contained inside the `html` element.

The `body` element contains the content that will be displayed in the browser. Here, we've just copied the HTML from earlier in the chapter.

HTML HIERARCHY

HTML elements have a clear hierarchy, or order, and can be thought of as a kind of upside-down tree. You can see how our document would look as a tree in Figure 5-7.

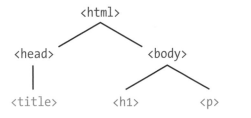

Figure 5-7: The elements from Figure 5-6, shown as a tree

The top element is the html element. It contains the head and body elements. The head contains the title element, and the body contains the h1 and p elements. The browser interprets your HTML according to this hierarchy. We'll look at how to change the document structure later, in Chapter 9.

Figure 5-8 shows another way of visualizing the HTML hierarchy, as a set of nested boxes.

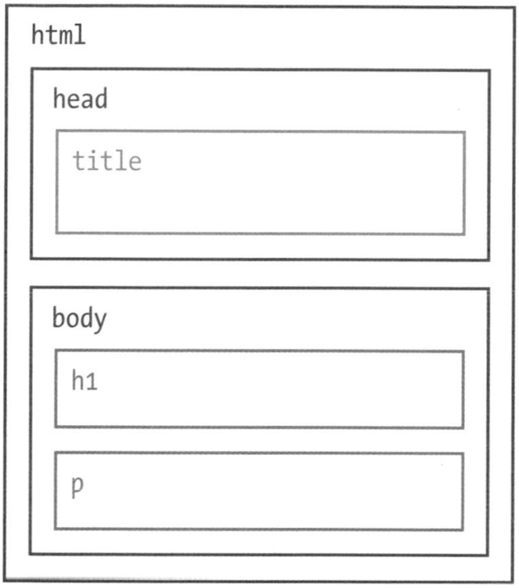

Figure 5-8: The HTML hierarchy, shown as nested boxes

ADDING LINKS TO YOUR HTML

Earlier in this chapter, we learned that the *HT* in *HTML* stands for HyperText, or linked text. HTML documents can contain *hyperlinks* (*links* for short) that take you to other web pages. The a element (for *anchor*) creates a link element.

Modify your HTML document to match the following example: delete the second p element and the <em> and <strong> tags, and then add the new colored code to create a link to *http://xkcd.com/*:

```
<!DOCTYPE html>
<html>
<head>
    <title>My first proper HTML page</title>
</head>
```

```
<body>
    <h1>Hello world!</h1>
    <p>My first web page.</p>
    <p><a href="http://xkcd.com">Click here</a> to read some excellent
comics.</p>
</body>
</html>
```

Now save and open your page in your browser, and it should look like Figure 5-9.

Figure 5-9: A web page containing a link to
http://xkcd.com/

If you click that link, your browser should go to the xkcd web-site, *http://xkcd.com/*. Once you've had your fill of geeky comics, click the back button to return to your page.

LINK ATTRIBUTES

Let's take a closer look at how we created that HTML link. To tell the browser where to go when you click the a element, we added something called an *attribute* to the anchor element. Attributes in HTML elements are similar to key-value pairs in JavaScript objects. Every attribute has a name and a value. Here's the xkcd link we created again:

```
<a href="http://xkcd.com">Click here</a>
```

In this case, the attribute name is href and the attribute value is "http://xkcd.com". The name href stands for *hypertext reference*, which is a fancy way of saying "web address."

Figure 5-10 shows all the parts of the link.

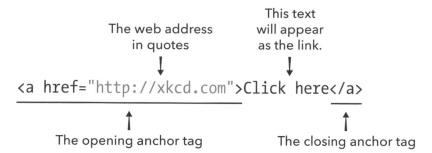

Figure 5-10: The basic syntax for creating a hyperlink

The link will take you to whatever web address is entered as the value of the href attribute.

TITLE ATTRIBUTES

Another attribute we can add to links is the title attribute. This attribute sets the text you see when you hover your mouse over a link. For example, change the opening <a> tag so it looks like this:

```
<a href="http://xkcd.com" title="xkcd: Land of geeky comics!">Click here</a>
```

Now reload the page. When you hover your cursor over the link, you should see the text "xkcd: Land of geeky comics!" floating above the page, as shown in Figure 5-11.

Figure 5-11: A web page containing a link to http://xkcd.com/ with a title attribute

WHAT YOU LEARNED

In this chapter, you learned the basics of HTML, the language
used to create web pages. We created a simple page containing a
link to another page.

In the next chapter, we'll look at how to embed JavaScript in
our web page. This will make it much easier to create larger programs as we explore more features of JavaScript in the next few
chapters.

This is a book on JavaScript, not HTML, so I've introduced
only the very basics of creating HTML documents. Here are some
resources where you can learn more about HTML:

- The Mozilla Developer Network's Introduction to HTML:
  *https://developer.mozilla.org/en-US/docs/Web/Guide/HTML/
  Introduction/*
- Codecademy's HTML and CSS course: *http://www.codecademy
  .com/tracks/web/*
- Mozilla Webmaker: *https://webmaker.org/*

6
CONDITIONALS AND LOOPS

Conditionals and loops are two of the most important concepts in JavaScript. A *conditional* says, "If something is true, do this. Otherwise, do that." For example, if you do your homework, you can have ice cream, but if you don't do your homework, you don't get the ice cream. A *loop* says, "As long as something is true, keep doing this." For example, as long as you are thirsty, keep drinking water.

Conditionals and loops are powerful concepts that are key to any sophisticated program. They are called *control structures* because they allow you to control which parts of your code are executed when and how often they're executed, based on certain conditions you define.

We first need to go over how to embed JavaScript in our HTML file so we can start creating longer programs than we've looked at so far.

EMBEDDING JAVASCRIPT IN HTML

Here is the HTML file we created in Chapter 5, with additions in color and the existing text in gray. (To make this example a little simpler, I've also deleted the link to xkcd.)

```
<!DOCTYPE html>
<html>
<head>
    <title>My first proper HTML page</title>
</head>

<body>
    <h1>Hello world!</h1>
    <p>My first web page.</p>
    <script>
    var message = "Hello world!";
    console.log(message);
    </script>
</body>
</html>
```

Here we've added a new element, called script. This is a special element in HTML. With most HTML elements, the content between the opening and closing tags is displayed on the page. With script, on the other hand, everything between the tags is treated as JavaScript and run by the JavaScript interpreter.

Now let's look at the code inside the script element:

```
var message = "Hello world!";
❶ console.log(message);
```

Running JavaScript in an HTML file is quite different from running it in the console. When you're using the JavaScript console, each line you type is run as soon as you press ENTER, and the value of that line is printed out to the console. In a web page, the JavaScript is all run from top to bottom at one time, and nothing is automatically printed to the console, unless we tell the browser otherwise. We can use `console.log` to print things out, which will make it easier to see what's going on as we run our programs. The `console.log` method takes any value and prints out, or *logs*, that value to the console. For example, if you load the HTML file from the beginning of this section with the JavaScript console open, you'll see this:

```
Hello world!
```

Calling `console.log(message)` at ❶ caused the string `"Hello world!"` to be printed to the console.

Now that you know how to write longer programs with JavaScript, you can start learning about conditionals.

CONDITIONALS

There are two forms of conditional statements in JavaScript: `if` statements and `if...else` statements. An `if` statement is used to execute a piece of code if something is true. For example, *if* you've been good, you get a treat. An `if...else` statement executes one piece of code if something is true and another if not. For example, *if* you've been good, you get a treat; *else*, you get grounded.

IF STATEMENTS

The `if` statement is the simplest of JavaScript's control structures. It's used to run code only if a condition is true. Return to your

HTML file and replace the two lines inside the `script` element with this:

```
❶ var name = "Nicholas";
❷ console.log("Hello " + name);
❸ if (name.length > 7) {
❹   console.log("Wow, you have a REALLY long name!");
  }
```

First, at ❶ we create a variable called `name` and set its value to the string `"Nicholas"`. Then we use `console.log` to log the string `"Hello Nicholas"` at ❷.

At ❸ we use an `if` statement to check whether the length of `name` is greater than 7. If it is, the console will display `"Wow, you have a REALLY long name!"`, using `console.log` at ❹.

As Figure 6-1 shows, an `if` statement has two main parts: the condition and the body. The *condition* should be a Boolean value. The *body* is one or more lines of JavaScript code, which are executed if the condition is true.

The `if` statement
checks whether this
condition is true.

```
if (condition) {
    console.log("Do something");
}
```

Some code to run
if the condition is true,
called the *body*

Figure 6-1: The general structure of an `if` statement

When you load your HTML page with this JavaScript in it, you should see the following in the console:

```
Hello Nicholas
Wow, you have a REALLY long name!
```

Because the name *Nicholas* has eight characters, `name.length` returns 8. Therefore, the condition `name.length > 7` is true, which causes the body of the `if` statement to be run, resulting in this somewhat startling message being logged. To avoid triggering the if condition, change the name *Nicholas* to *Nick* (leaving the rest of the code as is):

```
var name = "Nick";
```

Now save the file and reload the page. This time, the condition `name.length > 7` is not true, because `name.length` is 4. That means that the body of the `if` statement is not run and all that gets printed to the console is this:

```
Hello Nick
```

The body of an `if` statement is executed only if the condition is true. When the condition is `false`, the interpreter simply skips over the `if` statement and moves on to the next line.

IF...ELSE STATEMENTS

As I said before, an `if` statement will execute its body only if the condition is `true`. If you want something else to happen when the condition is `false`, you need to use an `if...else` statement.

Let's extend the example from earlier:

```
var name = "Nicholas";
console.log("Hello " + name);
if (name.length > 7) {
  console.log("Wow, you have a REALLY long name!"),
} else {
  console.log("Your name isn't very long.");
}
```

This does the same thing as before, except that if the name *isn't* longer than seven characters, it prints out an alternative message.

As Figure 6-2 shows, `if...else` statements look like `if` statements, but with two bodies. The keyword `else` is placed between the two bodies. In an `if...else` statement, the first body is run if the condition is `true`; otherwise, the second body is run.

Something that is
either true or false

↓

Some code to run if the
condition is true

↙

```
if (condition) {
  console.log("Do something");
} else {
  console.log("Do something else!");
}
```

↖

Some code to run
if the condition is false

Figure 6-2: The general structure of an if...else statement

CHAINING IF...ELSE STATEMENTS

Often we need to check a sequence of conditions and do something when one of them is true. For example, say you're ordering Chinese food and you're choosing what to eat. Your favorite Chinese dish is lemon chicken, so you'll have that if it's on the menu. If it's not, you'll have beef with black bean sauce. If *that*'s not on the menu, you'll have sweet and sour pork. In the rare case that none of those options is available, you'll have egg fried rice, because you know all the Chinese restaurants you go to will have that.

```
var lemonChicken = false;
var beefWithBlackBean = true;
var sweetAndSourPork = true;

if (lemonChicken) {
  console.log("Great! I'm having lemon chicken!");
} else if (beefWithBlackBean) {
  console.log("I'm having the beef.");
} else if (sweetAndSourPork) {
  console.log("OK, I'll have the pork.");
} else {
  console.log("Well, I guess I'll have rice then.");
}
```

To create a chain of if...else statements, start with a normal if statement and, after the closing brace of its body, enter the keywords else if, followed by another condition and another body. You can keep doing this until you run out of conditions; there's no limit to the number of conditions. The final else section will run if none of the conditions is true. Figure 6-3 shows a generic chain of if...else statements.

Each condition has code to run
if the condition is true.

```
if (condition1) {
  console.log("Do this if condition 1 is true");
} else if (condition2) {
  console.log("Do this if condition 2 is true");
} else if (condition3) {
  console.log("Do this if condition 3 is true");
} else {
  console.log("Do this otherwise");
}
```

Some code to run
if all the conditions are false

Figure 6-3: Chaining multiple if...else statements

You can read this as follows:

1. If the first condition is true, execute the first body.
2. Otherwise, if the second condition is true, execute the second body.
3. Otherwise, if the third condition is true, execute the third body.
4. Otherwise, execute the else body.

When you have a chain of if...else statements like this with a final else section, you can be sure that one (and only one) of the bodies will be run. As soon as a true condition is found, its associated body is run, and none of the other conditions is checked. If we run the code in the previous example, I'm having the beef will be printed to the console, because beefWithBlackBean is the first condition that's found to be true in the if...else chain. If none of the conditions is true, the else body is run.

There's one other thing to note: you don't necessarily have to include the final else. If you don't, though, and none of the conditions is true, then nothing inside the if...else chain will be executed.

```
var lemonChicken = false;
var beefWithBlackBean = false;
var sweetAndSourPork = false;

if (lemonChicken) {
  console.log("Great! I'm having lemon chicken!");
} else if (beefWithBlackBean) {
  console.log("I'm having the beef.");
} else if (sweetAndSourPork) {
  console.log("OK, I'll have the pork.");
}
```

In this example, we've left out the final else section. Because none of your favorite foods is available, nothing gets printed out (and it looks like you're not going to have anything to eat!).

TRY IT OUT!

Write a program with a name variable. If name is your name, print out Hello me!; otherwise, print Hello stranger!. (Hint: Use === to compare name to your name.)

Next, rewrite the program so it'll say hi to your dad if name is set to your dad's name or hi to your mom if name is your mom's name. If it's neither of them, say Hello stranger! as before.

LOOPS

As we've seen, conditionals allow you to run a piece of code once if a condition is true. Loops, on the other hand, allow you to run a piece of code multiple times, depending on whether a condition remains true. For example, while there's food on your plate, you should keep eating; or, while you still have dirt on your face, you should keep washing.

WHILE LOOPS

The simplest kind of loop is a while loop. A while loop repeatedly executes its body until a particular condition stops being true. By writing a while loop, you are saying, "Keep doing this while this condition is true. Stop when the condition becomes false."

As Figure 6-4 shows, while loops start with the while keyword, followed by a condition in parentheses and then a body in braces.

This condition is checked
each time the loop repeats.

```
while (condition) {
  console.log("Do something");
  i++;
}
```

Some code to run and repeat
as long as the condition is true
(something in here should change things
so the condition is eventually false)

Figure 6-4: The general structure of a while loop

Like an if statement, the body of a while loop is executed if the condition is true. *Unlike* an if statement, after the body is executed, the condition is checked again, and if it's still true, the body runs again. This cycle goes on until the condition is false.

COUNTING SHEEP WITH A WHILE LOOP

Say you're having trouble sleeping and you want to count sheep. But you're a programmer, so why not write a program to count sheep for you?

```
var sheepCounted = 0;
❶ while (sheepCounted < 10) {
❷ console.log("I have counted " + sheepCounted + " sheep!");
    sheepCounted++;
  }
  console.log("Zzzzzzzzzz");
```

We create a variable called sheepCounted and set its value to 0. When we reach the while loop ❶, we check to see whether sheepCounted is less than 10. Because 0 is less than 10, the code inside the braces (the body of the loop) ❷ runs, and "I have counted " + sheepCounted + " sheep!" is logged as "I have counted 0 sheep!" Next, sheepCounted++ adds 1 to the value of sheepCounted, and we go back to the start of the loop, over and over:

```
I have counted 0 sheep!
I have counted 1 sheep!
I have counted 2 sheep!
I have counted 3 sheep!
I have counted 4 sheep!
I have counted 5 sheep!
I have counted 6 sheep!
I have counted 7 sheep!
I have counted 8 sheep!
I have counted 9 sheep!
Zzzzzzzzzzz
```

This repeats until sheepCounted becomes 10, at which point the condition becomes false (10 is *not* less than 10), and the program moves on to whatever comes after the loop. In this case, it prints Zzzzzzzzzzz.

PREVENTING INFINITE LOOPS

Keep this in mind when you're using loops: if the condition you set never becomes false, your loop will loop forever (or at least until you quit your browser). For example, if you left out the line sheepCounted++;, then sheepCounted would remain 0, and the output would look like this:

```
I have counted 0 sheep!
I have counted 0 sheep!
I have counted 0 sheep!
I have counted 0 sheep!
...
```

Because there's nothing to stop it, the program would keep doing this forever! This is called an *infinite loop*.

FOR LOOPS

for loops make it easier to write loops that create a variable, loop until a condition is true, and update the variable at the end of each turn around the loop. When setting up a for loop, you create a variable, specify the condition, and say how the variable should change after each cycle—all before you reach the body of the loop. For example, here's how we could use a for loop to count sheep:

```
for (var sheepCounted = 0; sheepCounted < 10; sheepCounted++) {
  console.log("I have counted " + sheepCounted + " sheep!");
}
console.log("Zzzzzzzzzzz");
```

As Figure 6-5 shows, there are three parts to this for loop, separated by semicolons: the setup, condition, and increment.

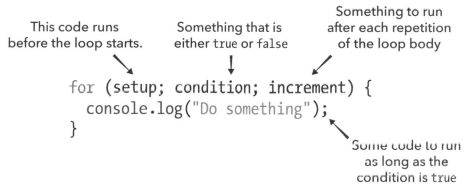

Figure 6-5: The general structure of a for loop

The *setup* (var sheepCounted = 0) is run before the loop starts. It's generally used to create a variable to track the number of times the loop has run. Here we create the variable sheepCounted with an initial value of 0.

The *condition* (sheepCounted < 10) is checked before each run of the loop body. If the condition is true, the body is executed; if it's false, the loop stops. In this case, the loop will stop once sheepCounted is no longer less than 10.

The *increment* (sheepCounted++) is run after every execution of the loop body. It's generally used to update the looping variable. Here, we use it to add 1 to sheepCounted each time the loop runs.

for loops are often used to do something a set number of times. For example, this program will say Hello! three times.

```javascript
var timesToSayHello = 3;
for (var i = 0; i < timesToSayHello; i++) {
  console.log("Hello!");
}
```

Here is the output:

```
Hello!
Hello!
Hello!
```

If we were the JavaScript interpreter running this code, we would first create a variable called timesToSayHello and set it to 3. When we reach the for loop, we run the setup, which creates a variable i and sets it to 0. Next, we check the condition. Because i is equal to 0 and timesToSayHello is 3, the condition is true, so we enter the loop body, which simply outputs the string "Hello!". We then run the increment, which increases i to 1.

Now we check the condition again. It's still true, so we run the body and increment again. This happens repeatedly until i is equal to 3. At this point, the condition is false (3 is not less than 3), so we exit the loop.

USING FOR LOOPS WITH ARRAYS AND STRINGS

One very common use of for loops is to do something with every element in an array or every character in a string. For example, here is a for loop that prints out the animals in a zoo:

```javascript
var animals = ["Lion", "Flamingo", "Polar Bear", "Boa Constrictor"];

for (var i = 0; i < animals.length; i++) {
  console.log("This zoo contains a " + animals[i] + ".");
}
```

In this loop, i starts at 0 and goes up to one less than animals.length, which in this case is 3. The numbers 0, 1, 2, and 3 are the indexes of the animals in the animals array. This means that every time around the loop, i is a different index, and animals[i] is another animal from the animals array. When i is 0, animals[i] is "Lion". When i is 1, animals[i] is "Flamingo", and so on.

Running this would output:

```
This zoo contains a Lion.
This zoo contains a Flamingo.
This zoo contains a Polar Bear.
This zoo contains a Boa Constrictor.
```

As you saw in Chapter 2, you can access individual characters in a string in the same way you can access individual elements in an array, using square brackets. This next example uses a for loop to print out the characters in a name:

```javascript
var name = "Nick";

for (var i = 0; i < name.length; i++) {
  console.log("My name contains the letter " + name[i] + ".");
}
```

This would output:

```
My name contains the letter N.
My name contains the letter i.
My name contains the letter c.
My name contains the letter k.
```

OTHER WAYS TO USE FOR LOOPS

As you might imagine, you don't always have to start the looping variable at 0 and increment it by 1. For example, here's a way to print all the powers of 2 below the number 10,000:

```javascript
for (var x = 2; x < 10000; x = x * 2) {
  console.log(x);
}
```

We set x to 2 and increment the value of x using x = x * 2;, which will double the value of x each time the loop runs. The result gets big very quickly, as you can see:

```
2
4
8
16
32
64
128
256
512
1024
2048
4096
8192
```

And voilà! This short for loop prints out all the powers of 2 below 10,000.

TRY IT OUT!

Write a loop to print the powers of 3 under 10,000 (it should print 3, 9, 27, etc.).

Rewrite this loop with a while loop. (Hint: Provide the setup *before* the loop.)

WHAT YOU LEARNED

In this chapter, you learned about conditionals and loops. Conditionals are used to run code only when a certain condition is true. Loops are used to run code multiple times and to keep running that code as long as a certain condition is true. You can use conditionals to make sure that the right code is run at the right time, and you can use loops to keep your program running as long as necessary. Having the ability to do these two things opens up a whole new world of programming possibilities.

In the next chapter, we'll use the power of conditionals and loops to make our first real game!

PROGRAMMING CHALLENGES

Try out these challenges to practice working with conditionals and loops.

#1: AWESOME ANIMALS

Write a for loop that modifies an array of animals, making them awesome! For example, if your starting array is . . .

```
var animals = ["Cat", "Fish", ↵
"Lemur", "Komodo Dragon"];
```

then after you run your loop, it should look like this:

```
["Awesome Cat", "Awesome Fish", "Awesome Lemur", "Awesome ↵
Komodo Dragon"]
```

Hint: You'll need to *reassign* values to the array at each index. This just means assigning a new value at an existing position in the array. For example, to make the first animal awesome, you could say:

```
animals[0] = "Awesome " + animals[0];
```

#2: RANDOM STRING GENERATOR

Make a random string generator. You'll need to start with a string containing all the letters in the alphabet:

```
var alphabet = "abcdefghijklmnopqrstuvwxyz";
```

To pick a random letter from this string, you can update the code we used for the random insult generator in Chapter 3: `Math.floor(Math.random() * alphabet.length)`. This will create a random index into the string. You can then use square brackets to get the character at that index.

(continued)

To create the random string, start with an empty string (var randomString = ""). Then, create a while loop that will continually add new random letters to this string, as long as the string length is less than 6 (or any length you choose). You could use the += operator to add a new letter to the end of the string. After the loop has finished, log it to the console to see your creation!

#3: H4CK3R SP34K

Turn text into h4ck3r sp34k! A lot of people on the Internet like to replace certain letters with numbers that look like those letters. Some numbers that look like letters are 4 for A, 3 for E, 1 for I, and 0 for O. Even though the numbers look more like capital letters, we'll be replacing the lowercase versions of those letters. To change normal text to h4ck3r sp34k, we'll need an input string and a new empty string:

```
var input = "javascript is awesome";
var output = "";
```

You'll then need to use a for loop to go through all the letters of the input string. If the letter is "a", add a "4" to the output string. If it's "e", add a "3". If it's "i", add a "1", and if it's "o", add a "0". Otherwise, just add the original letter to the new string. As before, you can use += to add each new letter to the output string.

After the loop, log the output string to the console. If it works correctly, you should see it log "j4v4scr1pt 1s 4w3s0m3".

7

CREATING A HANGMAN GAME

In this chapter we'll build a Hangman game! We'll learn how to use dialogs to make the game interactive and take input from someone playing the game.

Hangman is a word-guessing game. One player picks a secret word, and the other player tries to guess it.

For example, if the word were *TEACHER*, the first player would write:

— — — — — — —

The guessing player tries to guess the letters in the word. Each time they guess a letter correctly, the first player fills in the blanks for each occurrence of that letter. For example, if the guessing player guessed the letter *E*, the first player would fill in the *E*s in the word *TEACHER* like so:

_ E _ _ _ E _

When the guessing player guesses a letter that isn't in the word, they lose a point and the first player draws part of a stickman for each wrong guess. If the first player completes the stickman before the guessing player guesses the word, the guessing player loses.

In our version of Hangman, the JavaScript program will choose the word and the human player will guess letters. We won't be drawing the stickman, because we haven't yet learned how to draw in JavaScript (we'll learn how to do that in Chapter 13).

INTERACTING WITH A PLAYER

To create this game, we have to have some way for the guessing player (human) to enter their choices. One way is to open a pop-up window (which JavaScript calls a *prompt*) that the player can type into.

CREATING A PROMPT

First, let's create a new HTML document. Using **File ▸ Save As**, save your *page.html* file from Chapter 5 as *prompt.html*. To create a prompt, enter this code between the `<script>` tags of *prompt.html* and refresh the browser:

```
var name = prompt("What's your name?");
console.log("Hello " + name);
```

Here we create a new variable, called `name`, and assign to it the value returned from calling `prompt("What's your name?")`. When `prompt` is called, a small window (or *dialog*) is opened, which should look like Figure 7-1.

Figure 7-1: A prompt dialog

Calling `prompt("What's your name?")` pops up a window with the text "What's your name?" along with a text box for input. At the bottom of the dialog are two buttons, Cancel and OK. In Chrome, the dialog has the heading *JavaScript*, to inform you that JavaScript opened the prompt.

When you enter text in the box and click OK, that text becomes the value that is returned by `prompt`. For example, if I were to enter my name into the text box and click OK, JavaScript would print this in the console:

```
Hello Nick
```

Because I entered *Nick* in the text box and clicked OK, the string `"Nick"` is saved in the variable `name` and `console.log` prints `"Hello " + "Nick"`, which gives us `"Hello Nick"`.

NOTE *The second time you open any kind of dialog in Chrome, it adds an extra line to the dialog with a checkbox saying, "Prevent this page from creating additional dialogs." This is Chrome's way of protecting users from web pages with lots of annoying pop-ups. Just leave the box unchecked for the exercises in this chapter.*

USING CONFIRM TO ASK A YES OR NO QUESTION

The confirm function is a way to take user input without a text box by asking for a yes or no (Boolean) answer. For example, here we use confirm to ask the user if they like cats (see Figure 7-2). If so, the variable likesCats is set to true, and we respond with "You're a cool cat!" If they don't like cats, likesCats is set to false, so we respond with "Yeah, that's fine. You're still cool!"

```javascript
var likesCats = confirm("Do you like cats?");
if (likesCats) {
  console.log("You're a cool cat!");
} else {
  console.log("Yeah, that's fine. You're still cool!");
}
```

Figure 7-2: A confirm dialog

The answer to the `confirm` prompt is returned as a Boolean value. If the user clicks OK in the confirm dialog shown in Figure 7-2, true is returned. If they click Cancel, `false` is returned.

USING ALERTS TO GIVE A PLAYER INFORMATION

If you want to just give the player some information, you can use an alert dialog to display a message with an OK button. For example, if you think that JavaScript is awesome, you might use this alert function:

```
alert("JavaScript is awesome!");
```

Figure 7-3 shows what this simple alert dialog would look like.

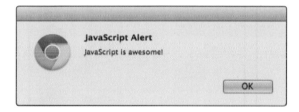

Figure 7-3: An alert dialog

Alert dialogs just display a message and wait until the user clicks OK.

WHY USE ALERT INSTEAD OF CONSOLE.LOG?

Why use an alert dialog in a game instead of using `console.log`? First, because if all you want to do is tell the player something, using alert means the player doesn't have to interrupt game play to open the console to see a status message. Second, calling alert (as well as `prompt` and `confirm`) pauses the JavaScript interpreter until the user clicks OK (or Cancel, in the case of prompt and confirm). That means the player has time to read the alert. On the other hand, when you use console.log, the text is displayed immediately and the interpreter moves on to the next line in your program.

DESIGNING YOUR GAME

Before we start writing the Hangman game, let's think about its structure. There are a few things we need our program to do:

1. Pick a random word.
2. Take the player's guess.
3. Quit the game if the player wants to.
4. Check that the player's guess is a valid letter.
5. Keep track of letters the player has guessed.
6. Show the player their progress.
7. Finish when the player has guessed the word.

Apart from the first and last tasks (picking a word for the player to guess and finishing the game), these steps all need to happen multiple times, and we don't know how many times (it depends on how well the player guesses). When you need to do the same thing multiple times, you know you'll need a loop.

But this simple list of tasks doesn't really give us any idea of what needs to happen when. To get a better idea of the structure of the code, we can use *pseudocode*.

USING PSEUDOCODE TO DESIGN THE GAME

Pseudocode is a handy tool that programmers often use to design programs. It means "fake code," and it's a way of describing how a program will work that looks like a cross between written English and code. Pseudocode has loops and conditionals, but other than that, everything is just plain English. Let's look at a pseudocode version of our game to get an idea:

```
Pick a random word

While the word has not been guessed {
  Show the player their current progress
  Get a guess from the player

  If the player wants to quit the game {
    Quit the game
  }
  Else If the guess is not a single letter {
    Tell the player to pick a single letter
  }
  Else {
    If the guess is in the word {
      Update the player's progress with the guess
    }
  }
}

Congratulate the player on guessing the word
```

As you can see, none of this is real code, and no computer could understand it. But it gives us an idea of how our program will be structured, before we get to actually writing the code and having to deal with the messy details, like *how* we're going to pick a random word.

TRACKING THE STATE OF THE WORD

In the previous pseudocode, one of the first lines says, "Show the player their current progress." For the Hangman game, this means filling in the letters that the player has guessed correctly and showing which letters in the secret word are still blank. How are we going to do this? We can actually keep track of the player's progress in a similar way to how traditional Hangman works: by keeping a collection of blank spaces and filling them in as the player guesses correct letters.

In our game, we'll do this using an array of blanks for each letter in the word. We'll call this the answer array, and we'll fill it with the player's correct guesses as they're made. We'll represent each blank with the string "_".

The answer array will start out as a group of these empty entries equal in number to the letters in the secret word. For example, if the secret word is *fish*, the array would look like this:

```
["_", "_", "_", "_"]
```

If the player correctly guessed the letter *i*, we'd change the second blank to an *i*:

```
["_", "i", "_", "_"]
```

Once the player guesses all the correct letters, the completed array would look like this:

```
["f", "i", "s", "h"]
```

We'll also use a variable to keep track of the number of remaining letters the player has to guess. For every occurrence of a correctly guessed letter, this variable will decrease by 1. Once it hits 0, we know the player has won.

DESIGNING THE GAME LOOP

The main game takes place inside a while loop (in our pseudo-code, this loop begins with the line "While the word has not been guessed"). In this loop we display the current state of the word being guessed (beginning with all blanks); ask the player for a guess (and make sure it's a valid, single-letter guess); and update the answer array with the chosen letter, if that letter appears in the word.

Almost all computer games are built around a loop of some kind, often with the same basic structure as the loop in our Hangman game. A game loop generally does the following:

1. Takes input from the player
2. Updates the game state
3. Displays the current state of the game to the player

Even games that are constantly changing follow this same kind of loop—they just do it *really* fast. In the case of our Hangman game, the program takes a guess from the player, updates the answer array if the guess is correct, and displays the new state of the answer array.

Once the player guesses all letters in the word, we show the completed word and a congratulatory message telling them that they won.

CODING THE GAME

Now that we know the general structure of our game, we can start to go over how the code will look. The following sections will walk you through all the code in the game. After that, you'll see the whole game code in one listing so you can type it up and play it yourself.

CHOOSING A RANDOM WORD

The first thing we have to do is to choose a random word. Here's how that will look:

```
❶ var words = [
    "javascript",
    "monkey",
    "amazing",
    "pancake"
  ];

❷ var word = words[Math.floor(Math.random() * words.length)];
```

We begin our game at ❶ by creating an array of words (*javascript*, *monkey*, *amazing*, and *pancake*) to be used as the source of our secret word, and we save the array in the words variable. The words should be all lowercase. At ❷ we use Math.random and Math.floor to pick a random word from the array, as we did with the random insult generator in Chapter 3.

CREATING THE ANSWER ARRAY

Next we create an empty array called answerArray and fill it with underscores (_) to match the number of letters in the word.

```
var answerArray = [];
❶ for (var i = 0; i < word.length; i++) {
    answerArray[i] = "_";
}

var remainingLetters = word.length;
```

The for loop at ❶ creates a looping variable i that starts at 0 and goes up to (but does not include) word.length. Each time around the loop, we add a new element to answerArray, at answerArray[i]. When the loop finishes, answerArray will be the same length as word. For example, if word is "monkey" (which has six letters), answerArray will be ["_", "_", "_", "_", "_", "_"] (six underscores).

Finally, we create the variable remainingLetters and set it to the length of the secret word. We'll use this variable to keep track of how many letters are left to be guessed. Every time the player guesses a correct letter, this value will be *decremented* (reduced) by 1 for each instance of that letter in the word.

CODING THE GAME LOOP

The skeleton of the game loop looks like this:

```
while (remainingLetters > 0) {
    // Game code goes here
    // Show the player their progress
    // Take input from the player
    // Update answerArray and remainingLetters for every correct guess
}
```

We use a while loop, which will keep looping as long as remainingLetters > 0 remains true. The body of the loop will have to update remainingLetters for every correct guess the player makes. Once the player has guessed all the letters, remainingLetters will be 0 and the loop will end.

The following sections explain the code that will make up the body of the game loop.

SHOWING THE PLAYER'S PROGRESS

The first thing we need to do inside the game loop is to show the player their current progress:

```
alert(answerArray.join(" "));
```

We do that by joining the elements of answerArray into a string, using the space character as the separator, and then using alert to show that string to the player. For example, let's say the word is *monkey* and the player has guessed *m*, *o*, and *e* so far. The answer array would look like this ["m", "o", "_", "_", "e", "_"], and answerArray.join(" ") would be "m o _ _ e _". The alert dialog would then look like Figure 7-4.

Figure 7-4: Showing the player's progress using alert

HANDLING THE PLAYER'S INPUT

Now we have to get a guess from the player and ensure that it's a single character.

```
❶ var guess = prompt("Guess a letter, or click Cancel to stop playing.");
❷ if (guess === null) {
    break;
❸ } else if (guess.length !== 1) {
    alert("Please enter a single letter.");
  } else {
❹    // Update the game state with the guess
  }
```

At ❶, prompt takes a guess from the player and saves it to the variable guess. One of four things will happen at this point.

First, if the player clicks the Cancel button, then guess will be null. We check for this condition at ❷ with if (guess === null). If this condition is true, we use break to exit the loop.

You can use the break keyword in any loop to immediately stop looping, no matter where the program is in the loop or whether the while condition is currently true.

The second and third possibilities are that the player enters either nothing or too many letters. If they enter nothing but click OK, guess will be the empty string "". In this case, guess.length will be 0. If they enter anything more than one letter, guess.length will be greater than 1.

At ❸, we use else if (guess.length !== 1) to check for these conditions, ensuring that guess is exactly one letter. If it's not, we display an alert saying, "Please enter a single letter."

The fourth possibility is that the player enters a valid guess of one letter. Then we have to update the game state with their guess using the else statement at ❹, which we'll do in the next section.

UPDATING THE GAME STATE

Once the player has entered a valid guess, we must update the game's answerArray according to the guess. To do that, we add the following code to the else statement:

```
❶ for (var j = 0; j < word.length; j++) {
❷   if (word[j] === guess) {
      answerArray[j] = guess;
❸     remainingLetters--;
    }
  }
```

At ❶, we create a for loop with a new looping variable called j, which runs from 0 up to word.length. (We're using j as the variable in this loop because we already used i in the previous for loop.) We use this loop to step through each letter of word. For example, let's say word is *pancake*. The first time around this loop, when j is 0, word[j] will be "p". The next time, word[j] will be "a", then "n", "c", "a", "k", and finally "e".

At ❷, we use if (word[j] === guess) to check whether the current letter we're looking at matches the player's guess. If it does, we use answerArray[j] = guess to update the answer array with the current guess. For each letter in the word that matches guess, we update the answer array at the corresponding point. This works because the looping variable j can be used as an index for answerArray just as it can be used as an index for word, as you can see in Figure 7-5.

Index (j)	0	1	2	3	4	5	6
word	" p	a	n	c	a	k	e "
answerArray	["_",	"_",	"_",	"_",	"_",	"_",	"_"]

Figure 7-5: The same index can be used for both word and answerArray.

For example, imagine we've just started playing the game and we reach the for loop at ❶. Let's say word is "pancake", guess is "a", and answerArray currently looks like this:

```
["_", "_", "_", "_", "_", "_", "_"]
```

The first time around the for loop at ❶, j is 0, so word[j] is "p". Our guess is "a", so we skip the if statement at ❷ (because "p" === "a" is false). The second time around, j is 1, so word[j] is "a". This *is* equal to guess, so we enter the if part of the statement. The line answerArray[j] = guess; sets the element at index 1 (the second element) of answerArray to guess, so answerArray now looks like this:

```
["_", "a", "_", "_", "_", "_", "_"]
```

The next two times around the loop, word[j] is "n" and then "c", which don't match guess. However, when j reaches 4, word[j] is "a" again. We update answerArray again, this time setting the element at index 4 (the fifth element) to guess. Now answerArray looks like this:

```
["_", "a", "_", "_", "a", "_", "_"]
```

The remaining letters don't match "a", so nothing happens the last two times around the loop. At the end of this loop, answerArray will be updated with all the occurrences of guess in word.

For every correct guess, in addition to updating `answerArray`, we also need to decrement `remainingLetters` by 1. We do this at ❸ using `remainingLetters--;`. Every time guess matches a letter in word, `remainingLetters` decreases by 1. Once the player has guessed all the letters correctly, `remainingLetters` will be 0.

ENDING THE GAME

As we've already seen, the main game loop condition is `remainingLetters > 0`, so as long as there are still letters to guess, the loop will keep looping. Once `remainingLetters` reaches 0, we leave the loop. We end with the following code:

```
alert(answerArray.join(" "));
alert("Good job! The answer was " + word);
```

The first line uses `alert` to show the answer array one last time. The second line uses `alert` again to congratulate the winning player.

THE GAME CODE

Now we've seen all the code for the game, and we just need to put it together. What follows is the full listing for our Hangman game. I've added comments throughout to make it easier for you to see what's happening at each point. It's quite a bit longer than any of the code we've written so far, but typing it out will help you to become more familiar with writing JavaScript. Create a new HTML file called *hangman.html* and type the following into it:

```
<!DOCTYPE html>
<html>
<head>
    <title>Hangman!</title>
</head>
```

```
<body>
    <h1>Hangman!</h1>

    <script>
    // Create an array of words
    var words = [
      "javascript",
      "monkey",
      "amazing",
      "pancake"
    ];

    // Pick a random word
    var word = words[Math.floor(Math.random() * words.length)];

    // Set up the answer array
    var answerArray = [];
    for (var i = 0; i < word.length; i++) {
      answerArray[i] = "_";
    }

    var remainingLetters = word.length;

    // The game loop
    while (remainingLetters > 0) {
      // Show the player their progress
      alert(answerArray.join(" "));

      // Get a guess from the player
      var guess - prompt("Guess a letter, or click Cancel to stop ↵
playing.");
      if (guess === null) {
        // Exit the game loop
        break;
      } else if (guess.length !== 1) {
        alert("Please enter a single letter.");
      } else {
        // Update the game state with the guess
        for (var j = 0; j < word.length; j++) {
          if (word[j] === guess) {
            answerArray[j] = guess;
            remainingLetters--;
          }
        }
      }
```

```
    // The end of the game loop
    }

    // Show the answer and congratulate the player
    alert(answerArray.join(" "));
    alert("Good job! The answer was " + word);
    </script>
</body>
</html>
```

If the game doesn't run, make sure that you typed in everything correctly. If you make a mistake, the JavaScript console can help you find it. For example, if you misspell a variable name, you'll see something like Figure 7-6 with a pointer to where you made your mistake.

```
⊗  ▶ Uncaught ReferenceError: remainingLetter is not defined          hangman.html:30
```

Figure 7-6: A JavaScript error in the Chrome console

If you click hangman.html:30, you'll see the exact line where the error is. In this case, it's showing us that we misspelled remainingLetters as remainingLetter at the start of the while loop.

Try playing the game a few times. Does it work the way you expected it to work? Can you imagine the code you wrote running in the background as you play it?

WHAT YOU LEARNED

In just a few pages, you've created your first JavaScript game! As you can see, loops and conditionals are essential for creating games or any other interactive computer program. Without these control structures, a program just begins and ends.

In Chapter 8, we'll use functions to package up code so you can run it from different parts of your programs.

PROGRAMMING CHALLENGES

Here are some challenges to build on and improve the Hangman game you created in this chapter.

#1: MORE WORDS

Add your own words to the words array. Remember to enter words in all lowercase.

#2: CAPITAL LETTERS

If a player guesses a capital letter, it won't match a lowercase letter in the secret word. To address this potential problem, convert the player's guess to lowercase. (Hint: You can use the toLowerCase method to convert a string to lowercase.)

#3: LIMITING GUESSES

Our Hangman game gives a player unlimited guesses. Add a variable to track the number of guesses and end the game if the player runs out of guesses. (Hint: Check this variable in the same while loop that checks whether remainingLetters > 0. As we did in Chapter 2, you can use && to check whether two Boolean conditions are true.)

#4: FIXING A BUG

There's a bug in the game: if you keep guessing the same correct letter, remainingLetters will keep decrementing. Can you fix it? (Hint: You could add another condition to check whether a value in answerArray is still an underscore. If it's not an underscore, then that letter must have been guessed already.)

8

FUNCTIONS

A *function* is a way to bundle code so that it can be reused. Functions allow us to run the same piece of code from multiple places in a program without having to copy and paste the code repeatedly. Also, by hiding long bits of code in a function and giving it an easy-to-understand name, you'll be better able to plan out your code because you can focus on organizing your functions rather than all of the little code details that make them up. Splitting up your code into smaller, more manageable pieces allows you to see the bigger picture and think about how your programs are structured at a higher level.

You'll find functions really useful when you need to repeatedly perform a calculation or action throughout a program. Earlier in the book, you used various functions such as `Math.random`, `Math.floor`, `alert`, `prompt`, and `confirm`. In this chapter, you'll learn how to create your own functions.

THE BASIC ANATOMY OF A FUNCTION

Figure 8-1 shows how a function is built. The code between the curly brackets is called the *function body*, just as the code between the curly brackets in a loop is called the *loop body*.

```
function () {
    console.log("Do something");
}
```

The function body
goes between curly brackets.

Figure 8-1: The syntax for creating a function

CREATING A SIMPLE FUNCTION

Let's create a simple function that prints `Hello world!`. Enter the following code in the browser console. Use SHIFT-ENTER to start each new line without executing the code.

```
var ourFirstFunction = function () {
  console.log("Hello world!");
};
```

This code creates a new function and saves it in the variable `ourFirstFunction`.

CALLING A FUNCTION

To run the code inside a function (the function body), we need to *call* the function. To call a function, you enter its name followed by a pair of opening and closing parentheses, as shown here.

```
ourFirstFunction();
Hello world!
```

Calling `ourFirstFunction` executes the body of the function, which is `console.log("Hello world!");`, and the text we asked to be printed is displayed on the next line: `Hello world!`.

But if you call this function in your browser, you'll notice that there's a third line, with a little left-facing arrow, as shown in Figure 8-2. This is the return value of the function.

```
> ourFirstFunction();
  Hello, world!
< undefined
```

Figure 8-2: Calling a function with an undefined return value

A *return value* is the value that a function outputs, which can then be used elsewhere in your code. In this case, the return value is undefined because we didn't tell the function to return any particular value in the body of the function. All we did was ask it to print a message to the console, which is not the same as returning a value. A function always returns undefined unless there is something in the function body that tells it to return a different value. (We'll look at how to specify a return value in "Returning Values from Functions" on page 129.)

NOTE *In the Chrome console and in the code listings throughout this book, return values are always color-coded based on data type, while text printed with `console.log` is always plain black.*

PASSING ARGUMENTS INTO FUNCTIONS

ourFirstFunction just prints the same line of text every time you call it, but you'll probably want your functions to be more flexible than that. Function *arguments* allow us to pass values into a function in order to change the function's behavior when it's called. Arguments always go between the function parentheses, both when you create the function and when you call it.

The following sayHelloTo function uses an argument (name) to say hello to someone you specify.

```
var sayHelloTo = function (name) {
  console.log("Hello " + name + "!");
};
```

We create the function in the first line and assign it to the variable sayHelloTo. When the function is called, it logs the string "Hello " + name + "!", replacing name with whatever value you pass to the function as an argument.

Figure 8-3 shows the syntax for a function with one argument.

An argument name

```
function ( argument ) {
    console.log("My argument was: " + argument);
}
```

This function body can use the argument.

Figure 8-3: The syntax for creating a function with one argument

To call a function that takes an argument, place the value you'd like to use for the argument between the parentheses following the function name. For example, to say hello to Nick, you would write:

```
sayHelloTo("Nick");
Hello Nick!
```

Or, to say hello to Lyra, write:

```
sayHelloTo("Lyra");
Hello Lyra!
```

Each time we call the function, the argument we pass in for name is included in the string printed by the function. So when we pass in "Nick", the console prints "Hello Nick!", and when we pass in "Lyra", it prints "Hello Lyra!".

PRINTING CAT FACES!

One reason to pass an argument into a function might be to tell it how many times to do something. For example, the function drawCats prints cat faces (like this: =^.^=) to the console. We tell the function how many cats to print using the argument howManyTimes:

```
var drawCats = function (howManyTimes) {
  for (var i = 0; i < howManyTimes; i++) {
    console.log(i + " =^.^=");
  }
};
```

The body of the function is a for loop that loops as many times as the howManyTimes argument tells it to (since the variable i starts at 0 and repeats until it increments to howManyTimes minus 1). Each time through the loop, the function logs the string i + " =^.^=".

Here's what happens when we call this function with the argument 5 for howManyTimes:

```
drawCats(5);
0 =^.^=
1 =^.^=
2 =^.^=
3 =^.^=
4 =^.^=
```

Try it out with howManyTimes equal to 100 to print 100 cat faces!

PASSING MULTIPLE ARGUMENTS TO A FUNCTION

You can pass more than one value into a function using multiple arguments. To add another argument, enter the arguments between the parentheses after the function keyword, separating them by commas. Figure 8-4 shows the syntax for a function with two arguments.

Each argument name is
separated by a comma.
↓

```
function (argument1, argument2) {
   console.log("My first argument was: " + argument1);
   console.log("My second argument was: " + argument2);
}
```
↑
The function body can
use both arguments.

Figure 8-4: The syntax for creating a function with two arguments

The following function, printMultipleTimes, is like drawCats except that it has a second argument called whatToDraw.

```
var printMultipleTimes = function (howManyTimes, whatToDraw) {
  for (var i = 0; i < howManyTimes; i++) {
    console.log(i + " " + whatToDraw);
  }
};
```

The printMultipleTimes function prints the string you enter for whatToDraw as many times as you specify with the argument howManyTimes. The second argument tells the function what to print, and the first argument tells the function how many times to print it.

When calling a function with multiple arguments, insert the values you wish to use between the parentheses following the function name, separated by commas.

For example, to print out cat faces using this new `printMultipleTimes` function, you'd call it like this:

```
printMultipleTimes(5, "=^.^=");
0 =^.^=
1 =^.^=
2 =^.^=
3 =^.^=
4 =^.^=
```

To have `printMultipleTimes` print a happy face four times, you could do this:

```
printMultipleTimes(4, "^_^");
0 ^_^
1 ^_^
2 ^_^
3 ^_^
```

When we call `printMultipleTimes`, we pass in the arguments 4 for `howManyTimes` and "^_^" for `whatToDraw`. As a result, the for loop loops four times (with i incrementing from 0 to 3), printing i + " " + "^_^" each time.

To draw the character (>_<) two times, you could write:

```
printMultipleTimes(2, "(>_<)");
0 (>_<)
1 (>_<)
```

In this case, we pass in 2 for `howManyTimes` and "(>_<)" for `whatToDraw`.

RETURNING VALUES FROM FUNCTIONS

The functions we've looked at so far have all printed text to the console using `console.log`. That's an easy and useful way to make JavaScript display values, but when we log a value to the console, we aren't able to use that value later in the program. What if you want your function to output that value so that you can keep using it in other parts of your code?

As mentioned earlier in this chapter, the output of a function is called the return value. When you call a function that returns a value, you can use that value in the rest of your code (you could save a return value in a variable, pass it to another function, or simply combine it with other code). For example, the following line of code adds 5 to the return value of the call to Math.floor(1.2345):

```
5 + Math.floor(1.2345);
6
```

Math.floor is a function that returns the number you pass to it, rounded down to the nearest whole number. When you see a function call like Math.floor(1.2345), imagine replacing it with the return value of that function call, which is the number 1.

Let's create a function that returns a value. The function double takes the argument number and returns the result of number * 2. In other words, the value returned by this function is twice the number supplied as its argument.

```
  var double = function (number) {
❶   return number * 2;
  };
```

To return a value from a function, use the keyword return, followed by the value you want to return. At ❶, we use the return keyword to return the value number * 2 from the double function.

Now we can call our double function to double numbers:

```
double(3);
6
```

Here, the return value (6) is shown on the second line. Even though functions can take multiple arguments, they can return only one value. If you don't tell the function to return anything, it will return undefined.

USING FUNCTION CALLS AS VALUES

When you call a function from within a larger piece of code, the function's return value is used wherever that function call was placed. For example, let's use our double function to determine the result of doubling two numbers and then adding the results:

```
double(5) + double(6);
22
```

In this example, we call the double function twice and add the two return values together. You can think of the call double(5) as the value 10 and the call double(6) as the value 12.

You can also pass a function call into another function as an argument, and the function call will be substituted with its return value. In this next example we call double, passing the result of calling double with 3 as an argument. We replace double(3) with 6 so that double(double(3)) simplifies to double(6), which then simplifies to 12.

```
double(double(3));
12
```

Here's how JavaScript calculates this:

```
double( double(3) );

❶   double( 3 * 2 )

❷       double(6)

❸       6 * 2

❹         12
```

The body of the double function returns number * 2, so at ❶ we replace double(3) with 3 * 2. At ❷ we replace 3 * 2 with 6. Then at ❸, we do the same thing and replace double(6) with 6 * 2. Finally, at ❹, we can replace 6 * 2 with 12.

USING FUNCTIONS TO SIMPLIFY CODE

In Chapter 3, we used the methods `Math.random` and `Math.floor` to pick random words from arrays and generate random insults. In this section, we'll re-create our insult generator and simplify it by creating functions.

A FUNCTION TO PICK A RANDOM WORD

Here is the code we used in Chapter 3 to choose a random word from an array:

```
randomWords[Math.floor(Math.random() * randomWords.length)];
```

If we turn this code into a function, we can reuse it to pick a random word from an array without having to enter the same code each time. For example, here's how we could define a `pickRandomWord` function.

```
var pickRandomWord = function (words) {
  return words[Math.floor(Math.random() * words.length)];
};
```

All we're doing here is wrapping the previous code in a function. Now, we can create this `randomWords` array . . .

```
var randomWords = ["Planet", "Worm", "Flower", "Computer"];
```

and pick a random word from this array using the `pickRandomWord` function, like this:

```
pickRandomWord(randomWords);
"Flower"
```

We can use this same function on any array. For example, here's how we would pick a random name from an array of names:

```
pickRandomWord(["Charlie", "Raj", "Nicole", "Kate", "Sandy"]);
"Raj"
```

A RANDOM INSULT GENERATOR

Now let's try re-creating our random insult generator, using our function that picks random words. First, here's a reminder of what the code from Chapter 3 looked like:

```
var randomBodyParts = ["Face", "Nose", "Hair"];
var randomAdjectives = ["Smelly", "Boring", "Stupid"];
var randomWords = ["Fly", "Marmot", "Stick", "Monkey", "Rat"];

// Pick a random body part from the randomBodyParts array:
var randomBodyPart = randomBodyParts[Math.floor(Math.random() * 3)];
// Pick a random adjective from the randomAdjectives array:
var randomAdjective = randomAdjectives[Math.floor(Math.random() * 3)];
// Pick a random word from the randomWords array:
var randomWord = randomWords[Math.floor(Math.random() * 5)];
// Join all the random strings into a sentence:
var randomString = "Your " + randomBodyPart + " is like a " + ↵
randomAdjective + " " + randomWord + "!!!";
randomString;
"Your Nose is like a Stupid Marmot!!!"
```

Notice that we end up repeating *words*[Math.floor(Math.random() * *length*)] quite a few times in this code. Using our pickRandomWord function, we could rewrite the program like this:

```
var randomBodyParts = ["Face", "Nose", "Hair"];
var randomAdjectives = ["Smelly", "Boring", "Stupid"];
var randomWords = ["Fly", "Marmot", "Stick", "Monkey", "Rat"];

// Join all the random strings into a sentence:
var randomString = "Your " + pickRandomWord(randomBodyParts) + ↵
" is like a " + pickRandomWord(randomAdjectives) + ↵
" " + pickRandomWord(randomWords) + "!!!";

randomString;
"Your Nose is like a Smelly Marmot!!!"
```

There are two changes here. First, we use the pickRandomWord function when we need a random word from an array, instead of using *words*[Math.floor(Math.random() * *length*)] each time. Also, instead of saving each random word in a variable before adding it to the final string, we're adding the return values from the function calls

directly together to form the string. A call to a function can be treated as the value that the function returns. So really, all we're doing here is adding together strings. As you can see, this version of the program is a lot easier to read, and it was easier to write too, since we reused some code by using a function.

MAKING THE RANDOM INSULT GENERATOR INTO A FUNCTION

We can take our random insult generator one step further by creating a larger function that produces random insults. Let's take a look:

```
generateRandomInsult = function () {
  var randomBodyParts = ["Face", "Nose", "Hair"];
  var randomAdjectives = ["Smelly", "Boring", "Stupid"];
  var randomWords = ["Fly", "Marmot", "Stick", "Monkey", "Rat"];

  // Join all the random strings into a sentence:
  var randomString = "Your " + pickRandomWord(randomBodyParts) + ↵
  " is like a " + pickRandomWord(randomAdjectives) + ↵
  " " + pickRandomWord(randomWords) + "!!!";

❶  return randomString;
};

generateRandomInsult();
"Your Face is like a Smelly Stick!!!"
generateRandomInsult();
"Your Hair is like a Boring Stick!!!"
generateRandomInsult();
"Your Face is like a Stupid Fly!!!"
```

Our new `generateRandomInsult` function is just the code from before placed inside a function with no arguments. The only addition is at ❶, where we have the function return `randomString` at the end. You can see a few sample runs of the preceding function, and it returns a new insult string each time.

Having the code in one function means we can keep calling that function to get a random insult, instead of having to copy and paste the same code every time we want a new insult.

LEAVING A FUNCTION EARLY WITH RETURN

As soon as the JavaScript interpreter reaches return in a function, it leaves the function, even if more code remains in the function body.

One common way to use return is to leave a function early if any of the arguments to the function are *invalid*; that is, if they're not the kind of arguments the function needs in order to run properly. For example, the following function returns a string telling you the fifth character of your name. If the name passed to the function has fewer than five characters, the function uses return to leave the function immediately. This means the return statement at the end, which tells you the fifth letter of your name, is never executed.

```
var fifthLetter = function (name) {
❶   if (name.length < 5) {
❷     return;
    }

    return "The fifth letter of your name is " + name[4] + ".";
};
```

At ❶ we check to see whether the length of the input name is less than five. If it is, we use return at ❷ to exit the function early.

Let's try calling this function.

```
fifthLetter("Nicholas");
"The fifth letter of your name is o."
```

The name *Nicholas* is longer than five characters, so fifthLetter completes and returns the fifth letter in the name

Nicholas, which is the letter *o*. Let's try calling it again on a shorter name:

```
fifthLetter("Nick");
undefined
```

When we call `fifthLetter` with the name *Nick*, the function knows that the name isn't long enough, so it exits early with the first return statement at ❷. Because there is no value specified after the return at ❷, the function returns `undefined`.

USING RETURN MULTIPLE TIMES INSTEAD OF IF...ELSE STATEMENTS

We can use multiple return keywords inside different if statements in a function body to have a function return a different value depending on the input. For example, say you're writing a game that awards players medals based on their score. A score of 3 or below is a bronze medal, scores between 3 and 7 are silver, and anything above 7 is gold. You could use a function like `medalForScore` to evaluate a score and return the right kind of medal, as shown here:

```
var medalForScore = function (score) {
    if (score < 3) {
❶      return "Bronze";
    }

❷   if (score < 7) {
        return "Silver";
    }

❸   return "Gold";
};
```

At ❶ we return "Bronze" and exit the function if the score is less than 3. If we reach ❷ we know that score must be at least 3, because if it was less than 3, we would have *returned* already (that is, we would have exited the function when we reached the return keyword in the first test). Finally, if we reach ❸, we know that score must be at least 7, so there's nothing left to check, and we can just return "Gold".

Although we're checking multiple conditions, we don't need to use chained if...else statements. We use if...else statements to ensure that only one of the options is executed. When each of the options has its own return statement, this also ensures that only one of the options will be executed (because functions can return only once).

SHORTHAND FOR CREATING FUNCTIONS

There's a longhand way and a shorthand way to write functions. I'm using the longhand way because it shows more clearly how a function is stored as a variable. Still, you should know what the shorthand looks like because lots of JavaScript code uses it. Once you're used to how functions work, you might want to use the shorthand version, too.

Here's an example of a longhand function:

```
var double = function (number) {
  return number * 2;
};
```

The shorthand version looks like this:

```
function double(number) {
  return number * 2;
}
```

As you can see, in the longhand version, we explicitly create a variable name and assign the function to the variable, so double appears before the function keyword. By contrast, the function keyword appears first in the shorthand version, followed by the function name. In this version, the variable double is created by JavaScript behind the scenes.

In technical terms, the longhand version is known as a function *expression*. The shorthand version is known as a function *declaration*.

WHAT YOU LEARNED

Functions allow us to reuse blocks of code. They can do different things depending on the arguments passed to them, and they can return values to the location in the code where the function was called. Functions also make it possible to give a piece of code a meaningful name. For example, the name of the function `pickRandomWord` makes clear that the function has something to do with picking a random word.

In the next chapter, we'll learn how to write JavaScript that can manipulate HTML documents.

PROGRAMMING CHALLENGES

Here are some challenges for you to practice working with functions.

#1: DOING ARITHMETIC WITH FUNCTIONS

Create two functions, `add` and `multiply`. Each should take two arguments. The `add` function should sum its arguments and return the result, and `multiply` should multiply its arguments.

Using only these two functions, solve this simple mathematical problem:

```
36325 * 9824 + 777
```

#2: ARE THESE ARRAYS THE SAME?

Write a function called `areArraysSame` that takes two arrays of numbers as arguments. It should return true if the two arrays are the same (that is, they have the same numbers in the same order) and `false` if they're different. Try running the following code to make sure your functions are working correctly:

```
areArraysSame([1, 2, 3], [4, 5, 6]);
false
```

```
areArraysSame([1, 2, 3], [1, 2, 3]);
true
areArraysSame([1, 2, 3], [1, 2, 3, 4]);
false
```

Hint 1: you'll need to use a for loop to go through each of the values in the first array to see whether they're the same in the second array. You can return false in the for loop if you find a value that's not equal.

Hint 2: you can leave the function early and skip the for loop altogether if the arrays are different lengths.

#3: HANGMAN, USING FUNCTIONS

Go back to your Hangman game from Chapter 7. We're going to rewrite it using functions.

I've rewritten the final Hangman code here, but with certain parts of the code replaced by function calls. All you need to do is write the functions!

```
// Write your functions here

var word = pickWord();
var answerArray = setupAnswerArray(word);
var remainingLetters = word.length;

while (remainingLetters > 0) {
  showPlayerProgress(answerArray);
  var guess = getGuess();
  if (guess === null) {
    break;
  } else if (guess.length !== 1) {
    alert("Please enter a single letter.");
  } else {
    var correctGuesses = updateGameState(guess, word, answerArray);
    remainingLetters -= correctGuesses;
  }
}

showAnswerAndCongratulatePlayer(answerArray);
```

(continued)

This version of the code using functions is almost as simple as the pseudocode version from Chapter 7. This should give you some idea of how useful functions can be for making code easier to understand.

Here are the functions you need to fill in:

```javascript
var pickWord = function () {
  // Return a random word
};

var setupAnswerArray = function (word) {
  // Return the answer array
};

var showPlayerProgress = function (answerArray) {
  // Use alert to show the player their progress
};

var getGuess = function () {
  // Use prompt to get a guess
};

var updateGameState = function (guess, word, answerArray) {
  // Update answerArray and return a number showing how many
  // times the guess appears in the word so remainingLetters
  // can be updated
};

var showAnswerAndCongratulatePlayer = function (answerArray) {
  // Use alert to show the answer and congratulate the player
};
```

PART II

ADVANCED JAVASCRIPT

9

THE DOM AND JQUERY

So far, we've been using JavaScript to do relatively simple things like print text to the browser console or display an alert or prompt dialog. But you can also use JavaScript to manipulate (control or modify) and interact with the HTML you write in web pages. In this chapter, we'll discuss two tools that will allow you to write much more powerful JavaScript: the DOM and jQuery.

The *DOM*, or *document object model*, is what allows JavaScript to access the content of a web page. Web browsers use the DOM to keep track of the elements on a page (such as paragraphs, headings, and other HTML elements), and JavaScript can manipulate DOM elements in various ways. For example, you'll soon see how you can use JavaScript to replace the main heading of the HTML document with input from a prompt dialog.

We'll also look at a useful tool called jQuery, which makes it much easier to work with the DOM. jQuery gives us a set of functions that we can use to choose which elements to work with and to make changes to those elements.

In this chapter, we'll learn how to use the DOM and jQuery to edit existing DOM elements and create new DOM elements, giving us full control over the content of our web pages from JavaScript. We'll also learn how to use jQuery to animate DOM elements—for example, fading elements in and out.

SELECTING DOM ELEMENTS

When you load an HTML document into a browser, the browser converts the elements into a tree-like structure. This tree is known as the *DOM tree*. Figure 9-1 shows a simple DOM tree—the same tree we used in Chapter 5 to illustrate the hierarchy of HTML. The browser gives JavaScript programmers a way to access and modify this tree structure using a collection of methods called the DOM.

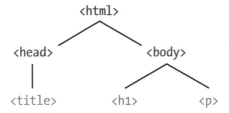

Figure 9-1: The DOM tree for a simple HTML document, like the one we made in Chapter 5

USING ID TO IDENTIFY ELEMENTS

The HTML id attribute lets you assign a unique name, or *identifier*, to an HTML element. For example, this h1 element has an id attribute:

```
<h1 id="main-heading">Hello world!</h1>
```

In this example, the id of "main-heading" will let us identify, and eventually change, this particular heading without affecting other elements or even other h1 headings.

SELECTING AN ELEMENT USING GETELEMENTBYID

Having uniquely identified an element with id (each id must have a unique value), we can use the DOM method document.getElementById to return the "main-heading" element:

```
var headingElement = document.getElementById("main-heading");
```

By calling document.getElementById("main-heading"), we tell the browser to look for the element with the id of "main-heading". This call returns a DOM object that corresponds to the id, and we save this DOM object to the variable headingElement.

Once we've selected an element, we can manipulate it with JavaScript. For example, we can use the innerHTML property to retrieve and replace the text inside the selected element:

```
headingElement.innerHTML;
```

This code returns the HTML contents of headingElement—the element we selected using getElementById. In this case, the content of this element is the text Hello world! that we entered between the <h1> tags.

REPLACING THE HEADING TEXT USING THE DOM

Here's an example of how to replace heading text using the DOM. First, we create a new HTML document called *dom.html* containing this code:

```
<!DOCTYPE html>
<html>
<head>
    <title>Playing with the DOM</title>
</head>

<body>
    <h1 id="main-heading">Hello world!</h1>

    <script>
❶    var headingElement = document.getElementById("main-heading");
❷    console.log(headingElement.innerHTML);
❸    var newHeadingText = prompt("Please provide a new heading:");
❹    headingElement.innerHTML = newHeadingText;
    </script>
</body>
</html>
```

At ❶ we use document.getElementById to get the h1 element (with the id of "main-heading") and save it into the variable headingElement. At ❷ we print the string returned by headingElement.innerHTML, which prints Hello world! to the console. At ❸ we use a prompt dialog to ask the user for a new heading and save the text the user enters in the variable newHeadingText. Finally, at ❹ we set the innerHTML property of headingElement to the text saved in newHeadingText.

When you load this page, you should see a prompt dialog like the one shown in Figure 9-2.

Figure 9-2: Our page with the dialog open

Enter the text **JAVASCRIPT IS AWESOME** into the dialog and click **OK**. The heading should update instantly with the new text, as shown in Figure 9-3.

Figure 9-3: Our page after the heading change

Using the innerHTML property, we can change the content of any DOM element using JavaScript.

USING JQUERY TO WORK WITH THE DOM TREE

The built-in DOM methods are great, but they're not very easy to use. Because of this, many developers use a set of tools called jQuery to access and manipulate the DOM tree. jQuery is a JavaScript *library*—a collection of related tools (mostly functions) that gives us, in this case, a simpler way to work with DOM elements. Once we load a library onto our page, we can use its functions and methods in addition to those built into JavaScript and those provided by the browser.

LOADING JQUERY ON YOUR HTML PAGE

To use the jQuery library, we first tell the browser to load it with this line of HTML:

```
<script src="https://code.jquery.com/jquery-2.1.0.js"></script>
```

Notice that the <script> tag here has no contents, and it has a src attribute. The src attribute lets us insert a JavaScript file into our page by including its *URL* (web address). In this case, *https://code.jquery.com/jquery-2.1.0.js* is the URL for a specific version of jQuery (version 2.1.0) on the jQuery website.

To see the jQuery library, visit that URL; you'll see the JavaScript that will be loaded when this <script> tag is added. The entire library is over 9,000 lines of complicated JavaScript, though, so don't expect to understand it all right now!

REPLACING THE HEADING TEXT USING JQUERY

In "Replacing the Heading Text Using the DOM" on page 146, you learned how to replace text using the built-in DOM methods. In this section, we'll update that code to use jQuery to replace the heading text instead. Open *dom.html* and make the changes shown.

```
<!DOCTYPE html>
<html>
<head>
    <title>Playing with the DOM</title>
</head>

<body>
    <h1 id="main-heading">Hello world!</h1>

❶  <script src="https://code.jquery.com/jquery-2.1.0.js"></script>

    <script>
    var newHeadingText = prompt("Please provide a new heading:");
❷  $("#main-heading").text(newHeadingText);
    </script>
</body>
</html>
```

At ❶ we add a new <script> tag to the page to load jQuery. With jQuery loaded, we use the jQuery function $ to select an HTML element.

The $ function takes one argument, called a *selector string*, which tells jQuery which element or elements to select from the DOM tree. In this case, we entered "#main-heading" as the argument. The # character in a selector string means "ID," so our selector string "#main-heading" means "the element with an id of main-heading."

The $ function returns a jQuery object that represents the elements you selected. For example, $("#main-heading") returns a jQuery object for the h1 element (which has an id of "main-heading").

We now have a jQuery object representing the h1 element. We can modify its text by calling the text method on the jQuery object at ❷, passing in the new text for that element, and replacing the text of the heading with the user input saved to the variable new-HeadingText. As before, when you load this page, a dialog should prompt you to enter replacement text for the old text in the h1 element.

CREATING NEW ELEMENTS WITH JQUERY

In addition to manipulating elements with jQuery, we can also use jQuery to create new elements and add them to the DOM tree. To do so, we call append on a jQuery object with a string containing HTML. The append method converts the string to a DOM element (using the HTML tags in the string) and adds the new element to the end of the original one.

For example, to add a p element to the end of the page, we could add this to our JavaScript:

```
$("body").append("<p>This is a new paragraph</p>");
```

The first part of this statement uses the $ function with the selector string "body" to select the body of our HTML document. The selector string doesn't have to be an id. The code $("body") selects the body element. Likewise, we could use the code $("p") to select all the p elements.

Next, we call the append method on the object returned by $("body"). The string passed to append is turned into a DOM element, and it is added inside the body element, just before the closing tag. Figure 9-4 shows what our revised page would look like.

Figure 9-4: Our document with a new element

We could also use append to add multiple elements in a for loop like this:

```
for (var i = 0; i < 3; i++) {
  var hobby = prompt("Tell me one of your hobbies!");
  $("body").append("<p>" + hobby + "</p>");
}
```

This loops three times. Each time through a loop, a prompt appears, asking users to enter one of their hobbies. Each hobby is then put inside a set of <p> tags and passed to the append method, which adds the hobby to the end of the body element. Try adding this code to your *dom.html* document, and then load it in a browser to test it. It should look like Figure 9-5.

Figure 9-5: Extra elements added in a loop

ANIMATING ELEMENTS WITH JQUERY

Lots of websites use animations to show and hide content. For example, if you were adding a new paragraph of text to your page, you might want to fade it in slowly so it doesn't appear all of a sudden.

jQuery makes it easy to animate elements. For example, to fade an element out, we can use the fadeOut method. To test this method, replace the contents of the second script element in *dom.html* with this:

```
$("h1").fadeOut(3000);
```

We use the $ function to select all h1 elements. Because *dom.html* has only one h1 element (the heading containing the text Hello world!), that heading is selected as a jQuery object. By calling .fadeOut(3000) on this jQuery object, we make the heading fade away until it disappears, over the course of 3 seconds. (The argument to fadeOut is in milliseconds, or thousandths of a second, so entering 3000 makes the animation last 3 seconds.)

As soon as you load the page with this code, the h1 element should start to fade away.

CHAINING JQUERY ANIMATIONS

When you call a method on a jQuery object, the method usually returns the original object that it was called on. For example, $("h1") returns a jQuery object representing all h1 elements, and $("h1").fadeOut(3000) returns the *same* jQuery object representing all h1 elements. To change the text of the h1 element and fade it out, you could enter:

```
$("h1").text("This will fade out").fadeOut(3000);
```

Calling multiple methods in a row like this is known as *chaining*.

We can chain multiple animations on the same element. For example, here's how we could chain a call to the fadeOut and fadeIn methods to fade an element out and then immediately fade it in again:

```
$("h1").fadeOut(3000).fadeIn(2000);
```

The fadeIn animation makes an invisible element fade back in. jQuery is smart enough to know that when you chain two animations in a row like this, you probably want them to happen one after the other. Therefore, this code fades the h1 element out over the course of 3 seconds and then fades it back in over 2 seconds.

jQuery provides two additional animation methods similar to fadeOut and fadeIn, called slideUp and slideDown. The slideUp method makes elements disappear by sliding them up, and slideDown makes them reappear by sliding them down. Replace the second script element in the *dom.html* document with the following, and reload the page to try it out:

```
$("h1").slideUp(1000).slideDown(1000);
```

Here we select the h1 element, slide it up over 1 second, and then slide it down over 1 second until it reappears.

We use `fadeIn` to make invisible elements visible. But what happens if you call `fadeIn` on an element that's already visible or an element that comes *after* the element you're animating?

For example, say you add a new `p` element to your *dom.html* document after the heading. Try using `slideUp` and `slideDown` to hide and show the `h1` element, and see what happens to the `p` element. What if you use `fadeOut` and `fadeIn`?

What happens if you call `fadeOut` and `fadeIn` on the same element without chaining the calls? For example:

```
$("h1").fadeOut(1000);
$("h1").fadeIn(1000);
```

Try adding the preceding code inside a `for` loop set to run five times. What happens?

What do you think the `show` and `hide` jQuery methods do? Try them out to see if you're right. How could you use `hide` to fade in an element that's already visible?

WHAT YOU LEARNED

In this chapter, you learned how to update HTML pages using JavaScript by manipulating DOM elements. As you've seen, jQuery gives us even more powerful ways to select elements and change or even animate them. You also learned a new HTML attribute, `id`, which allows you to give an element a unique identifier.

In the next chapter, you'll learn how to control when your JavaScript is run—for example, once a timer has run out or when you click a button. We'll also look at how to run the same piece of code multiple times with a time delay in between—for example, updating a clock once every second.

PROGRAMMING CHALLENGES

Try these challenges to practice more things you can do with jQuery and DOM elements.

#1: LISTING YOUR FRIENDS WITH JQUERY (AND MAKING THEM SMELL!)

Create an array containing the names of a few friends. Using a for loop, create a p element for each of your friends and add it to the end of the body element using the jQuery append method. Use jQuery to change the h1 element so it says My friends instead of Hello world!. Use the hide method followed by the fadeIn method to fade in each name as it's provided.

Now, modify the p elements you created to add the text smells! after each friend. Hint: If you select the p elements using $("p"), the append method will apply to all the p elements.

#2: MAKING A HEADING FLASH

How could you use fadeOut and fadeIn to cause the heading to flash five times, once a second? How could you do this using a for loop? Try modifying your loop so it fades out and fades in over 1 second the first time, over 2 seconds the second time, over 3 seconds the third time, and so on.

#3: DELAYING ANIMATIONS

The delay method can be used to delay animations. Using delay, fadeOut, and fadeIn, make an element on your page fade out and then fade back in again after 5 seconds.

#4: USING FADETO

Try using the fadeTo method. Its first argument is a number of milliseconds, as in all the other animation methods. Its second argument is a number between 0 and 1. What happens when you run the following code?

```
$("h1").fadeTo(2000, 0.5);
```

What do you think the second argument means? Try using different values between 0 and 1 to figure out what the second argument is used for.

10

INTERACTIVE PROGRAMMING

Until now, the JavaScript code on our web pages has run as soon as the page is loaded, pausing only if we include a call to a function like alert or confirm. But we don't always necessarily want all of our code to run as soon as the page loads—what if we want some code to run after a delay or in response to something the user does?

In this chapter, we'll look at different ways of modifying *when* our code is run. Programming in this way is called *interactive programming*. This will let us create interactive web pages that change over time and respond to actions by the user.

DELAYING CODE WITH SETTIMEOUT

Instead of having JavaScript execute a function immediately, you can tell it to execute a function after a certain period of time. Delaying a function like this is called *setting a timeout*. To set a timeout in JavaScript, we use the function setTimeout. This function takes two arguments (as shown in Figure 10-1): the function to call after the time has elapsed and the amount of time to wait (in milliseconds).

The function to call after
timeout milliseconds have passed
↓

setTimeout(func, timeout)
↑

The number of milliseconds to wait
before calling the function

Figure 10-1: The arguments for setTimeout

The following listing shows how we could use setTimeout to display an alert dialog.

```
❶ var timeUp = function () {
     alert("Time's up!");
   };

❷ setTimeout(timeUp, 3000);
   1
```

At ❶ we create the function timeUp, which opens an alert dialog that displays the text "Time's up!". At ❷ we call setTimeout with two arguments: the function we want to call (timeUp) and the number of milliseconds (3000) to wait before calling that function. We're essentially saying, "Wait 3 seconds and then call timeUp." When setTimeout(timeUp, 3000) is first called, nothing happens, but after 3 seconds timeUp is called and the alert dialog pops up.

Notice that calling `setTimeout` returns 1. This return value is called the *timeout ID*. The timeout ID is a number that's used to identify this particular timeout (that is, this particular delayed function call). The actual number returned could be any number, since it's just an identifier. Call `setTimeout` again, and it should return a different timeout ID, as shown here:

```
setTimeout(timeUp, 5000);
2
```

You can use this timeout ID with the `clearTimeout` function to cancel that specific timeout. We'll look at that next.

CANCELING A TIMEOUT

Once you've called `setTimeout` to set up a delayed function call, you may find that you don't actually want to call that function after all. For example, if you set an alarm to remind you to do your homework, but you end up doing your homework early, you'd want to cancel that alarm. To cancel a timeout, use the function `clearTimeout` on the timeout ID returned by `setTimeout`. For example, say we create a "do your homework" alarm like this:

```
var doHomeworkAlarm = function () {
  alert("Hey! You need to do your homework!");
};
```

❶ `var timeoutId = setTimeout(doHomeworkAlarm, 60000);`

The function `doHomeworkAlarm` pops up an alert dialog telling you to do your homework. When we call `setTimeout(doHomeworkAlarm, 60000)` we're telling JavaScript to execute that function after 60,000 milliseconds (or 60 seconds) has passed. At ❶ we make this call to `setTimeout` and save the timeout ID in a new variable called `timeoutId`.

To cancel the timeout, pass the timeout ID to the `clearTimeout` function like this:

```
clearTimeout(timeoutId);
```

Now `setTimeout` won't call the `doHomeworkAlarm` function after all.

CALLING CODE MULTIPLE TIMES WITH SETINTERVAL

The setInterval function is like setTimeout, except that it repeatedly calls the supplied function after regular pauses, or *intervals*. For example, if you wanted to update a clock display using JavaScript, you could use setInterval to call an update function every second. You call setInterval with two arguments: the function you want to call and the length of the interval (in milliseconds), as shown in Figure 10-2.

```
            The function to call
       every interval milliseconds
                     ↓
setInterval(func, interval)
                       ↑
       The number of milliseconds to wait
              between each call
```

Figure 10-2: The arguments for setInterval

Here's how we could write a message to the console every second:

```
❶ var counter = 1;

❷ var printMessage = function () {
     console.log("You have been staring at your console for " + counter ↵
   + " seconds");
❸   counter++;
   };

❹ var intervalId = setInterval(printMessage, 1000);
   You have been staring at your console for 1 seconds
   You have been staring at your console for 2 seconds
   You have been staring at your console for 3 seconds
   You have been staring at your console for 4 seconds
   You have been staring at your console for 5 seconds
   You have been staring at your console for 6 seconds
❺ clearInterval(intervalId);
```

At ❶ we create a new variable called counter and set it to 1. We'll be using this variable to keep track of the number of seconds you've been looking at your console.

At ❷ we create a function called printMessage. This function does two things. First, it prints out a message telling you how long you have been staring at your console. Then, at ❸, it increments the counter variable.

Next, at ❹, we call setInterval, passing the printMessage function and the number 1000. Calling setInterval like this means "call printMessage every 1,000 milliseconds." Just as setTimeout returns a timeout ID, setInterval returns an *interval ID*, which we save in the variable intervalId. We can use this interval ID to tell JavaScript to stop executing the printMessage function. This is what we do at ❺, using the clearInterval function.

TRY IT OUT!

Modify the preceding example to print the message every five seconds instead of every second.

ANIMATING ELEMENTS WITH SETINTERVAL

As it turns out, we can use setInterval to animate elements in a browser. Basically, we need to create a function that moves an element by a small amount, and then pass that function to setInterval with a short interval time. If we make the movements small enough and the interval short enough, the animation will look very smooth.

Let's animate the position of some text in an HTML document by moving the text horizontally in the browser window. Create a document called *interactive.html*, and fill it with this HTML:

```
<!DOCTYPE html>
<html>
<head>
    <title>Interactive programming</title>
</head>

<body>
    <h1 id="heading">Hello world!</h1>

    <script src="https://code.jquery.com/jquery-2.1.0.js"></script>

    <script>
    // We'll fill this in next
    </script>
</body>
</html>
```

Now let's look at the JavaScript. As always, put your code inside the <script> tags of the HTML document.

```
❶ var leftOffset = 0;

❷ var moveHeading = function () {
❸     $("#heading").offset({ left: leftOffset });

❹     leftOffset++;

❺     if (leftOffset > 200) {
         leftOffset = 0;
       }
   };

❻ setInterval(moveHeading, 30);
```

When you open this page, you should see the heading element gradually move across the screen until it travels 200 pixels; at that point, it will jump back to the beginning and start again. Let's see how this works.

At ❶ we create the variable leftOffset, which we'll use later to position our Hello world! heading. It starts with a value of 0, which means the heading will start on the far left side of the page.

Next, at ❷, we create the function moveHeading, which we'll
call later with setInterval. Inside the moveHeading function, at ❸, we
use $("#heading") to select the element with the id of "heading" (our
h1 element) and use the offset method to set the left offset of the
heading—that is, how far it is from the left side of the screen.

The offset method takes an object that can contain a left
property, which sets the left offset of the element, or a top property,
which sets the top offset of the element. In this example we use
the left property and set it to our leftOffset variable. If we wanted
a static offset (that is, an offset that doesn't change), we could set
the property to a numeric value. For example, calling $("#heading")
.offset({ left: 100 }) would place the heading element 100 pixels
from the left side of the page.

At ❹ we increment the leftOffset variable by 1. To make sure
the heading doesn't move too far, at ❺ we check to see if leftOffset
is greater than 200, and if it is, we reset it to 0. Finally, at ❻ we
call setInterval, and for its arguments we pass in the function
moveHeading and the number 30 (for 30 milliseconds).

This code calls the moveHeading function every 30 milliseconds,
or about 33 times every second. Each time moveHeading is called, the
leftOffset variable is incremented, and the value of this variable
is used to set the position of the heading element. Because the
function is constantly being called and leftOffset is incremented
by 1 each time, the heading gradually moves across the screen by
1 pixel every 30 milliseconds.

TRY IT OUT!

You can speed up this animation by raising the amount
that leftOffset is increased every time moveHeading is called
or by reducing the time that setInterval waits between calls
to moveHeading.

How would you *double* the speed that the heading moves?
Try it with both techniques. What difference do you see?

RESPONDING TO USER ACTIONS

As you've seen, one way to control when code is run is with the functions setTimeout and setInterval, which run a function once a fixed amount of time has passed. Another way is to run code only when a user performs certain actions, such as clicking, typing, or even just moving the mouse. This will let users interact with your web page so that your page responds according to what they do.

In a browser, every time you perform an action such as clicking, typing, or moving your mouse, something called an *event* is triggered. An event is the browser's way of saying, "This thing happened!" You can listen to these events by adding an *event handler* to the element where the event happened. Adding an event handler is your way of telling JavaScript, "If this event happens on this element, call this function." For example, if you want a function to be called when the user clicks a heading element, you could add a click event handler to the heading element. We'll look at how to do that next.

RESPONDING TO CLICKS

When a user clicks an element in the browser, this triggers a *click event*. jQuery makes it easy to add a handler for a click event. Open the *interactive.html* document you created earlier, use **File ▸ Save As** to save it as *clicks.html*, and replace its second script element with this code:

```
❶ var clickHandler = function (event) {
❷   console.log("Click! " + event.pageX + " " + event.pageY);
  };

❸ $("h1").click(clickHandler);
```

At ❶ we create the function clickHandler with the single argument event. When this function is called, the event argument will be an object holding information about the click event, such as the location of the click. At ❷, inside the handler function, we use console.log to output the properties pageX and pageY from the event object. These properties tell us the event's *x*- and *y*-coordinates—in other words, they say where on the page the click occurred.

Finally, at ❸ we activate the click handler. The code $("h1") selects the h1 element, and calling $("h1").click(clickHandler) means "When there is a click on the h1 element, call the clickHandler function and pass it the event object." In this case, the click handler retrieves information from the event object to output the *x*- and *y*-coordinates of the click location.

Reload your modified page in your browser and click the heading element. Each time you click the heading, a new line should be output to the console, as shown in the following listing. Each line shows two numbers: the *x*- and *y*-coordinates of the clicked location.

```
Click! 88 43
Click! 63 53
Click! 24 53
Click! 121 46
Click! 93 55
Click! 103 48
```

BROWSER COORDINATES

In the web browser and in most programming and graphics environments, the 0 position of the *x*- and *y*-coordinates is at the top-left corner of the screen. As the *x*-coordinate increases, you move right across the page, and as the *y*-coordinate increases, you move down the page (see Figure 10-3).

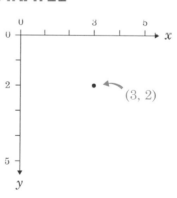

Figure 10-3: Coordinates in the browser, showing a click at the coordinate (3, 2)

THE MOUSEMOVE EVENT

The mousemove event is triggered every time the mouse moves. To try it out, create a file called *mousemove.html* and enter this code:

```
<!DOCTYPE html>
<html>
<head>
    <title>Mousemove</title>
</head>

<body>
    <h1 id="heading">Hello world!</h1>

    <script src="https://code.jquery.com/jquery-2.1.0.js"></script>

    <script>
➊    $("html").mousemove(function (event) {
➋      $("#heading").offset({
          left: event.pageX,
          top: event.pageY
        });
      });
    </script>
</body>
</html>
```

At ➊ we add a handler for the mousemove event using $("html") .mousemove(*handler*). In this case, the *handler* is the entire function that appears after mousemove and before </script>. We use $("html") to select the html element so that the handler is triggered by mouse movements that occur anywhere on the page. The function that we pass into the parentheses after mousemove will be called every time the user moves the mouse.

In this example, instead of creating the event handler separately and passing the function name to the mousemove method (as we did with our clickHandler function earlier), we're passing the handler function directly to the mousemove method. This is a very common way of writing event handlers, so it's good to be familiar with this type of syntax.

At ➋, inside the event handler function, we select the heading element and call the offset method on it. As I

mentioned before, the object passed to offset can have left and top properties. In this case, we set the left property to event.pageX and the top property to event.pageY. Now, every time the mouse moves, the heading will move to that location. In other words, wherever you move the mouse, the heading follows it!

WHAT YOU LEARNED

In this chapter, you learned how to write JavaScript that runs only when you want it to. The setTimeout and setInterval functions are great for timing code to run after a delay or at certain intervals. If you want to run code when the user does something in the browser, you can use events like click and mousemove, but there are many others.

In the next chapter, we'll put what you've just learned to good use to make a game!

PROGRAMMING CHALLENGES

Here are a few challenges to explore more ways to use interactive programming.

#1: FOLLOW THE CLICKS

Modify the previous mousemove program so that instead of following your mouse, the heading will follow just your clicks. Whenever you click the page, the heading should move to the click location.

#2: CREATE YOUR OWN ANIMATION

Use setInterval to animate an h1 heading element around the page, in a square. It should move 200 pixels to the right, 200 pixels down, 200 pixels to the left, 200 pixels up, and then start again. Hint: You'll need to keep track of your current direction (right, down, left, or up) so that you know whether to increase or decrease the left or top offset of the heading. You'll also need to change the direction when you reach a corner of the square.

(continued)

#3: CANCEL AN ANIMATION WITH A CLICK

Building upon Challenge #2, add a click handler to the moving `h1` element that cancels the animation. Hint: You can cancel intervals with the `clearInterval` function.

#4: MAKE A "CLICK THE HEADER" GAME!

Modify Challenge #3 so that every time a player clicks the heading, instead of stopping, the heading speeds up, making it harder and harder to click. Keep track of the number of times the heading has been clicked and update the heading text so it shows this number. When the player has reached 10 clicks, stop the animation and change the text of the heading to "You Win." Hint: To speed up, you'll have to cancel the current interval and then start a new one with a shorter interval time.

11

FIND THE BURIED TREASURE!

Let's put what we've learned so far to good use and make a game! The aim of this game is to find the hidden treasure. In this game, the web page will display a treasure map. Inside that map, the program will pick a single pixel location, which represents where the hidden treasure is buried. Every time the player clicks the map, the web page will tell them how close to the treasure they are. When they click the location of the treasure (or very close to it), the game congratulates them on finding the treasure and says how many clicks it took to find it. Figure 11-1 shows what the game will look like after a player clicks the map.

Figure 11-1: The buried treasure game

DESIGNING THE GAME

Before we start writing the code, let's break down the overall structure of this game. Here is a list of steps we need to take to set up the game so it can respond accordingly when a player clicks the treasure map.

1. Create a web page with an image (the treasure map) and a place to display messages to the player.
2. Pick a random spot on the map picture to hide the treasure.

3. Create a click handler. Each time the player clicks the map, the click handler will do the following:

   a. Add 1 to a click counter.

   b. Calculate how far the click location is from the treasure location.

   c. Display a message on the web page to tell the player whether they're hot or cold.

   d. Congratulate the player if they click on the treasure or very close to it, and say how many clicks it took to find the treasure.

I'll show you how to implement each of these features in the game, and then we'll go through the full code.

CREATING THE WEB PAGE WITH HTML

Let's look at the HTML for the game. We'll use a new element called img for the treasure map and add a p element where we can display messages to the player. Enter the following code into a new file called *treasure.html*.

```
<!DOCTYPE html>
<html>
<head>
    <title>Find the buried treasure!</title>
</head>

<body>
    <h1 id="heading">Find the buried treasure!</h1>

➊   <img id="map" width=400 height=400 ↵
➋     src="http://nostarch.com/images/treasuremap.png">

➌   <p id="distance"></p>

    <script src="https://code.jquery.com/jquery-2.1.0.js"></script>

    <script>
    // Game code goes here
    </script>
</body>
</html>
```

The img element is used to include images in HTML documents. Unlike the other HTML elements we've looked at, img doesn't use a closing tag. All you need is an opening tag, which, like other HTML tags, can contain various attributes. At ❶ we've added an img element with an id of "map". We set the width and height of this element using the width and height attributes, which are both set to 400. This means our image will be 400 pixels tall and 400 pixels wide.

To tell the document which image we want to display, we use the src attribute to include the web address of the image at ❷. In this case, we're linking to an image called *treasuremap.png* on the No Starch Press website.

Following the img element is an empty p element at ❸, which we give an id of "distance". We'll add text to this element by using JavaScript to tell the player how close they are to the treasure.

PICKING A RANDOM TREASURE LOCATION

Now let's build the JavaScript for our game. First we need to pick a random location for the hidden treasure inside the treasure map image. Since the dimensions of the map are 400 by 400 pixels, the coordinates of the top-left pixel will be { x: 0, y: 0 }, and the bottom-right pixel will be { x: 399, y: 399 }.

PICKING RANDOM NUMBERS

To set a random coordinate point within the treasure map, we pick a random number between 0 and 399 for the x value and a random number between 0 and 399 for the y value. To generate these random values, we'll write a function that takes a size argument as input and picks a random number from 0 up to (but not including) size:

```
var getRandomNumber = function (size) {
  return Math.floor(Math.random() * size);
};
```

This code is similar to the code we've used to pick random words in earlier chapters. We generate a random number between

0 and 1 using `Math.random`, multiply that by the `size` argument, and then use `Math.floor` to round that number down to a whole number. Then we output the result as the return value of the function. Calling `getRandomNumber(400)` will return a random number from 0 to 399, which is just what we need!

SETTING THE TREASURE COORDINATES

Now let's use the `getRandomNumber` function to set the treasure coordinates:

```
❶ var width = 400;
   var height = 400;

❷ var target = {
     x: getRandomNumber(width),
     y: getRandomNumber(height)
   };
```

The section of code at ❶ sets the `width` and `height` variables, which represent the width and height of the `img` element that we're using as a treasure map. At ❷ we create an object called target, which has two properties, x and y, that represent the coordinates of the buried treasure. The x and y properties are both set by getRandomNumber. Each time we run this code, we get a new random location on the map, and the chosen coordinates will be saved in the x and y properties of the target variable.

THE CLICK HANDLER

The click handler is the function that will be called when the player clicks the treasure map. Start building this function with this code:

```
$("#map").click(function (event) {
  // Click handler code goes here
});
```

First we use `$("#map")` to select the treasure map area (because the `img` element has an `id` of `"map"`), and then we go into the click handler function. Each time the player clicks the map, the function body between the curly brackets will be executed. Information about the click is passed into that function body as an object through the event argument.

This click handler function needs to do quite a bit of work: it has to increment the click counter, calculate how far each click is from the treasure, and display messages. Before we fill in the code for the click handler function, we'll define some variables and create some other functions that will help execute all these steps.

COUNTING CLICKS

The first thing our click handler needs to do is track the total number of clicks. To set this up, we create a variable called clicks at the beginning of the program (outside the click handler) and initialize it to zero:

```
var clicks = 0;
```

Inside the click handler, we'll include clicks++ so that we increment clicks by 1 each time the player clicks the map.

CALCULATING THE DISTANCE BETWEEN THE CLICK AND THE TREASURE

To figure out whether the player is hot or cold (close to the treasure or far away), we need to measure the distance between where the player clicked and the location of the hidden treasure. To do this, we'll write a function called getDistance, like so:

```
var getDistance = function (event, target) {
  var diffX = event.offsetX - target.x;
  var diffY = event.offsetY - target.y;
  return Math.sqrt((diffX * diffX) + (diffY * diffY));
};
```

The getDistance function takes two objects as arguments: event and target. The event object is the object passed to the click handler, and it comes with lots of built-in information about the player's click. In particular, it contains two properties called offsetX and offsetY, which tell us the x- and y-coordinates of the click, and that's exactly the information we need.

Inside the function, the variable diffX stores the horizontal distance between the clicked location and the target, which we calculate by subtracting target.x (the x-coordinate of the treasure) from event.offsetX (the x-coordinate of the click). We calculate the vertical distance between the points in the same way, and store the result as diffY. Figure 11-2 shows how we would calculate diffX and diffY for two points.

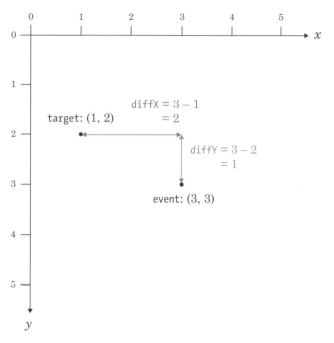

Figure 11-2: Calculating the horizontal and vertical distances between event and target

USING THE PYTHAGOREAN THEOREM

Next, the getDistance function uses the *Pythagorean theorem* to calculate the distance between two points. The Pythagorean theorem says that for a right triangle, where a and b represent the lengths of the two sides bordering the right angle and c represents the length of the diagonal side (the *hypotenuse*), $a^2 + b^2 = c^2$. Given the lengths of a and b, we can calculate the length of the hypotenuse by calculating the square root of $a^2 + b^2$.

To calculate the distance between the event and the target, we treat the two points as if they're part of a right triangle, as shown in Figure 11-3. In the getDistance function, diffX is the length of the horizontal edge of the triangle, and diffY is the length of the vertical edge.

To calculate the distance between the click and the treasure, we need to calculate the length of the hypotenuse, based on the lengths diffX and diffY. A sample calculation is shown in Figure 11-3.

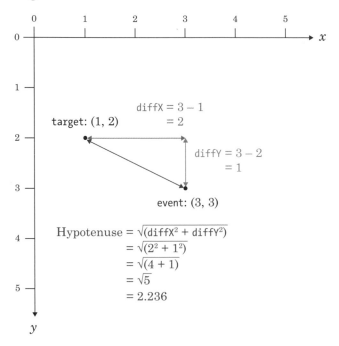

Figure 11-3: Calculating the hypotenuse to find out the distance between event and target

To get the length of the hypotenuse, we first have to square diffX and diffY. We then add these squared values together, and get the square root using the JavaScript function Math.sqrt. So our complete formula for calculating the distance between the click and the target looks like this:

```
Math.sqrt((diffX * diffX) + (diffY * diffY))
```

The getDistance function calculates this and returns the result.

TELLING THE PLAYER HOW CLOSE THEY ARE

Once we know the distance between the player's click and the treasure, we want to display a hint telling the player how close they are to the treasure, without telling them exactly how far away the treasure is. For this, we use the getDistanceHint function shown here:

```
var getDistanceHint = function (distance) {
  if (distance < 10) {
    return "Boiling hot!";
  } else if (distance < 20) {
    return "Really hot";
  } else if (distance < 40) {
    return "Hot";
  } else if (distance < 80) {
    return "Warm";
  } else if (distance < 160) {
    return "Cold";
  } else if (distance < 320) {
    return "Really cold";
  } else {
    return "Freezing!";
  }
};
```

This function returns different strings depending on the calculated distance from the treasure. If the distance is less than 10, the function returns the string "Boiling hot!". If the distance is between 10 and 20, the function returns "Really hot". The strings get colder as the distance increases, up to the point where we return "Freezing!" if the distance is greater than 320 pixels.

We display the message to the player by adding it as text in the p element of the web page. The following code will go inside our click handler to calculate the distance, pick the appropriate string, and display that string to the player:

```
var distance = getDistance(event, target);
var distanceHint = getDistanceHint(distance);
$("#distance").text(distanceHint);
```

As you can see, we first call getDistance and then save the result as the variable distance. Next we pass that distance to the getDistanceHint function to pick the appropriate string and save it as distanceHint.

The code `$("#distance").text(distanceHint);` selects the element with the id of `"distance"` (in this case the p element) and sets its text to `distanceHint` so that each time the player clicks the map, our web page tells them how close they are to the target.

CHECKING IF THE PLAYER WON

Finally, our click handler needs to check whether the player has won. Because pixels are so small, instead of making the player click the exact location of the treasure, we'll let them win if they click within 8 pixels.

This code checks the distance to the treasure and displays a message telling the player that they've won:

```
if (distance < 8) {
  alert("Found the treasure in " + clicks + " clicks!");
}
```

If the distance is less than 8 pixels, this code uses `alert` to tell the player they found the treasure and how many clicks it took them to do so.

PUTTING IT ALL TOGETHER

Now that we have all the pieces, let's combine them to make one script.

```
// Get a random number from 0 to size
var getRandomNumber = function (size) {
  return Math.floor(Math.random() * size);
};

// Calculate distance between click event and target
var getDistance = function (event, target) {
  var diffX = event.offsetX - target.x;
  var diffY = event.offsetY - target.y;
  return Math.sqrt((diffX * diffX) + (diffY * diffY));
};

// Get a string representing the distance
var getDistanceHint = function (distance) {
  if (distance < 10) {
    return "Boiling hot!";
```

```
      } else if (distance < 20) {
        return "Really hot";
      } else if (distance < 40) {
        return "Hot";
      } else if (distance < 80) {
        return "Warm";
      } else if (distance < 160) {
        return "Cold";
      } else if (distance < 320) {
        return "Really cold";
      } else {
        return "Freezing!";
      }
    };

    // Set up our variables
❶  var width = 400;
    var height = 400;
    var clicks = 0;

    // Create a random target location
❷  var target = {
      x: getRandomNumber(width),
      y: getRandomNumber(height)
    };

    // Add a click handler to the img element
❸  $("#map").click(function (event) {
      clicks++;

      // Get distance between click event and target
❹    var distance = getDistance(event, target);
      // Convert distance to a hint
❺    var distanceHint = getDistanceHint(distance);

      // Update the #distance element with the new hint
❻    $("#distance").text(distanceHint);

      // If the click was close enough, tell them they won
❼    if (distance < 8) {
        alert("Found the treasure in " + clicks + " clicks!");
      }
    });
```

First, we have the three functions getRandomNumber, getDistance, and getDistanceHint, which we've already looked at. Then, at ❶, we set up the variables we'll need: `width`, `height`, and `clicks`. After that, at ❷, we create the random location for the treasure.

At ❸ we create a click handler on the `map` element. The first thing this does is increment the `clicks` variable by 1. Then, at ❹, it works out the distance between `event` (the click location) and `target` (the treasure location). At ❺ we use the function `getDistanceHint` to convert this distance into a string representing the distance (`"Cold"`, `"Warm"`, and so on). We update the display at ❻ so the user can see how far they are. Finally, at ❼, we check to see whether the distance is under 8, and if so, we tell the player they've won and in how many clicks.

This is the entire JavaScript for our game. If you add this to the second `<script>` tag in *treasure.html*, you should be able to play it in your browser! How many clicks does it take you to find the treasure?

WHAT YOU LEARNED

In this chapter, you used your new event-handling skills to create a game. You also learned about the `img` element, which can be used to add images to a web page. Finally, you learned how to measure the distance between two points using JavaScript.

In the next chapter, we'll learn about object-oriented programming, which will give us more tools for organizing our code.

PROGRAMMING CHALLENGES

Here are a few ways you could change the game and add more features.

#1: INCREASING THE PLAYING AREA

You could make the game harder by increasing the size of the playing area. How would you make it 800 pixels wide by 800 pixels tall?

#2: ADDING MORE MESSAGES

Try adding some extra messages to display to the player (like "Really really cold!"), and modify the distances to make the game your own.

#3: ADDING A CLICK LIMIT

Add a limit to the number of clicks and show the message "GAME OVER" if the player exceeds this limit.

#4: DISPLAYING THE NUMBER OF REMAINING CLICKS

Show the number of remaining clicks as an extra piece of text after the distance display so the player knows if they're about to lose.

12
OBJECT-ORIENTED PROGRAMMING

Chapter 4 discussed JavaScript objects—collections of keys paired with values. In this chapter, we'll look at ways to create and use objects as we explore *object-oriented programming*. Object-oriented programming is a way to design and write programs so that all of the program's important parts are represented by objects. For example, when building a racing game, you could use object-oriented programming techniques to represent each car as an object and then create multiple car objects that share the same properties and functionality.

A SIMPLE OBJECT

In Chapter 4, you learned that objects are made up of properties, which are simply pairs of keys and values. For example, in the following code the object dog represents a dog with the properties name, legs, and isAwesome:

```
var dog = {
  name: "Pancake",
  legs: 4,
  isAwesome: true
};
```

Once we create an object, we can access its properties using dot notation (discussed in "Accessing Values in Objects" on page 66). For example, here's how we could access the name property of our dog object:

```
dog.name;
"Pancake"
```

We can also use dot notation to add properties to a JavaScript object, like this:

```
dog.age = 6;
```

This adds a new key-value pair (age: 6) to the object, as you can see below:

```
dog;
Object {name: "Pancake", legs: 4, isAwesome: true, age: 6}
```

ADDING METHODS TO OBJECTS

In the preceding example, we created several properties with different kinds of values saved to them: a string ("Pancake"), numbers (4 and 6), and a Boolean (true). In addition to strings, numbers, and Booleans, you can save a *function* as a property inside an object. When you save a function as a property in an object, that property is called a *method*. In fact, we've already used several built-in JavaScript methods, like the join method on arrays and the toUpperCase method on strings.

Now let's see how to create our own methods. One way to add a method to an object is with dot notation. For example, we could add a method called bark to the dog object like this:

```
❶ dog.bark = function () {
❷   console.log("Woof woof! My name is " + this.name + "!");
};

❸ dog.bark();
Woof woof! My name is Pancake!
```

At ❶ we add a property to the dog object called bark and assign a function to it. At ❷, inside this new function, we use console.log to log Woof woof! My name is Pancake!. Notice that the function uses this.name, which retrieves the value saved in the object's name property. Let's take a closer look at how the this keyword works.

USING THE THIS KEYWORD

You can use the this keyword inside a method to refer to the object on which the method is currently being called. For example, when you call the bark method on the dog object, this refers to the dog object, so this.name refers to dog.name. The this keyword makes methods more versatile, allowing you to add the same method to multiple objects and have it access the properties of whatever object it's currently being called on.

SHARING A METHOD BETWEEN MULTIPLE OBJECTS

Let's create a new function called speak that we can use as a method in multiple objects that represent different animals. When speak is called on an object, it will use the object's name (this.name) and the sound the animal makes (this.sound) to log a message.

```
var speak = function () {
  console.log(this.sound + "! My name is " + this.name + "!");
};
```

Now let's create another object so we can add speak to it as a method:

```
var cat = {
  sound: "Miaow",
  name: "Mittens",
❶  speak: speak
};
```

Here we create a new object called cat, with sound, name, and speak properties. We set the speak property at ❶ and assign it the speak function we created earlier. Now cat.speak is a method that we can call by entering cat.speak(). Since we used the this keyword in the method, when we call it on cat, it will access the cat object's properties. Let's see that now:

```
cat.speak();
Miaow! My name is Mittens!
```

When we call the cat.speak method, it retrieves two properties from the cat object: this.sound (which is "Miaow") and this.name (which is "Mittens").

We can use the same speak function as a method in other objects too:

```
var pig = {
  sound: "Oink",
  name: "Charlie",
  speak: speak
};

var horse = {
  sound: "Neigh",
  name: "Marie",
  speak: speak
};

pig.speak();
Oink! My name is Charlie!

horse.speak();
Neigh! My name is Marie!
```

Again, each time this appears inside a method, it refers to the object on which the method is called. In other words, when you call horse.speak(), this will refer to horse, and when you call pig.speak(), this refers to pig.

To share methods between multiple objects, you can simply add them to each object, as we just did with speak. But if you have lots of methods or objects, adding the same methods to each object individually can become annoying, and it can make your code messier, too. Just imagine if you needed a whole zoo full of 100 animal objects and you wanted each to share a set of 10 methods and properties.

JavaScript object constructors offer a better way to share methods and properties between objects, as we'll see next.

CREATING OBJECTS USING CONSTRUCTORS

A JavaScript *constructor* is a function that creates objects and gives them a set of built-in properties and methods. Think of it as a specialized machine for creating objects, kind of like a factory that can churn out tons of copies of the same item. Once you've set up a constructor, you can use it to make as many of the same object as you want. To try it out, we'll build the beginnings of a racing game, using a Car constructor to create a fleet of cars with similar basic properties and methods for steering and acceleration.

ANATOMY OF THE CONSTRUCTOR

Each time you call a constructor, it creates an object and gives the new object built-in properties. To call a normal function, you enter the function name followed by a pair of parentheses. To call a constructor, you enter the keyword new (which tells JavaScript that you want to use your function as a constructor), followed by the constructor name and parentheses. Figure 12-1 shows the syntax for calling a constructor.

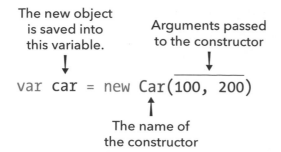

The new object is saved into this variable.

Arguments passed to the constructor

var car = new Car(100, 200)

The name of the constructor

Figure 12-1: The syntax for calling a constructor named Car with two arguments

Most JavaScript programmers start constructor names with a capital letter so it's easy to see at a glance that they're different from other functions.

CREATING A CAR CONSTRUCTOR

Now let's create a Car constructor that will add an x and y property to each new object it creates. These properties will be used to set each car's onscreen position when we draw it.

CREATING THE HTML DOCUMENT

Before we can build our constructor, we need to create a new HTML document. Make a new file called *cars.html* and enter this HTML into it:

```
<!DOCTYPE html>
<html>
<head>
    <title>Cars</title>
</head>

<body>
    <script src="https://code.jquery.com/jquery-2.1.0.js"></script>

    <script>
    // Code goes here
    </script>
</body>
</html>
```

THE CAR CONSTRUCTOR FUNCTION

Now add this code to the empty <script> tags in *cars.html* (replacing the comment // Code goes here) to create the Car constructor that gives each car a set of coordinates.

```
<script>
var Car = function (x, y) {
  this.x = x;
  this.y = y;
};
</script>
```

Our new constructor Car takes the arguments x and y. We've added the properties this.x and this.y to store the x and y values passed to Car in our new object. This way, each time we call Car as a constructor, a new object is created with its x and y properties set to the arguments we specify.

CALLING THE CAR CONSTRUCTOR

As I mentioned earlier, the keyword new tells JavaScript that we're calling a constructor to create a new object. For example, to create a car object named tesla, open *cars.html* in a web browser and then enter this code in the Chrome JavaScript console:

```
var tesla = new Car(10, 20);
tesla;
Car {x: 10, y: 20}
```

The code new Car(10, 20) tells JavaScript to create an object using Car as a constructor, pass in the arguments 10 and 20 for its x and y properties, and return that object. We assign the returned object to the tesla variable with var tesla.

Then when we enter tesla, the Chrome console returns the name of the constructor and its x and y values: Car {x: 10, y: 20}.

DRAWING THE CARS

To show the objects created by the Car constructor, we'll create a function called drawCar to place an image of a car at each car object's (*x*, *y*) position in a browser window. Once we've seen how this function works, we'll rewrite it in a more object-oriented way in "Adding a draw Method to the Car Prototype" on page 191. Add this code between the `<script>` tags in *cars.html*:

```
<script>
var Car = function (x, y) {
  this.x = x;
  this.y = y;
};

var drawCar = function (car) {
❶   var carHtml = '<img src="http://nostarch.com/images/car.png">';

❷   var carElement = $(carHtml);

❸   carElement.css({
      position: "absolute",
      left: car.x,
      top: car.y
    });

❹   $("body").append(carElement);
};
</script>
```

At ❶ we create a string containing HTML that points to an image of a car. (Using single quotes to create this string lets us use double quotes in the HTML.) At ❷ we pass carHTML to the $ function, which converts it from a string to a jQuery element. That means the carElement variable now holds a jQuery element with the information for our `<img>` tag, and we can tweak this element before adding it to the page.

At ❸ we use the css method on carElement to set the position of the car image. This code sets the left position of the image to the car object's x value and its top position to the y value. In other words, the left edge of the image will be x pixels from the left edge of the browser window, and the top edge of the image will be y pixels down from the top edge of the window.

In this example, the css method works like the offset method we used in Chapter 10 to move elements around the page. Unfortunately, offset doesn't work as well with multiple elements, and since we want to draw multiple cars, we're using css here instead.

Finally, at ❹ we use jQuery to append the carElement to the body element of the web page. This final step makes the carElement appear on the page. (For a reminder on how append works, see "Creating New Elements with jQuery" on page 150.)

TESTING THE DRAWCAR FUNCTION

Let's test the drawCar function to make sure it works. Add this code to your *cars.html* file (after the other JavaScript code) to create two cars.

```
    $("body").append(carElement);
};
var tesla = new Car(20, 20);
var nissan = new Car(100, 200);

drawCar(tesla);
drawCar(nissan);
</script>
```

Here, we use the Car constructor to create two car objects, one at the coordinates (20, 20) and the other at (100, 200), and then we use drawCar to draw each of them in the browser. Now when you open *cars.html*, you should see two car images in your browser window, as shown in Figure 12-2.

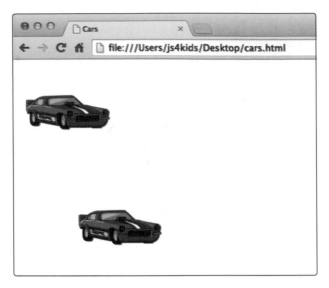

Figure 12-2: Drawing cars using drawCar

CUSTOMIZING OBJECTS WITH PROTOTYPES

A more object-oriented way to draw our cars would be to give each car object a draw method. Then, instead of writing drawCar(tesla), you'd write tesla.draw(). In object-oriented programming, we want objects to have their own functionality built in as methods. In this case, the drawCar function is always meant to be used on car objects, so instead of saving drawCar as a separate function, we should include it as part of each car object.

JavaScript *prototypes* make it easy to share functionality (as methods) between different objects. All constructors have a prototype property, and we can add methods to it. Any method that we add to a constructor's prototype property will be available as a method to all objects created by that constructor.

Figure 12-3 shows the syntax for adding a method to a prototype property.

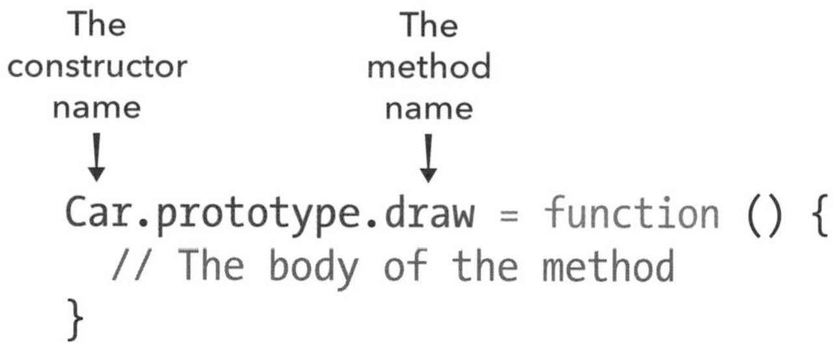

```
      The                      The
  constructor                 method
     name                      name
       │                         │
       ↓                         ↓
  Car.prototype.draw = function () {
    // The body of the method
  }
```

Figure 12-3: The syntax for adding a method to a prototype property

ADDING A DRAW METHOD TO THE CAR PROTOTYPE

Let's add a draw method to Car.prototype so that all objects we create using Car will have the draw method. Using **File ▸ Save As**, save your *cars.html* file as *cars2.html*. Then replace all of the JavaScript in your second set of <script> tags in *cars2.html* with this code:

```
❶ var Car = function (x, y) {
     this.x = x;
     this.y = y;
   };

❷ Car.prototype.draw = function () {
     var carHtml = '<img src="http://nostarch.com/images/car.png">';

❸   this.carElement = $(carHtml);

     this.carElement.css({
       position: "absolute",
❹     left: this.x,
       top: this.y
     });

     $("body").append(this.carElement);
   };

   var tesla = new Car(20, 20);
   var nissan = new Car(100, 200);

   tesla.draw();
   nissan.draw();
```

After creating our Car constructor at ❶, we add a new method called draw to Car.prototype at ❷. This makes the draw method part of all of the objects created by the Car constructor.

The contents of the draw method are a modified version of our drawCar function. First, we create an HTML string and save it as carHTML. At ❸ we create a jQuery element representing this HTML, but this time we save it as a property of the object by assigning it to this.carElement. Then at ❹, we use this.x and this.y to set the coordinates of the top-left corner of the current car image. (Inside a constructor, this refers to the new object currently being created.)

When you run this code, the result should look like Figure 12-2. We haven't changed the code's functionality, only its organization. The advantage to this approach is that the code for drawing the car is part of the car, instead of a separate function.

ADDING A MOVERIGHT METHOD

Now let's add some methods to move the cars around, beginning with a moveRight method to move the car 5 pixels to the right of its current position. Add the following code after your definition of Car.prototype.draw:

```
  this.carElement.css({
    position: "absolute",
    left: this.x,
    top: this.y
  });

  $("body").append(this.carElement);
};

Car.prototype.moveRight = function () {
  this.x += 5;

  this.carElement.css({
    left: this.x,
    top: this.y
  });
};
```

We save the moveRight method in Car.prototype to share it with all objects created by the Car constructor. With this.x += 5 we add 5 to the car's x value, which moves the car 5 pixels to the right. Then we use the css method on this.carElement to update the car's position in the browser.

Try the moveRight method in the browser console. First, refresh *cars2.html*, and then open the console and enter these lines:

```
tesla.moveRight();
tesla.moveRight();
tesla.moveRight();
```

Each time you enter tesla.moveRight, the top car should move 5 pixels to the right. You could use this method in a racing game to show the car moving down the racetrack.

TRY IT OUT!

Try moving nissan to the right. How many times do you need to call moveRight on nissan to make it line up with tesla?

Use setInterval and moveRight to animate nissan so that it drives across the browser window.

ADDING THE LEFT, UP, AND DOWN MOVE METHODS

Now we'll add the remaining directions to our code so that we can move our cars around the screen in any direction. These methods are basically the same as moveRight, so we'll write them all at once.

Add the following methods to *cars2.html* just after the code for moveRight:

```
Car.prototype.moveRight = function () {
  this.x += 5;

  this.carElement.css({
    left: this.x,
    top: this.y
  });
};
```

```
Car.prototype.moveLeft = function () {
  this.x -= 5;

  this.carElement.css({
    left: this.x,
    top: this.y
  });
};

Car.prototype.moveUp = function () {
  this.y -= 5;

  this.carElement.css({
    left: this.x,
    top: this.y
  });
};

Car.prototype.moveDown = function () {
  this.y += 5;

  this.carElement.css({
    left: this.x,
    top: this.y
  });
};
```

Each of these methods moves the car by 5 pixels in the specified direction by adding or subtracting 5 from each car's x or y value.

WHAT YOU LEARNED

In this chapter, you learned the basics of object-oriented programming in JavaScript, including how to create constructors to build new objects and how to modify the prototype property of those constructors to share methods between objects.

In object-oriented programs, most functions are written as methods. For example, to draw the car, we call the draw method on the car, and to move the car to the right, we call the moveRight method. Constructors and prototypes are JavaScript's built-in way of letting you create objects that share the same set of methods, but there are many ways to write object-oriented JavaScript. (For more on object-oriented JavaScript, see Nicholas C. Zakas's *The Principles of Object-Oriented JavaScript* [No Starch Press, 2014].)

Writing JavaScript in an object-oriented way can help you structure your code. Having well-structured code means that when you come back to it later to make changes, it should be easier to figure out how your program works if you don't remember (this is particularly important with bigger programs or when you start to work with other programmers who may need to access your code). For example, in the final project in this book, we'll build a Snake game that requires quite a bit of code, and we'll use objects and methods to organize our game and handle a lot of the important functionality.

In the next chapter, we'll go over how to draw and animate lines and shapes on a web page using the canvas element.

PROGRAMMING CHALLENGES

Try these challenges to practice working with objects and prototypes.

#1: DRAWING IN THE CAR CONSTRUCTOR

Add a call to the draw method from inside the Car constructor so that car objects automatically appear in the browser as soon as you create them.

(continued)

#2: ADDING A SPEED PROPERTY

Modify the Car constructor to add a new speed property with a value of 5 to the constructed objects. Then use this property instead of the value 5 inside the movement methods.

Now try out different values for speed to make the cars move faster or slower.

#3: RACING CARS

Modify the moveLeft, moveRight, moveUp, and moveDown methods so they take a single distance argument, the number of pixels to move, instead of always moving 5 pixels. For example, to move the nissan car 10 pixels to the right, you would call nissan.moveRight(10).

Now, use setInterval to move the two cars (nissan and tesla) to the right every 30 milliseconds by a different random distance between 0 and 5. You should see the two cars animate across the screen, jumping along at varying speeds. Can you guess which car will make it to the edge of the window first?

PART III

CANVAS

13

THE CANVAS ELEMENT

JavaScript isn't all about playing with text and numbers. You can also use JavaScript to draw pictures with the HTML canvas element, which you can think of as a blank canvas or sheet of paper. You can draw almost anything that you want on this canvas, such as lines, shapes, and text. The only limit is your imagination!

In this chapter, you'll learn the basics of drawing on the canvas. In the following chapters, we'll build on our knowledge to create a canvas-based JavaScript game.

CREATING A BASIC CANVAS

As our first step in using the canvas, create a new HTML document for the canvas element, as shown in the following listing. Save this document as *canvas.html*:

```
<!DOCTYPE html>
<html>
<head>
    <title>Canvas</title>
</head>

<body>
❶    <canvas id="canvas" width="200" height="200"></canvas>

    <script>
    // We'll fill this in next
    </script>
</body>
</html>
```

As you can see at ❶, we create a canvas element and give it an id property of "canvas", which we'll use to select the element in our code. The width and height properties set the dimensions of the canvas element in pixels. Here we set both dimensions to 200.

DRAWING ON THE CANVAS

Now that we've built a page with a canvas element, let's draw some rectangles with JavaScript. Enter this JavaScript between the <script> tags in *canvas.html*.

```
var canvas = document.getElementById("canvas");
var ctx = canvas.getContext("2d");
ctx.fillRect(0, 0, 10, 10);
```

We'll go over this code line by line in the following sections.

SELECTING AND SAVING THE CANVAS ELEMENT

First, we select the canvas element using document.getElementById("canvas"). As we saw in Chapter 9, the getElementById method returns a DOM object representing the element with the supplied id. This object is assigned to the canvas variable with the code var canvas = document.getElementById("canvas").

GETTING THE DRAWING CONTEXT

Next, we get the *drawing context* from the canvas element. A drawing context is a JavaScript object that includes all the methods and properties for drawing on a canvas. To get this object, we call getContext on canvas and pass it the string "2d" as an argument. This argument says that we want to draw a two-dimensional image on our canvas. We save this drawing context object in the variable ctx using the code var ctx = canvas.getContext("2d").

DRAWING A SQUARE

Finally, on the third line, we draw a rectangle on the canvas by calling the method fillRect on the drawing context. The fillRect method takes four arguments. In order, these are the *x*- and *y*-coordinates of the top-left corner of the rectangle (0, 0) and the width and height of the rectangle (10, 10). In this case, we're saying, "Draw a 10-pixel-by-10-pixel rectangle at coordinates (0, 0)," which are at the top-left corner of the canvas.

When you run this code, you should see a small black square on your screen, as shown in Figure 13-1.

Figure 13-1: Our first canvas drawing

DRAWING MULTIPLE SQUARES

How about trying something a bit more interesting? Rather than drawing just one square, let's use a loop to draw multiple squares running diagonally down the screen. Replace the code in the `<script>` tags with the following. When you run this code, you should see a set of eight black squares, as shown in Figure 13-2:

```
var canvas = document.getElementById("canvas");
var ctx = canvas.getContext("2d");
for (var i = 0; i < 8; i++) {
  ctx.fillRect(i * 10, i * 10, 10, 10);
}
```

The first two lines are the same as in the earlier listing. In the third line, we create a for loop that runs from 0 to 8. Next, inside this loop, we call `fillRect` on the drawing context.

Figure 13-2: Drawing multiple squares using a for loop

The x and y positions for the top-left corner of each square are based on the loop variable, i. The first time around the loop, when i is 0, the coordinates are (0, 0) because 0 × 10 is equal to 0. This means that when we run the code `ctx.fillRect(i * 10, i * 10, 10, 10)`, we will draw a square at the coordinates (0, 0), with a width and height of 10 pixels by 10 pixels. This is the top-left square in Figure 13-2.

The second time around the loop, when i is 1, the coordinates are (10, 10) because 1 × 10 is equal to 10. This time, the code `ctx.fillRect(i * 10, i * 10, 10, 10)` draws a square at the coordinates (10, 10),

but the square's size is still 10 pixels by 10 pixels (because we're not changing the width and height arguments). This is the second square down in Figure 13-2.

Since i increments by 1 each time through the loop, the *x*- and *y*-coordinates keep increasing by 10 pixels each time through the loop, but the width and height of the square stay fixed at 10. The remaining six squares are drawn over the remaining six times around the loop.

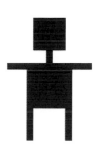

TRY IT OUT!

Now that you know how to draw squares and rectangles on the canvas, try drawing this little robot using the fillRect method.

Hint: You'll need to draw six separate rectangles. I made the head using a 50-pixel-by-50-pixel rectangle. The neck, arms, and legs are all 10 pixels wide.

CHANGING THE DRAWING COLOR

By default, when you call fillRect, JavaScript draws a black rectangle. To use a different color, you can change the fillStyle property of the drawing context. When you set fillStyle to a new color, everything you draw will be drawn in that color until you change fillStyle again.

The easiest way to set a color for fillStyle is to give it the name of a color as a string. For example:

```
var canvas = document.getElementById("canvas");
var ctx = canvas.getContext("2d");
❶ ctx.fillStyle = "Red";
ctx.fillRect(0, 0, 100, 100);
```

At ❶ we tell the drawing context that everything we draw from now on should be colored red. Running this code should draw a bright red square on the screen, as shown in Figure 13-3.

Figure 13-3: A red square

NOTE *JavaScript understands more than 100 color names, including Green, Blue, Orange, Red, Yellow, Purple, White, Black, Pink, Turquoise, Violet, SkyBlue, PaleGreen, Lime, Fuchsia, DeepPink, Cyan, and Chocolate. You'll find a full list on the CSS-Tricks website:* http://css-tricks.com/snippets/ css/named-colors-and-hex-equivalents/.

TRY IT OUT!

Look at the CSS-Tricks website (*http://css-tricks.com/ snippets/css/named-colors-and-hex-equivalents/*) and choose three colors you like. Draw three rectangles using these colors. Each rectangle should be 50 pixels wide and 100 pixels tall. Don't include any space between them. You should end up with something like this:

. . . although I'm sure you can find some more interesting colors than red, green, and blue!

DRAWING RECTANGLE OUTLINES

As we've seen, the `fillRect` method draws a filled-in rectangle. That's fine if that's what you want, but sometimes you might want to draw just the outline, as if you were using a pen or pencil. To draw just the outline of a rectangle, we use the `strokeRect` method. (The word *stroke* is another word for outline.) For example, running this code should draw the outline of small rectangle, as shown in Figure 13-4:

```
var canvas = document.getElementById("canvas");
var ctx = canvas.getContext("2d");
ctx.strokeRect(10, 10, 100, 20);
```

Figure 13-4: Using strokeRect to draw the outline of a rectangle

The `strokeRect` method takes the same arguments as `fillRect`: first the *x*- and *y*-coordinates of the top-left corner, followed by the width and height of the rectangle. In this example, we see that a rectangle is drawn starting at 10 pixels from the top left of the canvas, and it is 100 pixels wide by 20 pixels tall.

Use the `strokeStyle` property to change the color of the rectangle's outline. To change the thickness of the line, use the `lineWidth` property. For example:

```
var canvas = document.getElementById("canvas");
var ctx = canvas.getContext("2d");
❶ ctx.strokeStyle = "DeepPink";
❷ ctx.lineWidth = 4;
ctx.strokeRect(10, 10, 100, 20);
```

Here, we set the color of the line to DeepPink at ❶ and the width of the line to 4 pixels at ❷. Figure 13-5 shows the resulting rectangle.

Figure 13-5: A deep pink rectangle with a 4-pixel-wide outline

DRAWING LINES OR PATHS

Lines on the canvas are called *paths*. To draw a path with the canvas, you use *x*- and *y*-coordinates to set where each line should begin and end. By using a careful combination of starting and stopping coordinates, you can draw specific shapes on the canvas. For example, here's how you might draw the turquoise *X* shown in Figure 13-6:

```
  var canvas = document.getElementById("canvas");
  var ctx = canvas.getContext("2d");
❶ ctx.strokeStyle = "Turquoise";
❷ ctx.lineWidth = 4;
❸ ctx.beginPath();
❹ ctx.moveTo(10, 10);
❺ ctx.lineTo(60, 60);
❻ ctx.moveTo(60, 10);
❼ ctx.lineTo(10, 60);
❽ ctx.stroke();
```

Figure 13-6: A turquoise X, drawn with moveTo and lineTo

At ❶ and ❷ we set the color and width of the line. At ❸ we call the beginPath method on the drawing context (saved as ctx) to tell the canvas that we want to start drawing a new path. At ❹ we call the moveTo method with two arguments: *x*- and *y*-coordinates. Calling `moveTo` picks up our virtual JavaScript pen off the canvas paper and moves it to those coordinates without drawing a line.

To start drawing a line, we call the `lineTo` method at ❺ with *x*- and *y*-coordinates, which places the virtual pen back on the canvas and traces a path to these new coordinates. Here, we draw a line from the point (10, 10) to the point (60, 60)—a diagonal line from the top left of the canvas to the bottom right, forming the first line of the *X*.

At ❻ we call `moveTo` again, which sets a new location to draw from. At ❼ we call `lineTo` again, to draw a line from (60, 10) to (10, 60)—a diagonal line from the top right of the canvas to the bottom left, completing the *X* shape.

But we're not done yet! So far we've only told the canvas what we'd like to draw; we haven't actually drawn anything. So at ❽, we call the `stroke` method, which finally makes the lines appear on the screen.

TRY IT OUT!

Try drawing this happy stickman using the `beginPath`, `moveTo`, `lineTo`, and `stroke` methods. You can use the `strokeRect` method for the head. The head is a 20-pixel-by-20-pixel square, and the line width is 4 pixels.

FILLING PATHS

So far we've looked at `strokeRect` for drawing rectangle outlines, `fillRect` for filling rectangles with color, and `stroke` for outlining a path. The equivalent of `fillRect` for paths is called `fill`. To fill a closed path with color instead of just drawing an outline, you can use the `fill` method instead of `stroke`. For example, you could use this code to draw the simple sky blue house shown in Figure 13-7.

```
var canvas = document.getElementById("canvas");
var ctx = canvas.getContext("2d");

ctx.fillStyle = "SkyBlue";
ctx.beginPath();
ctx.moveTo(100, 100);
ctx.lineTo(100, 60);
ctx.lineTo(130, 30);
ctx.lineTo(160, 60);
ctx.lineTo(160, 100);
ctx.lineTo(100, 100);
❶ ctx.fill();
```

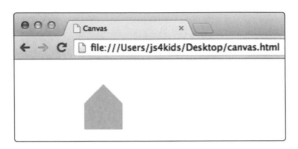

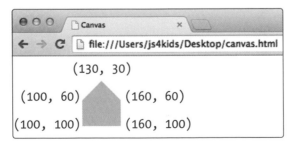

Figure 13-7: A sky blue house, drawn with a path and filled with the fill method

Here's how this code works. After setting our drawing color to SkyBlue, we begin our path with beginPath and then move to our starting point of (100, 100) using moveTo. Next we call lineTo five times for each corner of the house, using five sets of coordinates. The final call to lineTo completes the path by going back to the starting point of (100, 100).

Figure 13-8 shows the same house, but with each coordinate labeled.

Figure 13-8: The house from Figure 13-7 with coordinates labeled

Finally, at ❶ we call the fill method, which fills our path with the chosen fill color, SkyBlue.

DRAWING ARCS AND CIRCLES

In addition to drawing straight lines on the canvas, you can use the arc method to draw arcs and circles. To draw a circle, you set the circle's center coordinates and *radius* (the distance between the circle's center and outer edge) and tell JavaScript how much of the circle to draw by providing a starting angle and ending angle as arguments. You can draw a full circle, or just a portion of a circle to create an arc.

The starting and ending angles are measured in *radians*. When measured in radians, a full circle starts at 0 (at the right side of the circle) and goes up to π × 2 radians. So to draw a full circle, you tell arc to draw from 0 radians to π × 2 radians. Figure 13-9 shows a circle labeled with radians and their equivalent in degrees. The values 360° and π × 2 radians both mean a full circle.

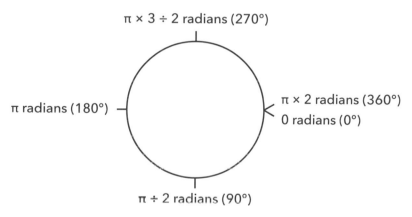

Figure 13-9: Degrees and radians, starting from the right side of the circle and moving clockwise

For example, the following code will create a quarter circle, a half circle, and a full circle, as shown in Figure 13-10.

```
ctx.lineWidth = 2;
ctx.strokeStyle = "Green";

ctx.beginPath();
❶ ctx.arc(50, 50, 20, 0, Math.PI / 2, false);
ctx.stroke();
```

```
  ctx.beginPath();
❷ ctx.arc(100, 50, 20, 0, Math.PI, false);
  ctx.stroke();

  ctx.beginPath();
❸ ctx.arc(150, 50, 20, 0, Math.PI * 2, false);
  ctx.stroke();
```

Figure 13-10: Drawing a quarter circle, a half circle, and a full circle

We'll go over all three shapes in the following sections.

DRAWING A QUARTER CIRCLE OR AN ARC

The first block of code draws a quarter circle. At ❶, after calling beginPath, we call the arc method. We set the center of the circle at the point (50, 50) and the radius to 20 pixels. The starting angle is 0 (which draws the arc starting from the right of the circle), and the ending angle is Math.PI / 2. Math.PI is how JavaScript refers to the number π (pi). Because a full circle is π × 2 radians, π radians means a half circle, and π ÷ 2 radians (which we're using for this first arc) gives us a quarter circle. Figure 13-11 shows the start and end angles.

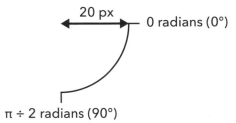

Figure 13-11: The start angle (0 radians, or 0°) and end angle (π ÷ 2 radians, or 90°) of the quarter-circle

We pass false for the final argument, which tells arc to draw in a clockwise direction. If you want to draw in a counterclockwise direction, pass true for this final argument.

DRAWING A HALF CIRCLE

Next we draw a half circle. The arc at ❷ has a center at (100, 50), which places it 50 pixels to the right of the first arc, which was at (50, 50). The radius is again 20 pixels. We also start at 0 radians again, but this time we end at Math.PI, drawing a half circle. Figure 13-12 shows the start and end angles.

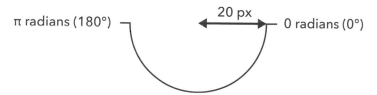

Figure 13-12: The start angle (0 radians, or 0°) and end angle (π radians, or 180°) of the half circle

DRAWING A FULL CIRCLE

At ❸ we draw a full circle. The center is at (150, 50), and the radius is 20 pixels. For this circle, we start the arc at 0 radians and end it at Math.PI * 2 radians, drawing a full circle. Figure 13-13 shows the start and end angles.

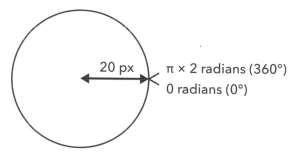

Figure 13-13: The start angle (0 radians, or 0°) and end angle (π × 2 radians, or 360°) of the full circle

DRAWING LOTS OF CIRCLES WITH A FUNCTION

If you just want to draw circles, the arc method is a bit complicated. For circles, you're always going to want to start the arc at 0 and end at π × 2, and the direction (clockwise or counterclockwise) doesn't matter. Also, to actually draw the circle you always need to call ctx.beginPath and ctx.stroke before and after calling the arc method. We can make a function to draw circles that lets us ignore those details so that we have to supply only the x, y, and radius arguments. Let's do that now.

```
var circle = function (x, y, radius) {
  ctx.beginPath();
  ctx.arc(x, y, radius, 0, Math.PI * 2, false);
  ctx.stroke();
};
```

As with the arc method, inside this function the first thing we have to do is call ctx.beginPath to tell the canvas we want to draw a path. Then, we call ctx.arc, passing the x, y, and radius variables from the function arguments. As before, we use 0 for the start angle, Math.PI * 2 for the end angle, and false to draw the circle clockwise.

Now that we have this function, we can draw lots of circles simply by filling in the center coordinates and radius as arguments. For example, this code would draw some colorful concentric circles:

```
ctx.lineWidth = 4;

ctx.strokeStyle = "Red";
circle(100, 100, 10);

ctx.strokeStyle = "Orange";
circle(100, 100, 20);

ctx.strokeStyle = "Yellow";
circle(100, 100, 30);

ctx.strokeStyle = "Green";
circle(100, 100, 40);

ctx.strokeStyle = "Blue";
circle(100, 100, 50);
```

```
ctx.strokeStyle = "Purple";
circle(100, 100, 60);
```

You can see what this should look like in Figure 13-14. First, we set the line width to a thick 4 pixels. Then we set the strokeStyle to "Red" and use the circle function to draw a circle at the coordinates (100, 100), with a radius of 10 pixels. This is the red center ring.

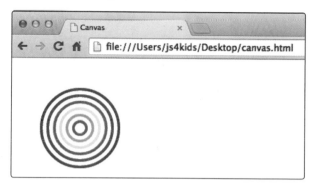

Figure 13-14: Colorful concentric circles, drawn using our circle function

We then use the same technique to draw an orange circle at the same location but with a radius of 20 pixels; we follow that with a yellow circle, again in the same location but with a radius of 30 pixels. The last three circles are also in the same location, but with increasingly larger radii and in green, blue, and purple.

TRY IT OUT!

How would you modify our circle function to make it fill the circle instead of outline it? Add a fourth argument, a Boolean, that says whether the circle should be filled or outlined. Passing true indicates that you want the circle to be filled. You can call the argument fillCircle.

Using your modified function, draw this snowman, using a mix of outlined and filled circles.

WHAT YOU LEARNED

In this chapter, you learned about a new HTML element called canvas. Using the canvas's drawing context, we can easily draw rectangles, lines, and circles, with full control over their location, line width, color, and so on.

In the next chapter, we'll learn how to animate our drawings, using some of the techniques we learned in Chapter 9.

PROGRAMMING CHALLENGES

Try these challenges to practice drawing to the canvas.

#1: A SNOWMAN-DRAWING FUNCTION

Building on your code for drawing a snowman (page 213), write a function that draws a snowman at a specified location, so that calling this . . .

```
drawSnowman(50, 50);
```

would draw a snowman at the point (50, 50).

#2: DRAWING AN ARRAY OF POINTS

Write a function that will take an array of points like this:

```
var points = [[50, 50], [50, 100], [100, 100], [100, 50], ↵
[50, 50]];
drawPoints(points);
```

and draw a line connecting the points. In this example, the function would draw a line from (50, 50) to (50, 100) to (100, 100) to (100, 50) and back to (50, 50).

Now use this function to draw the following points:

```
var mysteryPoints = [[50, 50], [50, 100], [25, 120], ↵
[100, 50], [70, 90], [100, 90], [70, 120]];
drawPoints(mysteryPoints);
```

Hint: You can use points[0][0] to get the first *x*-coordinate and points[0][1] to get the first *y*-coordinate.

#3: PAINTING WITH YOUR MOUSE

Using jQuery and the mousemove event, draw a filled circle with a radius of 3 pixels at the mouse position whenever you move your mouse over the canvas. Because this event is triggered by every tiny movement of the mouse, these circles will join into a line as you move the mouse over the canvas.

Hint: Refer to Chapter 10 for a reminder of how to respond to mousemove events.

#4: DRAWING THE MAN IN HANGMAN

In Chapter 7 we created our own version of the game Hangman. Now you can make it closer to the real game by drawing part of a stick man every time the player gets a letter wrong.

Hint: Keep track of the number of times the player has guessed incorrectly. Write a function that takes this number as an argument and draws a different part of the body depending on the number passed in.

14
MAKING THINGS MOVE ON THE CANVAS

Creating canvas animations in JavaScript is a lot like creating a stop-motion animation. You draw a shape, pause, erase the shape, and then redraw it in a new position. This may sound like a lot of steps, but JavaScript can update the position of the shape very quickly in order to create a smooth animation. In Chapter 10, we learned how to animate DOM elements. In this chapter, we'll animate our canvas drawings.

MOVING ACROSS THE PAGE

Let's use `canvas` and `setInterval` to draw a square and move it slowly across a page. Create a new file called *canvasanimation.html* and add the following HTML:

```
<!DOCTYPE html>
<html>
<head>
    <title>Canvas Animation</title>
</head>

<body>
    <canvas id="canvas" width="200" height="200"></canvas>

    <script>
    // We'll fill this in next
    </script>
</body>
</html>
```

Now add the following JavaScript to the `script` element:

```
var canvas = document.getElementById("canvas");
var ctx = canvas.getContext("2d");

var position = 0;

setInterval(function () {
❶   ctx.clearRect(0, 0, 200, 200);
❷   ctx.fillRect(position, 0, 20, 20);

❸   position++;
❹   if (position > 200) {
      position = 0;
    }
❺ }, 30);
```

The first two lines in this code create the canvas and the context. Next, we create the variable `position` and set it to 0, with the code `var position = 0`. We'll use this variable to control the left-to-right movement of the square.

Now we call `setInterval` to start our animation. The first argument to `setInterval` is a function, which draws a new square each time it's called.

CLEARING THE CANVAS

Inside the function we passed to `setInterval`, we call `clearRect` at ❶, which clears a rectangular area on the canvas. The `clearRect` method takes four arguments, which set the position and size of the rectangle to be cleared. As with `fillRect`, the first two arguments represent the *x*- and *y*-coordinates of the top-left corner of the rectangle, and the last two represent the width and height. Calling `ctx.clearRect(0, 0, 200, 200)` erases a 200-by-200-pixel rectangle, starting at the very top-left corner of the canvas. Because our canvas is exactly 200 by 200 pixels, this will clear the entire canvas.

DRAWING THE RECTANGLE

Once we've cleared the canvas, at ❷ we use `ctx.fillRect` (`position, 0, 20, 20`) to draw a 20-pixel square at the point (`position`, 0). When our program starts, the square will be drawn at (0, 0) because `position` starts off set to `0`.

CHANGING THE POSITION

Next, we increase `position` by 1, using `position++` at ❸. Then at ❹ we ensure that `position` doesn't get larger than 200 with the check `if (position > 200)`. If it is, we reset it to `0`.

VIEWING THE ANIMATION IN THE BROWSER

When you load this page in your browser, `setInterval` will call the supplied function once every 30 milliseconds, or about 33 times a second (this time interval is set by the second argument to `setInterval`, at ❺). Each time the supplied function is called, it clears the canvas, draws a square at (`position`, 0), and increments the variable `position`. As a result, the square gradually moves across the canvas. When the square reaches the end of the canvas (200 pixels to the right), its position is reset to 0.

Figure 14-1 shows the first four steps of the animation, zoomed in to the top-left corner of the canvas.

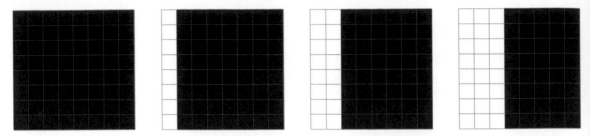

Figure 14-1: A close-up of the top-left corner of the canvas for the first four steps of the animation. At each step, position is incremented by 1 and the square moves 1 pixel to the right.

ANIMATING THE SIZE OF A SQUARE

By making only three changes to the code in the previous section, we can create a square that grows larger instead of moving. Here's what that code would look like:

```
var canvas = document.getElementById("canvas");
var ctx = canvas.getContext("2d");

var size = 0;

setInterval(function () {
  ctx.clearRect(0, 0, 200, 200);
  ctx.fillRect(0, 0, size, size);

  size++;
  if (size > 200) {
    size = 0;
  }
}, 30);
```

As you can see, we've done two things. First, instead of a position variable, we now have a variable named size, which will control the dimensions of the square. Second, instead of using this variable to set the square's horizontal position, we're using it to set the square's width and height with the code ctx.fillRect(0, 0, size, size). This will draw a square at the top-left corner of the canvas, with the width and height both set to match

size. Because size starts at 0, the square will start out invisible. The next time the function is called, size will be 1, so the square will be 1 pixel wide and tall. Each time the square is drawn, it grows a pixel wider and a pixel taller. When you run this code, you should see a square appear at the top-left corner of the canvas and grow until it fills the entire canvas. Once it fills the entire canvas—that is, if (size > 200)—the square will disappear and start growing again from the top-left corner.

Figure 14-2 shows a close-up of the top-left corner of the canvas for the first four steps of this animation.

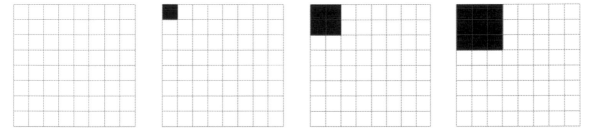

Figure 14-2: In each step of this animation, size is incremented by 1 and the width and height of the square grow by 1 pixel.

A RANDOM BEE

Now that we know how to move and grow objects on our screen, let's try something a bit more fun. Let's make a bee that flies randomly around the canvas! We'll draw our bee using a number of circles, like this:

The animation will work very similarly to the moving square animation: we'll set a position, and then for every step of the animation, we'll clear the canvas, draw the bee at that position, and modify the position. The difference is that to make the bee move randomly, we'll need to use more complex logic for updating the bee's position than we used for the square animation. We'll build up the code for this animation in a few sections.

A NEW CIRCLE FUNCTION

We'll draw our bee using a few circles, so first we'll make a circle function to fill or outline circles:

```
var circle = function (x, y, radius, fillCircle) {
  ctx.beginPath();
❶ ctx.arc(x, y, radius, 0, Math.PI * 2, false);
❷ if (fillCircle) {
❸   ctx.fill();
  } else {
❹   ctx.stroke();
  }
};
```

The function takes four arguments: x, y, radius, and fillCircle. We used a similar circle function in Chapter 13, but here we've added fillCircle as an extra argument. When we call this function, this argument should be set to true or false, which determines whether the function draws a filled circle or just an outline.

Inside the function, we use the arc method at ❶ to create the circle with its center at the position (x, y) and a radius of radius. After this, we check to see if the fillCircle argument is true at ❷. If it is true, we fill the circle using ctx.fill at ❸. Otherwise, we outline the circle using ctx.stroke at ❹.

DRAWING THE BEE

Next, we create the drawBee function to draw the bee. The drawBee function uses the circle function to draw a bee at the coordinates specified by its x and y arguments. It looks like this:

```
var drawBee = function (x, y) {
❶ ctx.lineWidth = 2;
  ctx.strokeStyle = "Black";
  ctx.fillStyle = "Gold";

❷ circle(x, y, 8, true);
  circle(x, y, 8, false);
  circle(x - 5, y - 11, 5, false);
  circle(x + 5, y - 11, 5, false);
  circle(x - 2, y - 1, 2, false);
  circle(x + 2, y - 1, 2, false);
};
```

In the first section of this code at ❶, we set the lineWidth, strokeStyle, and fillStyle properties for our drawing. We set the lineWidth to 2 pixels and the strokeStyle to Black. This means that our outlined circles, which we'll use for the bee's body, wings, and eyes, will have thick black borders. The fillStyle is set to Gold, which will fill the circle for our bee body with a nice yellow color.

In the second section of the code at ❷, we draw a series of circles to create our bee. Let's go through those one at a time.

The first circle draws the bee's body using a filled circle with a center at the point (x, y) and a radius of 8 pixels:

```
circle(x, y, 8, true);
```

Because we set the fillStyle to Gold, this circle will be filled in with yellow like so:

This second circle draws a black outline around the bee's body that's the same size and in the same place as the first circle:

```
circle(x, y, 8, false);
```

Added to the first circle, it looks like this:

Next, we use circles to draw the bee's wings. The first wing is an outlined circle with its center 5 pixels to the left and 11 pixels above the center of the body, with a radius of 5 pixels. The second wing is the same, except it's 5 pixels to the *right* of the body's center.

```
circle(x - 5, y - 11, 5, false);
circle(x + 5, y - 11, 5, false);
```

With those circles added, our bee looks like this:

Finally, we draw the eyes. The first one is 2 pixels to the left of the center of the body and 1 pixel above, with a radius of 2 pixels. The second one is the same, except it's 2 pixels right of center.

```
circle(x - 2, y - 1, 2, false);
circle(x + 2, y - 1, 2, false);
```

Together, these circles create a bee, with its body centered around the (x, y) coordinate passed into the drawBee function.

UPDATING THE BEE'S LOCATION

We'll create an update function to randomly change the bee's *x*- and *y*-coordinates in order to make it appear to buzz around the canvas. The update function takes a single coordinate; we update the *x*- and *y*-coordinates one at a time so that the bee will move randomly left and right and up and down. The update function looks like this:

```
  var update = function (coordinate) {
❶   var offset = Math.random() * 4 - 2;
❷   coordinate += offset;

❸   if (coordinate > 200) {
      coordinate = 200;
    }
❹   if (coordinate < 0) {
      coordinate = 0;
    }

❺   return coordinate;
  };
```

CHANGING THE COORDINATE WITH AN OFFSET VALUE

At ❶, we create a variable called offset, which will determine how much to change the current coordinate. We generate the offset value by calculating Math.random() * 4 - 2. This will give us a random number between −2 and 2. Here's how: calling Math.random() on its own gives us a random number between 0 and 1, so Math.random() * 4 produces a random number between 0 and 4. Then we subtract 2 to get a random number between −2 and 2.

At ❷ we use coordinate += offset to modify our coordinate with this offset number. If offset is a positive number, coordinate will increase, and if it's a negative number, coordinate will decrease. For example, if coordinate is set to 100 and offset is 1, then after we run the line at ❷, coordinate will be 101. However, if coordinate is 100 and offset is -1, this would change coordinate to 99.

CHECKING IF THE BEE REACHES THE EDGE

At ❸ and ❹ we prevent the bee from leaving the canvas by making sure coordinate never increases above 200 or shrinks below 0. If coordinate gets bigger than 200, we set it back to 200, and if it goes below 0, we reset it to 0.

RETURNING THE UPDATED COORDINATE

Finally, at ❺ we return coordinate. Returning the new value of coordinate lets us use that value in the rest of our code. Later we'll use this return value from the update method to modify the x and y values like this:

```
x = update(x);
y = update(y);
```

ANIMATING OUR BUZZING BEE

Now that we have the circle, drawBee, and update functions, we can write the animation code for our buzzing bee.

```
var canvas = document.getElementById("canvas");
var ctx = canvas.getContext("2d");

var x = 100;
var y = 100;

setInterval(function () {
❶  ctx.clearRect(0, 0, 200, 200);

❷  drawBee(x, y);
❸  x = update(x);
   y = update(y);

❹  ctx.strokeRect(0, 0, 200, 200);
}, 30);
```

As usual, we start with the var canvas and var ctx lines to get the drawing context. Next, we create the variables x and y and set both to 100. This sets the bee's starting position at the point (100, 100), which puts it in the middle of the canvas, as shown in Figure 14-3.

Next we call setInterval, passing a function to call every 30 milliseconds. Inside this function, the first thing we do is call clearRect at ❶ to clear the canvas. Next, at ❷ we draw the bee at the point (x, y). The first time the function is called, the bee is drawn at the point (100, 100), as you can see in Figure 14-3, and each time the function is called after that, it will draw the bee at a new, updated (x, y) position.

Figure 14-3: The bee drawn at the point (100, 100)

Next we update the x and y values starting at ❸. The update function takes a number, adds a random number between –2 and 2 to it, and returns that updated number. So the code x = update(x) basically means "change x by a small, random amount."

Finally, we call strokeRect at ❹ to draw a line around the edge of the canvas. This makes it easier for us to see when the bee is getting close to it. Without the border, the edge of the canvas is invisible.

Figure 14-4: The random bee animation

When you run this code, you should see the yellow bee randomly buzz around the canvas. Figure 14-4 shows a few frames from our animation.

BOUNCING A BALL!

Now let's make a ball that bounces around the canvas. Whenever the ball hits one of the walls, it will bounce off at an angle, as a rubber ball would.

First, we'll create a JavaScript object to represent our ball with a Ball constructor. This object will store the ball's speed and direction using two properties, xSpeed and ySpeed. The ball's horizontal speed will be controlled by xSpeed, and the vertical speed will be controlled by ySpeed.

We'll make this animation in a new file. Create a new HTML file called *ball.html*, and add the following HTML:

```
<!DOCTYPE html>
<html>
<head>
    <title>A Bouncing Ball</title>
</head>

<body>
    <canvas id="canvas" width="200" height="200"></canvas>

    <script>
    // We'll fill this in next
    </script>
</body>
</html>
```

THE BALL CONSTRUCTOR

First we'll create the Ball constructor, which we'll use to create our bouncing ball. Type the following code into the <script> tags in *ball.html*:

```
var Ball = function () {
  this.x = 100;
  this.y = 100;
  this.xSpeed = -2;
  this.ySpeed = 3;
};
```

Our constructor is very straightforward: it simply sets the starting position of the ball (this.x and this.y), the ball's horizontal speed (this.xSpeed), and its vertical speed (this.ySpeed). We set the starting position to the point (100, 100), which is the center of our 200-by-200-pixel canvas.

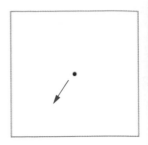

this.xSpeed is set to -2. This will make the ball move 2 pixels to the left for every step of the animation. this.ySpeed is set to 3. This will make the ball move 3 pixels down for every step of the animation. Therefore, the ball will move diagonally down (3 pixels) and to the left (2 pixels) between every frame.

Figure 14-5 shows the starting position of the ball and its direction of movement.

Figure 14-5: The starting position of the ball, with an arrow indicating its direction

DRAWING THE BALL

Next we'll add a draw method to draw the ball. We'll add this method to the Ball prototype so that any objects created by the Ball constructor can use it:

```
var circle = function (x, y, radius, fillCircle) {
  ctx.beginPath();
  ctx.arc(x, y, radius, 0, Math.PI * 2, false);
  if (fillCircle) {
    ctx.fill();
  } else {
    ctx.stroke();
  }
};

Ball.prototype.draw = function () {
  circle(this.x, this.y, 3, true);
};
```

First we include our circle function, the same one we used earlier in "A New circle Function" on page 222. We then add the draw method to Ball.prototype. This method simply calls circle(this.x, this.y, 3, true) to draw a circle. The circle's center will be at (this.x, this.y): the location of the ball. It will have a radius of 3 pixels. We pass true as the final argument to tell the circle function to fill the circle.

MOVING THE BALL

To move the ball, we just have to update the x and y properties based on the current speed. We'll do that using the following move method:

```
Ball.prototype.move = function () {
  this.x += this.xSpeed;
  this.y += this.ySpeed;
};
```

We use this.x += this.xSpeed to add the horizontal speed of the ball to this.x. Then this.y += this.ySpeed adds the vertical speed to this.y. For example, at the beginning of the animation, the ball will be at the point (100, 100), with this.xSpeed set to -2 and this.ySpeed set to 3. When we call the move method, it subtracts 2 from the x value and adds 3 to the y value, which places the ball at the point (98, 103). This moves the ball's location to the left 2 pixels and down 3 pixels, as illustrated in Figure 14-6.

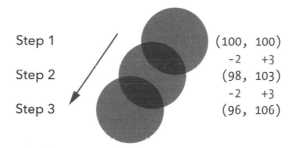

Step 1   (100, 100)

              -2 +3

Step 2   (98, 103)

              -2 +3

Step 3   (96, 106)

Figure 14-6: The first three steps of the animation, showing how the x and y properties change

BOUNCING THE BALL

At every step of the animation, we check to see if the ball has hit one of the walls. If it has, we update the xSpeed or ySpeed property by *negating* it (multiplying it by −1). For example, if the ball hits the bottom wall, we negate this.ySpeed. So if this.ySpeed is 3, negating it will make it -3. If this.ySpeed is -3, negating it will set it back to 3.

We'll call this method checkCollision, because it checks to see if the ball has collided with (hit) the wall.

```
Ball.prototype.checkCollision = function () {
❶    if (this.x < 0 || this.x > 200) {
       this.xSpeed = -this.xSpeed;
     }
❷    if (this.y < 0 || this.y > 200) {
       this.ySpeed = -this.ySpeed;
     }
};
```

At ❶, we determine whether the ball has hit the left wall or the right wall by checking to see if its x property is either less than 0 (meaning it hit the left edge) or greater than 200 (meaning it hit the right edge). If either of these is true, the ball has started to move off the edge of the canvas, so we have to reverse its horizontal direction. We do this by setting this.xSpeed equal to -this.xSpeed. For example, if this.xSpeed was -2 and the ball hit the left wall, this.xSpeed would become 2.

At ❷, we do the same thing for the top and bottom walls. If this.y is less than 0 or greater than 200, we know the ball has hit the top wall or the bottom wall, respectively. In that case, we set this.ySpeed to be equal to -this.ySpeed.

Figure 14-7 shows what happens when the ball hits the left wall. this.xSpeed starts as -2, but after the collision it is changed to 2. However, this.ySpeed remains unchanged at 3.

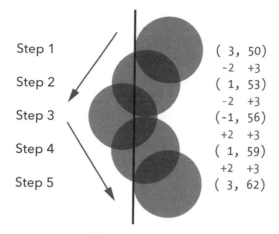

Step 1   (3, 50)
              -2 +3
Step 2   (1, 53)
              -2 +3
Step 3   (-1, 56)
              +2 +3
Step 4   (1, 59)
              +2 +3
Step 5   (3, 62)

Figure 14-7: How this.xSpeed changes after a collision with the left wall

As you can see in Figure 14-7, in this case the center of the ball goes off the edge of the canvas at step 3 when it collides with a wall. During that step, part of the ball will disappear, but this happens so quickly that it's barely noticeable when the animation is running.

ANIMATING THE BALL

Now we can write the code that gets the animation running. This code sets up the object that represents the ball, and it uses setInterval to call the methods that draw and update the ball for each animation step.

```
var canvas = document.getElementById("canvas");
var ctx = canvas.getContext("2d");

❶ var ball = new Ball();

❷ setInterval(function () {
❸   ctx.clearRect(0, 0, 200, 200);

❹   ball.draw();
    ball.move();
    ball.checkCollision();

❺   ctx.strokeRect(0, 0, 200, 200);
❻ }, 30);
```

We get the canvas and drawing context as usual on the first two lines. Then we create a ball object using new Ball() and save it in the variable ball at ❶. Next, we call setInterval at ❷, passing a function and the number 30 at ❻. As you've seen before, this means "call this function every 30 milliseconds."

The function we pass to setInterval does several things. First, it clears the canvas, using ctx.clearRect(0, 0, 200, 200) at ❸. After this, it calls the draw, move, and checkCollision methods at ❹ on the ball object. The draw method draws the ball at its current x- and y-coordinates. The move method updates the position of the ball based on its xSpeed and ySpeed properties. Finally, the checkCollision method updates the direction of the ball, if it hits a wall.

The last thing we do in the function passed to setInterval is call ctx.strokeRect(0, 0, 200, 200) at ❺ to draw a line around the edge of the canvas, so we can see the walls the ball is hitting.

When you run this code, the ball should immediately start moving down and to the left. It should hit the bottom wall first, and bounce up and to the left. It will continue to bounce around the canvas as long as you leave the browser window open.

WHAT YOU LEARNED

In this chapter, we combined our knowledge of animation from Chapter 11 with our knowledge of the canvas element to create various canvas-based animations. We began simply by moving and growing squares on the canvas. Next, we made a bee buzz randomly around the screen, and we ended with an animation of a bouncing ball.

All of these animations work in basically the same way: we draw a shape of a particular size in a particular position, then we update that size or position, and then we clear the canvas and draw the shape again. For elements moving around a 2D canvas, we generally have to keep track of the *x*- and *y*-coordinates of the element. For the bee animation, we added or subtracted a random number from the *x*- and *y*-coordinates. For the bouncing ball, we added the current xSpeed and ySpeed to the *x*- and *y*-coordinates. In the next chapter, we'll add interactivity to our canvas, which will let us control what's drawn to the canvas using the keyboard.

PROGRAMMING CHALLENGES

Here are some ways you can build on the bouncing ball animation from this chapter.

#1: BOUNCING THE BALL AROUND A LARGER CANVAS

Our 200-by-200-pixel canvas is a bit small. What if you wanted to increase the canvas size to 400 by 400 pixels or some other arbitrary size?

Instead of entering the width and height of the canvas manually throughout your program, you can create width and height variables and set the variables using the canvas object. Use the following code:

```
var width = canvas.width;
var height = canvas.height;
```

Now if you use these variables throughout your program, you only have to change the properties on the canvas element in the HTML if you want to try out a new size. Try changing the size of the canvas to 500 pixels by 300 pixels. Does your program still work?

#2: RANDOMIZING THIS.XSPEED AND THIS.YSPEED

To make the animation more interesting, set this.xSpeed and this.ySpeed to different random numbers (between −5 and 5) in the Ball constructor.

(continued)

#3: ANIMATING MORE BALLS

Instead of creating just one ball, create an empty array of balls, and use a for loop to add 10 balls to the array. Now, in the setInterval function, use a for loop to draw, move, and check collisions on each of the balls.

#4: MAKING THE BALLS COLORFUL

How about making some colored bouncing balls? Set a new property in the Ball constructor called color and use it in the draw method. Use the pickRandomWord function from Chapter 8 to give each ball a random color from this array:

```
var colors = ["Red", "Orange", "Yellow", "Green", "Blue", ↵
"Purple"];
```

15

CONTROLLING ANIMATIONS
WITH THE KEYBOARD

Now that you know how to work with the canvas;
draw and color objects; and make objects move, bounce,
and grow in size, let's liven things up by adding some
interactivity!

In this chapter, you'll learn how to make your canvas animations respond when a user presses a key on
the keyboard. This way, a player can control an animation by pressing an arrow key or one of a few assigned

letters on their keyboard (like the classic W, A, S, D game controls). For example, instead of just having a ball bounce across a screen, we can have a player control the movement of the ball using the arrow keys.

KEYBOARD EVENTS

JavaScript can monitor the keyboard through *keyboard events*. Each time a user presses a key on the keyboard, they generate a keyboard event, which is a lot like the mouse events we saw in Chapter 10. With mouse events, we used jQuery to determine where the cursor was when the event took place. With keyboard events, you can use jQuery to determine which key was pressed and then use that information in your code. For example, in this chapter we'll make a ball move left, right, up, or down when the user presses the left, right, up, or down arrow key.

We'll use the keydown event, which is triggered whenever a user presses a key, and we'll use jQuery to add an event handler to the keydown event. That way, every time a keydown event occurs, our event handler function can find out which key was pressed and respond accordingly.

SETTING UP THE HTML FILE

To begin, create a clean HTML file containing the following code and save it as *keyboard.html*.

```
<!DOCTYPE html>
<html>
<head>
    <title>Keyboard input</title>
</head>

<body>
    <canvas id="canvas" width="400" height="400"></canvas>

    <script src="https://code.jquery.com/jquery-2.1.0.js"></script>

    <script>
    // We'll fill this in next
    </script>
</body>
</html>
```

ADDING THE KEYDOWN EVENT HANDLER

Now let's add some JavaScript to respond to keydown events. Enter this code inside the empty <script> tags in your *keyboard.html* file.

```
$("body").keydown(function (event) {
  console.log(event.keyCode);
});
```

In the first line, we use the jQuery $ function to select the body element in our HTML and then call the keydown method. The argument to the keydown method is a function that will be called whenever a key is pressed. Information about the keydown event is passed in to the function through the event object. For this program, we want to know which key was pressed, and that information is stored in the event object as event.keyCode.

Inside the function, we use console.log to output the event object's keyCode property: a number representing the pressed key. Each key on your keyboard has a unique keycode. For example, the keycode for the spacebar is 32, and the left arrow is 37.

Once you've edited your *keyboard.html* file, save it and then open it in a browser. Now open the console so you can see the output, and click in the main browser window to have JavaScript register your keypresses. Now, if you start pressing keys, the corresponding keycodes should be printed to the console.

For example, if you type hi there, you should see the following output in the console:

```
72
73
32
84
72
69
82
69
```

Every key you press has a different keycode. The H key is 72, the I key is 73, and so on.

USING AN OBJECT TO CONVERT KEYCODES INTO NAMES

To make it easier to work with keys, we'll use an object to convert the keycodes into names so that the keypresses will be easier to recognize. In this next example, we create an object called keyNames, where the object keys are keycodes and the values are the names of those keys. Delete the JavaScript in *keyboard.html* and replace it with this:

```
var keyNames = {
  32: "space",
  37: "left",
  38: "up",
  39: "right",
  40: "down"
};

$("body").keydown(function (event) {
❶   console.log(keyNames[event.keyCode]);
});
```

First, we create the keyNames object and fill it with the keycodes 32, 37, 38, 39, and 40. The keyNames object uses key-value pairs to match keycodes (such as 32, 37, and so on) with corresponding labels (such as "space" for the spacebar and "left" for the left arrow).

We can then use this object to find out the name of a key based on its keycode. For example, to look up the keycode 32, enter keyNames[32]. That returns the string "space".

At ❶, we use the keyNames object in the keydown event handler to get the name of the key that was just pressed. If the event keycode referenced by event.keyCode matches one of the keys in the keyNames object, this function will log the name of that key. If no key matches, this code will log undefined.

Load *keyboard.html* in your browser. Open the console, click in the main browser window, and try pressing a few keys. If you press one of the five keys in the keyName object (the arrow keys or space-bar), the program should print the name of the key. Otherwise, it will print undefined.

TRY IT OUT!

Add more key-value pairs to the keyNames object so that it can convert more keys to names. Insert the keycodes and names for SHIFT, ENTER/RETURN, and ALT/OPTION.

MOVING A BALL WITH THE KEYBOARD

Now that we can determine which key is being pressed, we can write a program to use the keyboard to control the movement of a ball. Our program will draw a ball and move it to the right. Pressing the arrow keys will change the ball's direction, and pressing the spacebar will stop it. If the ball goes off the edge of the canvas, it will wrap around to the opposite side. For example, if the ball goes off the right edge of the canvas, it will show up again on the left edge while continuing to move in the same direction, as shown in Figure 15-1.

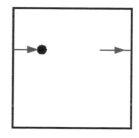

Figure 15-1: If the ball moves off the right side of the canvas, it will reappear on the left.

We'll use an object called keyActions to find out which key was pressed and then use that information to set the direction of the ball's movement. We'll use setInterval to continually update the ball's position and redraw it at its new position.

SETTING UP THE CANVAS

First we need to set up the canvas and the context object. Open *keyboard.html* and replace the JavaScript between the second set of <script> tags with this code:

```
var canvas = document.getElementById("canvas");
var ctx = canvas.getContext("2d");
var width = canvas.width;
var height = canvas.height;
```

On the first line, we use document.getElementById to select the canvas element. On the second line, we call getContext on the canvas to get the context object. Then, in the var width and var height lines, we store the width and height of the canvas element in the variables width and height. This way, when we need the canvas dimensions, we can use these variables instead of having to enter the numbers manually. Now, if we choose to change the size of the canvas, we can simply edit the HTML, and the JavaScript code should still work.

DEFINING THE CIRCLE FUNCTION

Next, we define the same circle function for the ball that we used in Chapter 14. Add this function after the code from the previous section:

```
var circle = function (x, y, radius, fillCircle) {
  ctx.beginPath();
  ctx.arc(x, y, radius, 0, Math.PI * 2, false);
  if (fillCircle) {
    ctx.fill();
  } else {
    ctx.stroke();
  }
};
```

CREATING THE BALL CONSTRUCTOR

Now we'll create a Ball constructor. We'll use this constructor to create the moving ball object. We'll be using the same technique for moving this ball as we did in Chapter 14—using the xSpeed and ySpeed properties to control the horizontal and vertical speed of the ball. Add this code after the circle function:

```
var Ball = function () {
  this.x = width / 2;
  this.y = height / 2;
  this.xSpeed = 5;
  this.ySpeed = 0;
};
```

We set the x and y values (the ball's position) to width / 2 and height / 2 so that the ball will start at the center of the canvas. We also set this.xSpeed to 5 and this.ySpeed to 0. This means that the ball will start the animation by moving to the right (that is, with each animation step, its x position will increase by 5 pixels and its y position will stay the same).

DEFINING THE MOVE METHOD

In this section, we'll define the move method. We'll add this method to Ball.prototype to move the ball to a new location based on its current location, xSpeed and ySpeed. Add this method after the Ball constructor:

```
Ball.prototype.move = function () {
  this.x += this.xSpeed;
  this.y += this.ySpeed;

❶  if (this.x < 0) {
    this.x = width;
  } else if (this.x > width) {
    this.x = 0;
  } else if (this.y < 0) {
    this.y = height;
  } else if (this.y > height) {
    this.y = 0;
  }
};
```

First we update this.x and this.y using this.xSpeed and this.ySpeed, just as we did in Chapter 14 (see "Moving the Ball" on page 229). After that is the code for when the ball reaches the edge of the canvas.

The if...else statement at ❶ checks the ball's position to see if it has moved off the edge of the canvas. If it has, this code makes the ball wrap around to the other side of the canvas. For example, if the ball goes off the left edge of the canvas, it should reappear from the right side of the canvas. In other words, if this.x is less than 0, we set this.x to width, which places it at the very right edge of the canvas. The rest of the if...else statement deals with the other three edges of the canvas in a similar way.

DEFINING THE DRAW METHOD

We'll use the draw method to draw the ball. Add this after the definition of the move method:

```
Ball.prototype.draw = function () {
  circle(this.x, this.y, 10, true);
};
```

This method calls the circle function. It uses the ball's x and y values to set the center of the ball, sets the radius to 10, and sets fillCircle to true. Figure 15-2 shows the resulting ball.

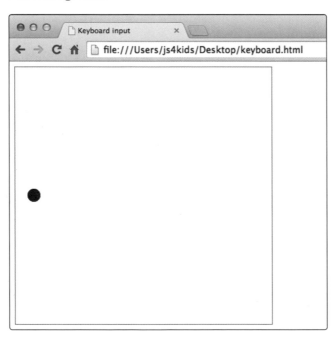

Figure 15-2: The ball is a filled circle with a radius of 10.

CREATING A SETDIRECTION METHOD

Now we have to create a way to set the direction of the ball. We'll do that with a method called setDirection. This method will be called by our keydown event handler, which you'll see in the next section. The keydown handler will tell setDirection which key was pressed by passing it a string ("left", "up", "right", "down", or "stop"). Based on that string, setDirection will change the xSpeed and ySpeed properties of the ball to make it move in the direction that matches the keypress. For example, if the string "down" is passed, we set this.xSpeed to 0 and this.ySpeed to 5. Add this code after the draw method:

```
Ball.prototype.setDirection = function (direction) {
  if (direction === "up") {
    this.xSpeed = 0;
    this.ySpeed = -5;
  } else if (direction === "down") {
    this.xSpeed = 0;
    this.ySpeed = 5;
  } else if (direction === "left") {
    this.xSpeed = -5;
    this.ySpeed = 0;
  } else if (direction === "right") {
    this.xSpeed = 5;
    this.ySpeed = 0;
  } else if (direction === "stop") {
    this.xSpeed = 0;
    this.ySpeed = 0;
  }
};
```

The entire body of this method is one long if...else statement. The new direction is passed into the method as the direction argument. If direction is equal to "up", we set the ball's xSpeed property to 0 and its ySpeed property to -5. The other directions are handled in the same way. Finally, if the direction is set to the string "stop", we set both this.xSpeed and this.ySpeed to 0, which means that the ball will stop moving.

REACTING TO THE KEYBOARD

This next snippet of code creates a `ball` object using the `Ball` constructor, and it listens for `keydown` events in order to set the ball's direction. Add this code after the `setDirection` method:

```
❶ var ball = new Ball();

❷ var keyActions = {
       32: "stop",
       37: "left",
       38: "up",
       39: "right",
       40: "down"
   };

❸ $("body").keydown(function (event) {
❹     var direction = keyActions[event.keyCode];
❺     ball.setDirection(direction);
   });
```

At ❶, we create a ball object by calling `new Ball()`. At ❷ we create a `keyActions` object, which we'll use to convert keycodes to their corresponding direction. This object is the same as the `keyNames` object we created on page 238, except that for 32 (the keycode for the spacebar) we replace the label `"space"` with `"stop"` since we want the spacebar to stop the ball from moving.

At ❸ we use the jQuery `$` function to select the body element and then call the `keydown` method to listen for `keydown` events. The function passed to the `keydown` method is called every time a key is pressed.

Inside this function, we use `keyActions[event.keyCode]` at ❹ to look up the label for the key that was pressed and assign that label to the `direction` variable. This sets the `direction` variable to a direction: `"left"` if the left arrow is pressed, `"right"` if the right arrow is pressed, `"up"` for the up arrow, `"down"` for the down arrow, and `"stop"` for the spacebar. If any other key is pressed, `direction` is set to `undefined`, and the animation won't be affected.

Finally, at ❺ we call the setDirection method on the ball object, passing the direction string. As you saw before, setDirection updates the ball's xSpeed and ySpeed properties based on the new direction.

ANIMATING THE BALL

All we have left to do now is animate the ball. The following code should look familiar, since it's quite similar to what we used in Chapter 14. It uses the setInterval function that we've seen in the animation code in previous chapters to update the ball's position at regular intervals. Add this code after the code from the previous section:

```
setInterval(function () {
  ctx.clearRect(0, 0, width, height);

  ball.draw();
  ball.move();

  ctx.strokeRect(0, 0, width, height);
}, 30);
```

We use setInterval to call our animation function every 30 milliseconds. The function first clears the entire canvas with clearRect and then calls the draw and move methods on the ball. As we've seen, the draw method simply draws a circle at the ball's current location, and the move method updates the ball's position based on its xSpeed and ySpeed properties. Finally, it draws a border with strokeRect so we can see the edge of the canvas.

PUTTING IT ALL TOGETHER

Now that we've gone through all the code, here's the full listing for your convenience.

```javascript
var canvas = document.getElementById("canvas");
var ctx = canvas.getContext("2d");
var width = canvas.width;
var height = canvas.height;

var circle = function (x, y, radius, fillCircle) {
  ctx.beginPath();
  ctx.arc(x, y, radius, 0, Math.PI * 2, false);
  if (fillCircle) {
    ctx.fill();
  } else {
    ctx.stroke();
  }
};

// The Ball constructor
var Ball = function () {
  this.x = width / 2;
  this.y = height / 2;
  this.xSpeed = 5;
  this.ySpeed = 0;
};

// Update the ball's position based on its speed
Ball.prototype.move = function () {
  this.x += this.xSpeed;
  this.y += this.ySpeed;

  if (this.x < 0) {
    this.x = width;
  } else if (this.x > width) {
    this.x = 0;
  } else if (this.y < 0) {
    this.y = height;
  } else if (this.y > height) {
    this.y = 0;
  }
};

// Draw the ball at its current position
Ball.prototype.draw = function () {
  circle(this.x, this.y, 10, true);
};
```

```javascript
// Set the ball's direction based on a string
Ball.prototype.setDirection = function (direction) {
  if (direction === "up") {
    this.xSpeed = 0;
    this.ySpeed = -5;
  } else if (direction === "down") {
    this.xSpeed = 0;
    this.ySpeed = 5;
  } else if (direction === "left") {
    this.xSpeed = -5;
    this.ySpeed = 0;
  } else if (direction === "right") {
    this.xSpeed = 5;
    this.ySpeed = 0;
  } else if (direction === "stop") {
    this.xSpeed = 0;
    this.ySpeed = 0;
  }
};

// Create the ball object
var ball = new Ball();

// An object to convert keycodes into action names
var keyActions = {
  32: "stop",
  37: "left",
  38: "up",
  39: "right",
  40: "down"
};

// The keydown handler that will be called for every keypress
$("body").keydown(function (event) {
  var direction = keyActions[event.keyCode];
  ball.setDirection(direction);
});

// The animation function, called every 30 ms
setInterval(function () {
  ctx.clearRect(0, 0, width, height);

  ball.draw();
  ball.move();

  ctx.strokeRect(0, 0, width, height);
}, 30);
```

RUNNING THE CODE

Now our program is complete. When you run the program, you should see a black ball moving across the canvas to the right, as shown in Figure 15-3. When it reaches the right side of the canvas, it should wrap around to the left side and keep moving to the right. When you press the arrow keys, the ball should change direction, and pressing the spacebar should make the ball stop.

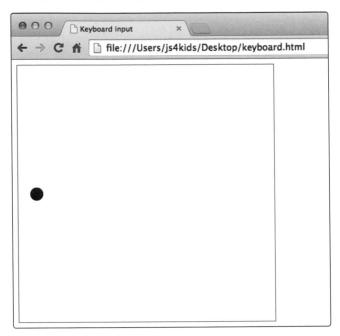

Figure 15-3: A screenshot from the moving ball animation

NOTE   *If the animation doesn't respond to keys as expected, click the page to make sure the program can access your keypresses.*

WHAT YOU LEARNED

In this chapter, you learned how to make programs that react to keyboard events. We used this knowledge to create a moving ball, where the ball's direction is set by the keyboard.

Now that we can draw to the canvas, create animations, and update those animations based on user input, we can create a simple canvas-based game! In the next chapter, we'll re-create the classic Snake game, combining everything we've learned up until now.

PROGRAMMING CHALLENGES

Here are a few ways you can build on the final animation to make it more sophisticated.

#1: BOUNCING OFF THE WALLS

Modify the code so the ball bounces off the side and top walls instead of wrapping around to the other side. Hint: Just reverse the direction when the ball hits the wall.

#2: CONTROLLING THE SPEED

The ball currently moves 5 pixels for every step of the animation. This is because setDirection always sets xSpeed or ySpeed to -5 or 5. Create a new property in the Ball constructor called speed and set it to 5. Then use this instead of the number 5 in setDirection.

Now, change your code so that you can use the number keys to set the speed from 1 to 9. Hint: Create an object called speeds, and use it to determine the new speed, if any, based on the keydown event.

#3: FLEXIBLE CONTROLS

Modify your code so that when you press the Z key, the ball slows down, and when you press the X key, it speeds up. Once that's working, use C to make the ball smaller and V to make it larger.

What happens if the speed goes below 0? What about the size? Add a check in the code to make sure the speed and size never go below 0.

16

MAKING A SNAKE GAME: PART 1

In this chapter and the next, we'll build our own version of the classic arcade game Snake. In Snake, the player uses the keyboard to control a snake by directing its movement up, down, left, or right. As the snake moves around the playing area, apples appear. When the snake reaches an apple, it eats the apple and grows longer. But if the snake hits a wall or runs into part of its own body, the game is over.

As you create this game, you'll combine many of the tools and techniques you've learned so far, including jQuery and the canvas as well as animation and interactivity. In this chapter, we'll look at the general structure of the game and go through the code for drawing the border and the score and ending the game. In Chapter 17, we'll write the code for the snake and the apple and then put everything together to complete the game.

THE GAME PLAY

Figure 16-1 shows what our finished game will look like. We'll need to keep track of and draw four items on the screen as the game runs: the border (in gray), the score (in black), the snake (in blue), and the apple (in lime green).

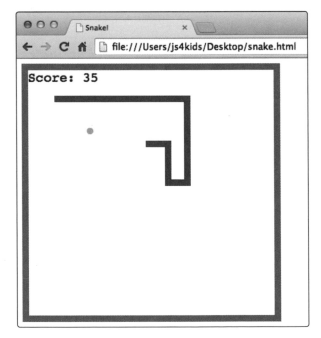

Figure 16-1: Our Snake game

THE STRUCTURE OF THE GAME

Before we start writing code, let's take a look at the overall structure of the game. This pseudocode describes what our program needs to do:

```
Set up the canvas
Set score to zero
Create snake
Create apple

Every 100 milliseconds {
  Clear the canvas
  Draw current score on the screen
  Move snake in current direction
  If snake collides with wall or itself {
    End the game
  } Else If snake eats an apple {
    Add one to score
    Move apple to new location
    Make snake longer
  }
  For each segment of the snake {
    Draw the segment
  }
  Draw apple
  Draw border
}

When the user presses a key {
  If the key is an arrow {
    Update the direction of the snake
  }
}
```

Over the course of this chapter and the next, we'll write the code to execute each of these steps. But first, let's talk through some of the major parts of this program and plan out some of the JavaScript tools we'll use for them.

USING SETINTERVAL TO ANIMATE THE GAME

As you can see in the pseudocode, every 100 milliseconds we need to call a series of functions and methods that update and draw everything to the game board. Just as we've done in Chapters 14 and 15, we'll use setInterval to animate the game by calling those functions at regular intervals. This is what our call to setInterval will look like in the final program:

```
var intervalId = setInterval(function () {
  ctx.clearRect(0, 0, width, height);
  drawScore();
  snake.move();
  snake.draw();
  apple.draw();
  drawBorder();
}, 100);
```

In the function that we pass to setInterval, the first line clears the canvas with clearRect so that we can draw the next step in the animation. Next we see several function and method calls. Notice that these all roughly match up with the steps in the pseudocode listing on the previous page.

Also notice that we save the interval ID in the variable intervalId. We'll need that interval ID when the game is over and we want to stop the animation (see "Ending the Game" on page 264).

CREATING THE GAME OBJECTS

For this program, we'll use the object-oriented programming style we learned about in Chapter 12 to represent the two main objects in the game: the snake and the apple. We'll create a constructor for each of these objects (called Snake and Apple), and we'll add methods (like move and draw) to the prototypes of these constructors.

We'll also divide the game board into a grid and then create a constructor called Block, which we'll use to create objects that represent squares in the grid. We'll use these block objects to represent the location of segments of the snake, and we'll use a single block object to store the apple's current location. These blocks will also have methods to let us draw the segments of the snake and the apple.

SETTING UP KEYBOARD CONTROL

In the earlier pseudocode, there's a section devoted to responding to keypresses by the user. To allow the player to control the snake using the arrow keys on the keyboard, we'll use jQuery to respond to keypresses, as we did in Chapter 15. We'll identify the key that was pressed by looking up the keycode, and then we'll set the snake's direction accordingly.

GAME SETUP

Now that we've gone through an overview of how the program will work, let's start writing some code! In this chapter, we'll start by setting up the HTML, the canvas, and some variables we'll need throughout the program. Then we'll tackle a few of the more straightforward functions we need for this game: one to draw the border around the board, one to draw the score on the screen, and one to end the game. In the next chapter, we'll create the constructors and methods for the snake and apple, create an event handler for arrow keypresses, and put it all together to complete the game.

CREATING THE HTML

To begin coding our game, enter the following into your text editor and save it as *snake.html*.

```
<!DOCTYPE html>
<html>
<head>
    <title>Snake!</title>
</head>

<body>
❶    <canvas id="canvas" width="400" height="400"></canvas>

❷    <script src="https://code.jquery.com/jquery-2.1.0.js"></script>

❸    <script>
    // We'll fill this in next
    </script>
</body>
</html>
```

At ❶ we create a canvas element that is 400 × 400 pixels. This is where we'll draw everything for our game. We include the jQuery library at ❷, followed by another pair of <script> tags at ❸, where we'll add our JavaScript code to control the game. Let's start writing that JavaScript now.

DEFINING THE CANVAS, CTX, WIDTH, AND HEIGHT VARIABLES

First we'll define the variables canvas and ctx, which will let us draw on the canvas, and the variables width and height, to get the width and height of the canvas element.

```
var canvas = document.getElementById("canvas");
var ctx = canvas.getContext("2d");

var width = canvas.width;
var height = canvas.height;
```

The code in the HTML sets the width and height to 400 pixels; if you change those dimensions in the HTML, width and height will match the new dimensions.

DIVIDING THE CANVAS INTO BLOCKS

Next, we'll create variables to help us think about our canvas as a grid of 10-by-10-pixel blocks, as shown in Figure 16-2. Although the grid will be invisible (that is, the game won't actually display it), everything in the game will be drawn to line up with it.

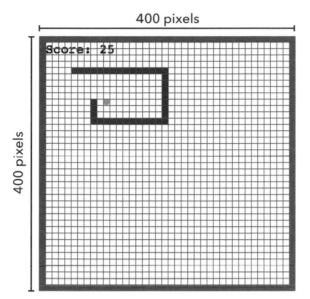

Figure 16-2: A 10-pixel grid showing the block layout of the game

The snake and apple will both be one block wide so that they fit within this grid. For every step of the animation, the snake will move exactly one block in its current direction.

We'll use these variables to create the blocks on our canvas:

```
❶ var blockSize = 10;
❷ var widthInBlocks = width / blockSize;
  var heightInBlocks = height / blockSize;
```

At ❶ we create a variable called `blockSize` and set it to 10, since we want our blocks to be 10 pixels tall and wide. At ❷ we create the variables `widthInBlocks` and `heightInBlocks`. We set `widthInBlocks` equal to the width of the canvas divided by the block size, which tells us how many blocks wide the canvas is. Similarly, `heightInBlocks` tells us how many blocks tall the canvas is. At the moment the canvas is 400 pixels wide and tall, so `widthInBlocks` and `heightInBlocks` will both be 40. If you count the number of squares in Figure 16-2 (including the border), you'll see that it's 40 blocks wide and tall.

DEFINING THE SCORE VARIABLE

Finally, we define the score variable.

```
var score = 0;
```

We'll use the score variable to keep track of the player's score. Because this is the beginning of the program, we set score equal to 0. We'll increment it by 1 every time the snake eats an apple.

DRAWING THE BORDER

Next, we'll create a drawBorder function to draw a border around the canvas. We'll make this border one block (10 pixels) thick.

Our function will draw four long, thin rectangles, one for each edge of the border. Each rectangle will be blockSize (10 pixels) thick and the full width or height of the canvas.

```
var drawBorder = function () {
  ctx.fillStyle = "Gray";
❶  ctx.fillRect(0, 0, width, blockSize);
❷  ctx.fillRect(0, height - blockSize, width, blockSize);
❸  ctx.fillRect(0, 0, blockSize, height);
❹  ctx.fillRect(width - blockSize, 0, blockSize, height);
};
```

First we set the fillStyle to gray, because we want the border to be gray. Then, at ❶, we draw the top edge of the border. Here we're drawing a rectangle starting at (0, 0)—the top-left corner of the canvas—with a width of width (400 pixels) and a height of blockSize (10 pixels).

Next, at ❷, we draw the bottom edge of the border. This will be a rectangle at the coordinates (0, height - blockSize), or (0, 390). This is 10 pixels up from the bottom of the canvas, on the left. Like the top border, this rectangle has a width of width and a height of blockSize.

Figure 16-3 shows what the top and bottom borders look like.

Figure 16-3: The top and bottom borders

At ❸ we draw the left border, and at ❹ we draw the right one. Figure 16-4 shows the addition of these two edges.

Figure 16-4: The left and right borders (with the top and bottom borders shown in a lighter gray)

DISPLAYING THE SCORE

Now let's write a drawScore function to display the score at the top left of the canvas, as shown in Figure 16-1 on page 252. This function will use the fillText context method to add text to the canvas. The fillText method takes a text string and the *x*- and *y*-coordinates where you want to display that text. For example,

```
ctx.fillText("Hello world!", 50, 50);
```

would write the string Hello world! at the coordinates (50, 50) on your canvas. Figure 16-5 shows how that would look.

Figure 16-5: The string Hello world! drawn at the point (50, 50)

Hey look, we've printed text to the canvas! But what if we want to have more control over how the text looks by tweaking the size and font or changing the alignment? For the score in our Snake game, we might want to use a different font, make the text bigger, and make sure the text appears precisely in the top-left corner, just below the border. So before we write our drawScore function, let's learn a little more about the fillText method and look at some ways to customize how text appears on the canvas.

SETTING THE TEXT BASELINE

The coordinate location that determines where the text appears is called the *baseline*. By default, the bottom-left corner of the text is lined up with the baseline point so that the text appears above and to the right of that point.

To change where the text appears in relation to the baseline, we can change the textBaseline property. The default value for this property is "bottom", but you can also set the textBaseline property to "top" or "middle". Figure 16-6 shows how the text is aligned for each of these options, in relation to the baseline point (shown as a red dot) that you pass to fillText.

Figure 16-6: The effect of changing textBaseline

For example, to run your text below the baseline, enter:

```
ctx.textBaseline = "top";
ctx.fillText("Hello world!", 50, 50);
```

Now, when you call fillText, the text will be below the point (50, 50), as you can see in Figure 16-7.

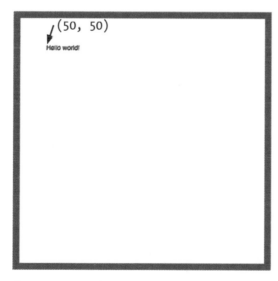

Figure 16-7: The string Hello world! with textBaseline set to "top"

Similarly, to change the horizontal position of the text relative to the baseline point, you can set the textAlign property to "left", "center", or "right". Figure 16-8 shows the results.

.left   cen.ter   right.

Figure 16-8: The effect of changing textAlign

SETTING THE SIZE AND FONT

We can change the size and font of the text we draw by setting the font property of the drawing context. This listing shows some examples of different fonts we could use:

```
❶ ctx.font = "20px Courier";
  ctx.fillText("Courier", 50, 50);

  ctx.font = "24px Comic Sans MS";
  ctx.fillText("Comic Sans", 50, 100);

  ctx.font = "18px Arial";
  ctx.fillText("Arial", 50, 150);
```

The font property takes a string that includes the size and the name of the font you want to use. For example, at ❶ we set the font property to "20px Courier", which means the text will be drawn at a size of 20 pixels in the font Courier. Figure 16-9 shows how these different fonts look when drawn on the canvas.

Figure 16-9: 20px Courier, 24px Comic Sans, and 18px Arial

WRITING THE DRAWSCORE FUNCTION

Now we can go ahead and write the drawScore function, which draws a string showing the current score on the canvas.

```
var drawScore = function () {
  ctx.font = "20px Courier";
  ctx.fillStyle = "Black";
  ctx.textAlign = "left";
  ctx.textBaseline = "top";
  ctx.fillText("Score: " + score, blockSize, blockSize);
};
```

This function sets the font to 20-pixel Courier (20px Courier), sets its color to black using fillStyle, left-aligns the text with the textAlign property, and then sets the textBaseline property to "top".

Next, we call fillText with the string "Score: " + score. The score variable holds the player's current score as a number. We set the starting score to 0 at the beginning of the game (in "Defining the score Variable" on page 258), so at first this will display "Score: 0".

When we call fillText, we set the x- and y-coordinates to blockSize. Since we set blockSize to 10, this sets the score's baseline point to (10, 10), which is just inside the top-left corner of the border. And since we set textBaseline to "top", the text will appear just below that baseline point, as shown in Figure 16-10.

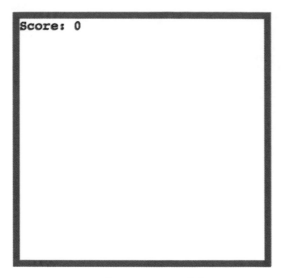

Score: 0

Figure 16-10: The position of the score text

ENDING THE GAME

We'll call the gameOver function to end the game when the snake hits the wall or runs into itself. The gameOver function uses clearInterval to stop the game and writes the text "Game Over" on the canvas. Here's what the gameOver function looks like:

```
var gameOver = function () {
  clearInterval(intervalId);
  ctx.font = "60px Courier";
  ctx.fillStyle = "Black";
  ctx.textAlign = "center";
  ctx.textBaseline = "middle";
  ctx.fillText("Game Over", width / 2, height / 2);
};
```

First we stop the game by calling clearInterval and passing in the variable intervalId. This cancels the setInterval animation function that we created in "Using setInterval to Animate the Game" on page 254.

Next, we set our font to 60-pixel Courier in black, center the text, and set the textBaseline property to "middle". We then call fillText and tell it to draw the string "Game Over" with width / 2 for the *x*-position and height / 2 for the *y*-position. The resulting "Game Over" text will be centered in the canvas, as shown in Figure 16-11.

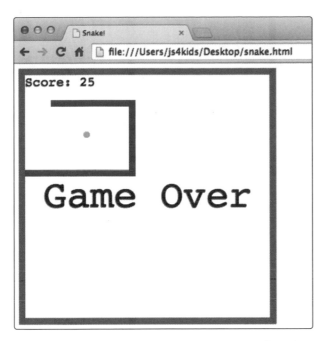

Figure 16-11: The "Game Over" screen, after the snake has hit the left wall

WHAT YOU LEARNED

In this chapter, we looked at the general outline of our Snake game and some of the functions we'll need to make the game. You learned how to draw text onto a canvas and how to customize its size, font, and position.

In the next chapter, we'll finish off our game by writing the code for the snake and the apple and to handle keyboard events.

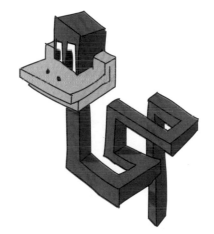

PROGRAMMING CHALLENGES

Here are a few exercises you can try before you go on to finish programming the game.

#1: PUTTING IT TOGETHER

Although I haven't shown all the code for the game yet, you can run the code for drawing the border and the score. Take your HTML file (from "Creating the HTML" on page 255) and add the code for setting up the canvas, creating the score, drawing the border, and drawing the score. Now you just need to call drawBorder and drawScore to see the border and score. It should look just like Figure 16-10. You can try out the gameOver function, too, but before you call that function, you'll need to delete the clearInterval(intervalId); line. You haven't created the intervalId variable yet, so for now, if you call the function without removing that line, it will produce an error.

#2: ANIMATING THE SCORE

Write your own call to setInterval with a function that increases the score by 1 and then draws the updated score using the drawScore function every 100 milliseconds. Remember that you'll need to clear the canvas each time, using the clearRect method on the canvas context.

#3: ADDING TEXT TO HANGMAN

Programming challenge #4 in Chapter 13 was to draw the man in our Hangman game using canvas. Try extending your Hangman game by using the fillText method to draw the current word underneath the hangman, as shown.

Hint: To underline each letter, I've used 30-pixel-long stroked lines, with 10 pixels between each one.

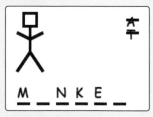

For even more of a challenge, draw the incorrect guesses crossed out, as shown to the right.

17

MAKING A SNAKE GAME: PART 2

In this chapter, we'll finish building our Snake game. In Chapter 16, we set up the playing area and covered how the game would work in general. Now we'll create the objects that represent the snake and apple in the game, and we'll program a keyboard event handler so that the player can control the snake with the arrow keys. Finally, we'll look at the complete code listing for the program.

As we create the snake and apple objects for this game, we'll use the object-oriented programming techniques we learned in Chapter 12 to create constructors and methods for each object. Both our snake and apple objects will rely on a more basic block object, which we'll use to represent one block on the game board grid. Let's start by building a constructor for that simple block object.

BUILDING THE BLOCK CONSTRUCTOR

In this section, we'll define a Block constructor that will create objects that represent individual blocks on our invisible game grid. Each block will have the properties col (short for *column*) and row, which will store the location of that particular block on the grid. Figure 17-1 shows this grid with some of the columns and rows numbered. Although this grid won't actually appear on the screen, our game is designed so that the apple and the snake segments will always line up with it.

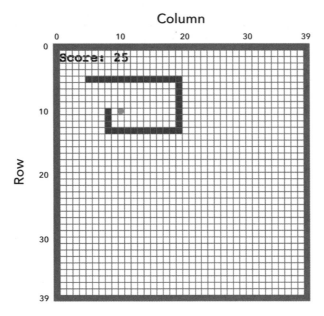

Figure 17-1: The column and row numbers used by the Block constructor

In Figure 17-1, the block containing the green apple is at column 10, row 10. The head of the snake (to the left of the apple) is at column 8, row 10.

Here's the code for the Block constructor:

```
var Block = function (col, row) {
  this.col = col;
  this.row = row;
};
```

Column and row values are passed into the Block constructor as arguments and saved in the col and row properties of the new object.

Now we can use this constructor to create an object representing a particular block on the game grid. For example, here's how we'd create an object that represents the block in column 5, row 5:

```
var sampleBlock = new Block(5, 5);
```

ADDING THE DRAWSQUARE METHOD

So far this block object lets us represent a location on the grid, but to actually make something appear at that location, we'll need to draw it on the canvas. Next, we'll add two methods, drawSquare and drawCircle, that will let us draw a square or a circle, respectively, in a particular block on the grid. First, here's the drawSquare method:

```
Block.prototype.drawSquare = function (color) {
❶  var x = this.col * blockSize;
❷  var y = this.row * blockSize;
   ctx.fillStyle = color;
   ctx.fillRect(x, y, blockSize, blockSize);
};
```

In Chapter 12 we learned that if you attach methods to the prototype property of a constructor, those methods will be available to any objects created with that constructor. So by adding the drawSquare method to Block.protoype, we make it available to any block objects.

This method draws a square at the location given by the block's col and row properties. It takes a single argument, color, which determines

the color of the square. To draw a square with canvas, we need to provide the *x*- and *y*-positions of the top-left corner of the square. At ❶ and ❷ we calculate these *x*- and *y*-values for the current block by multiplying the col and row properties by blockSize. We then set the fillStyle property of the drawing context to the method's color argument.

Finally, we call ctx.fillRect, passing our computed *x*- and *y*-values and blockSize for both the width and height of the square.

Here's how we would create a block in column 3, row 4, and draw it:

```
var sampleBlock = new Block(3, 4);
sampleBlock.drawSquare("LightBlue");
```

Figure 17-2 shows this square drawn on the canvas and how the measurements for the square are calculated.

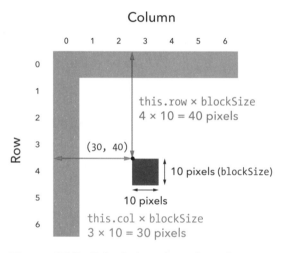

Figure 17-2: Calculating the values for drawing a square

ADDING THE DRAWCIRCLE METHOD

Now for the drawCircle method. It is very similar to the drawSquare method, but it draws a filled circle instead of a square.

```
Block.prototype.drawCircle = function (color) {
  var centerX = this.col * blockSize + blockSize / 2;
  var centerY = this.row * blockSize + blockSize / 2;
  ctx.fillStyle = color;
  circle(centerX, centerY, blockSize / 2, true);
};
```

First we calculate the location of the circle's center by creating two new variables, centerX and centerY. As before, we multiply the col and row properties by blockSize, but this time we also have to add blockSize / 2, because we need the pixel coordinates for the circle's center, which is in the middle of a block (as shown in Figure 17-3).

We set the context fillStyle to the color argument as in drawSquare and then call our trusty circle function, passing centerX and centerY for the *x*- and *y*-coordinates, blockSize / 2 for the radius, and true to tell the function to fill the circle. This is the same circle function we defined in Chapter 14, so we'll have to include the definition for that function once again in this program (as you can see in the final code listing).

Here's how we could draw a circle in column 4, row 3:

```
var sampleCircle = new Block(4, 3);
sampleCircle.drawCircle("LightGreen");
```

Figure 17-3 shows the circle, with the calculations for the center point and radius.

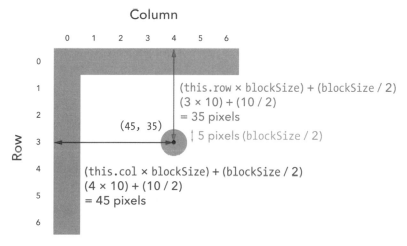

Figure 17-3: Calculating the values for drawing a circle

ADDING THE EQUAL METHOD

In our game, we'll need to know whether two blocks are in the same location. For example, if the apple and the snake's head are in the same location, that means the snake has eaten the apple. On the other hand, if the snake's head and tail are in the same location, then the snake has collided with itself.

To make it easier to compare block locations, we'll add a method, equal, to the Block constructor prototype. When we call equal on one block object and pass another object as an argument, it will return true if they are in the same location (and false if not). Here's the code:

```
Block.prototype.equal = function (otherBlock) {
  return this.col === otherBlock.col && this.row === otherBlock.row;
};
```

This method is pretty straightforward: if the two blocks (this and otherBlock) have the same col and row properties (that is, if this.col is equal to otherBlock.col and this.row is equal to otherBlock.row), then they are in the same place, and the method returns true.

For example, let's create two new blocks called apple and head and see if they're in the same location:

```
var apple = new Block(2, 5);
var head = new Block(3, 5);
head.equal(apple);
false
```

Although apple and head have the same row property (5), their col properties are different. If we set the head to a new block object one column to the left, now the method will tell us that the two objects are in the same location:

```
head = new Block(2, 5);
head.equal(apple);
true
```

Note that it doesn't make any difference whether we write head.equal(apple) or apple.equal(head); in both cases we're making the same comparison.

We'll use the equal method later to check whether the snake has eaten the apple or collided with itself.

CREATING THE SNAKE

Now we'll create the snake. We'll store the snake's position as an array called *segments*, which will contain a series of block objects. To move the snake, we'll add a new block to the beginning of the *segments* array and remove the block at the end of the array. The first element of the *segments* array will represent the head of the snake.

WRITING THE SNAKE CONSTRUCTOR

First we need a constructor to create our snake object:

```
var Snake = function () {
❶   this.segments = [
      new Block(7, 5),
      new Block(6, 5),
      new Block(5, 5)
    ];

❷   this.direction = "right";
❸   this.nextDirection = "right";
};
```

DEFINING THE SNAKE SEGMENTS

The *segments* property at ❶ is an array of block objects that each represent a segment of the snake's body. When we start the game, this array will contain three blocks at (7, 5), (6, 5), and (5, 5). Figure 17-4 shows these initial three segments of the snake.

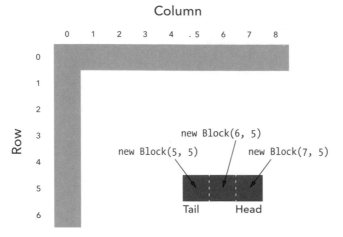

Figure 17-4: The initial blocks that make up the snake

SETTING THE DIRECTION OF MOVEMENT

The `direction` property at ❷ stores the current direction of the snake. Our constructor also adds the `nextDirection` property at ❸, which stores the direction in which the snake will move for the next animation step. This property will be updated by our `keydown` event handler when the player presses an arrow key (see "Adding the `keydown` Event Handler" on page 281). For now, the constructor sets both of these properties to `"right"`, so at the beginning of the game our snake will move to the right.

DRAWING THE SNAKE

To draw the snake, we simply have to loop through each of the blocks in its `segments` array, calling the `drawSquare` method we created earlier on each block. This will draw a square for each segment of the snake.

```
Snake.prototype.draw = function () {
  for (var i = 0; i < this.segments.length; i++) {
    this.segments[i].drawSquare("Blue");
  }
};
```

The `draw` method uses a `for` loop to operate on each block object in the `segments` array. Each time around the loop, this code takes the current segment (`this.segments[i]`) and calls `drawSquare("Blue")` on it, which draws a blue square in the corresponding block.

If you want to test out the draw method, you can run the following code, which creates a new object using the Snake constructor and calls its draw method:

```
var snake = new Snake();
snake.draw();
```

MOVING THE SNAKE

We'll create a move method to move the snake one block in its current direction. To move the snake, we add a new head segment (by adding a new block object to the beginning of the segments array) and then remove the tail segment from the end of the segments array.

The move method will also call a method, checkCollision, to see whether the new head has collided with the rest of the snake or with the wall, and whether the new head has eaten the apple. If the new head has collided with the body or the wall, we end the game by calling the gameOver function we created in Chapter 16. If the snake has eaten the apple, we increase the score and move the apple to a new location.

ADDING THE MOVE METHOD

The move method looks like this:

```
Snake.prototype.move = function () {
❶   var head = this.segments[0];
❷   var newHead;

❸   this.direction = this.nextDirection;

❹   if (this.direction === "right") {
      newHead = new Block(head.col + 1, head.row);
    } else if (this.direction === "down") {
      newHead = new Block(head.col, head.row + 1);
    } else if (this.direction === "left") {
      newHead = new Block(head.col - 1, head.row);
    } else if (this.direction === "up") {
      newHead = new Block(head.col, head.row - 1);
    }
```

```
❺   if (this.checkCollision(newHead)) {
      gameOver();
      return;
    }

❻   this.segments.unshift(newHead);

❼   if (newHead.equal(apple.position)) {
      score++;
      apple.move();
    } else {
      this.segments.pop();
    }
};
```

Let's walk through this method piece by piece.

CREATING A NEW HEAD

At ❶ we save the first element of the this.segments array in the variable head. We'll refer to this first segment of the snake many times in this method, so using this variable will save us some typing and make the code a bit easier to read. Now, instead of repeating this.segments[0] over and over again, we can just type head.

At ❷ we create the variable newHead, which we'll use to store the block representing the new head of the snake (which we're about to add).

At ❸ we set this.direction equal to this.nextDirection, which updates the direction of the snake's movement to match the most recently pressed arrow key. (We'll see how this works in more detail when we look at the keydown event handler.)

Beginning at ❹, we use a chain of if...else statements to determine the snake's direction. In each case, we create a new head for the snake and save it in the variable newHead. Depending on the direction of movement, we add or subtract one from the row or column of the existing head to place this new head directly next to the old one (either right, left, up, or down depending on the snake's direction of movement). For example, Figure 17-5 shows how the new head is added to the snake when this.nextDirection is set to "down".

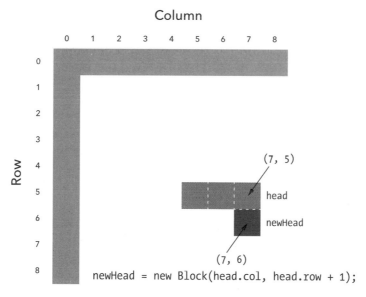

Figure 17-5: Creating newHead when this.nextDirection is "down"

CHECKING FOR COLLISIONS AND ADDING THE HEAD

At ❺ we call the checkCollision method to find out whether the snake has collided with a wall or with itself. We'll see the code for this method in a moment, but as you might guess, this method will return true if the snake has collided with something. If that happens, the body of the if statement calls the gameOver function to end the game and print "Game Over" on the canvas.

The return keyword that follows the call to gameOver exits the move method early, skipping any code that comes after it. We reach the return keyword only if checkCollision returns true, so if the snake hasn't collided with anything, we execute the rest of the method.

As long as the snake hasn't collided with something, we add the new head to the front of the snake at ❻ by using unshift to add newHead to the beginning of the segments array. For more about how the unshift method works on arrays, see "Adding Elements to an Array" on page 47.

EATING THE APPLE

At ❼, we use the equal method to compare newHead and apple.position. If the two blocks are in the same location, the equal method will return true, which means that the snake has eaten the apple.

If the snake has eaten the apple, we increase the score and then call move on the apple to move it to a new location. If the snake has not eaten the apple, we call pop on this.segments. This removes the snake's tail while keeping the snake the same size (since move already added a segment to the snake's head). When the snake eats an apple, it grows by one segment because we add a segment to its head without removing the tail.

We haven't defined apple yet, so this method won't fully work in its current form. If you want to test it out, you can delete the whole if...else statement at ❼ and replace it with this line:

```
this.segments.pop();
```

Then all you need to do is define the checkCollision method, which we'll do next.

ADDING THE CHECKCOLLISION METHOD

Each time we set a new location for the snake's head, we have to check for collisions. Collision detection, a very common step in game mechanics, is often one of the more complex aspects of game programming. Fortunately, it's relatively straightforward in our Snake game.

We care about two types of collisions in our Snake game: collisions with the wall and collisions with the snake itself. A wall collision happens if the snake hits a wall. The snake can collide with itself if you turn the head so that it runs into the body. At the start of the game, the snake is too short to collide with itself, but after eating a few apples, it can.

Here is the checkCollision method:

```
Snake.prototype.checkCollision = function (head) {
❶    var leftCollision = (head.col === 0);
     var topCollision - (head.row --- 0);
     var rightCollision = (head.col === widthInBlocks - 1);
     var bottomCollision = (head.row === heightInBlocks - 1);

❷    var wallCollision = leftCollision || topCollision || ↵
       rightCollision || bottomCollision;

❸    var selfCollision = false;

❹    for (var i = 0; i < this.segments.length; i++) {
       if (head.equal(this.segments[i])) {
❺        selfCollision = true;
       }
     }

❻    return wallCollision || selfCollision;
};
```

CHECKING FOR WALL COLLISIONS

At ❶ we create the variable leftCollision and set it to the value of head.col === 0. This variable will be true if the snake collides with the left wall; that is, when it is in column 0. Similarly, the variable topCollision in the next line checks the row of the snake's head to see if it has run into the top wall.

After that, we check for a collision with the right wall by checking whether the column value of the head is equal to widthInBlocks - 1. Since widthInBlocks is set to 40, this checks whether the head is in column 39, which corresponds to the right wall, as you can see back in Figure 17-1. Then we do the same thing for bottomCollision, checking whether the head's row property is equal to heightInBlocks - 1.

At ❷, we determine whether the snake has collided with a wall by checking to see if leftCollision *or* topCollision *or* rightCollision *or* bottomCollision is true, using the || (or) operator. We save the Boolean result in the variable wallCollision.

CHECKING FOR SELF-COLLISIONS

To determine whether the snake has collided with itself, we create a variable at ❸ called selfCollision and initially set it to false. Then at ❹ we use a for loop to loop through all the segments of the snake to determine whether the new head is in the same place as any segment, using head.equal(this.segments[i]). The head and all of the other segments are blocks, so we can use the equal method that we defined for block objects to see whether they are in the same place. If we find that any of the snake's segments are in the same place as the new head, we know that the snake has collided with itself, and we set selfCollision to true (at ❺).

Finally, at ❻, we return wallCollision || selfCollision, which will be true if the snake has collided with either the wall or itself.

SETTING THE SNAKE'S DIRECTION WITH THE KEYBOARD

Next we'll write the code that lets the player set the snake's direction using the keyboard. We'll add a keydown event handler to detect when an arrow key has been pressed, and we'll set the snake's direction to match that key.

ADDING THE KEYDOWN EVENT HANDLER

This code handles keyboard events:

```
❶ var directions = {
    37: "left",
    38: "up",
    39: "right",
    40: "down"
};

❷ $("body").keydown(function (event) {
    var newDirection = directions[event.keyCode];
❸  if (newDirection !== undefined) {
      snake.setDirection(newDirection);
    }
});
```

At ❶ we create an object to convert the arrow keycodes into strings indicating the direction they represent (this object is quite similar to the keyActions object we used in "Reacting to the Keyboard" on page 244). At ❷ we attach an event handler to the keydown event on the body element. This handler will be called when the user presses a key (as long as they've clicked inside the web page first).

This handler first converts the event's keycode into a direction string, and then it saves the string in the variable newDirection. If the keycode is not 37, 38, 39, or 40 (the keycodes for the arrow keys we care about), directions[event.keyCode] will be undefined.

At ❸ we check to see if newDirection is not equal to undefined. If it's not undefined, we call the setDirection method on the snake, passing the newDirection string. (Because there is no else case in this if statement, if newDirection is undefined, then we just ignore the keypress.)

This code won't work yet because we haven't defined the setDirection method on the snake. Let's do that now.

ADDING THE SETDIRECTION METHOD

The `setDirection` method takes the new direction from the keyboard handler we just looked at and uses it to update the snake's direction. This method also prevents the player from making turns that would have the snake immediately run into itself. For example, if the snake is moving right, and then it suddenly turns left without moving up or down to get out of its own way, it will collide with itself. We'll call these *illegal* turns because we do not want to allow the player to make them. For example, Figure 17-6 shows the valid directions and the one illegal direction when the snake is moving right.

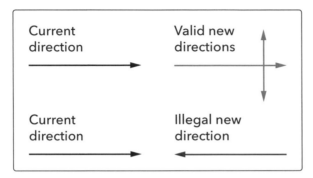

Figure 17-6: Valid new directions based on the current direction

The `setDirection` method checks whether the player is trying to make an illegal turn. If they are, the method uses `return` to end early; otherwise, it updates the `nextDirection` property on the snake object.

Here's the code for the `setDirection` method.

```
Snake.prototype.setDirection = function (newDirection) {
❶    if (this.direction === "up" && newDirection === "down") {
      return;
    } else if (this.direction === "right" && newDirection === "left") {
      return;
    } else if (this.direction === "down" && newDirection === "up") {
      return;
    } else if (this.direction === "left" && newDirection === "right") {
      return;
    }

❷    this.nextDirection = newDirection;
};
```

The if...else statement at ❶ has four parts to deal with the four illegal turns we want to prevent. The first part says that if the snake is moving up (this.direction is "up") and the player presses the down arrow (newDirection is "down"), we should exit the method early with return. The other parts of the statement deal with the other illegal turns in the same way.

The setDirection method will reach the final line only if newDirection is a valid new direction; otherwise, one of the return statements will stop the method.

If newDirection *is* allowed, we set it as the snake's nextDirection property, at ❷.

CREATING THE APPLE

In this game, we'll represent the apple as an object with three components: a position property, which holds the apple's position as a block object; a draw method, which we'll use to draw the apple; and a move method, which we'll use to give the apple a new position once it's been eaten by the snake.

WRITING THE APPLE CONSTRUCTOR

The constructor simply sets the apple's position property to a new block object.

```
var Apple = function () {
  this.position = new Block(10, 10);
};
```

This creates a new block object in column 10, row 10, and assigns it to the apple's position property. We'll use this constructor to create an apple object at the beginning of the game.

DRAWING THE APPLE

We'll use this draw method to draw the apple:

```
Apple.prototype.draw = function () {
  this.position.drawCircle("LimeGreen");
};
```

The apple's draw method is very simple, as all the hard work is done by the drawCircle method (created in "Adding the drawCircle Method" on page 270). To draw the apple, we simply call the drawCircle method on the apple's position property, passing the color "LimeGreen" to tell it to draw a green circle in the given block.

To test out drawing the apple, run the following code:

```
var apple = new Apple();
apple.draw();
```

MOVING THE APPLE

The move method moves the apple to a random new position within the game area (that is, any block on the canvas other than the border). We'll call this method whenever the snake eats the apple so that the apple reappears in a new location.

```
Apple.prototype.move = function () {
❶    var randomCol = Math.floor(Math.random() * (widthInBlocks - 2)) + 1;
     var randomRow = Math.floor(Math.random() * (heightInBlocks - 2)) + 1;
❷    this.position = new Block(randomCol, randomRow);
};
```

At ❶ we create the variables randomCol and randomRow. These variables will be set to a random column and row value within the playable area. As you saw in Figure 17-1, the columns and rows for the playable area range from 1 to 38, so we need to pick two random numbers in that range.

To generate these random numbers, we can call Math.floor (Math.random() * 38), which gives us a random number from 0 to 37, and then add 1 to the result to get a number between 1 and 38 (for more about how Math.floor and Math.random work, see "Decision Maker" on page 56).

This is exactly what we do at ❶ to create our random column value, but instead of writing 38, we write (widthInBlocks - 2). This means that if we later change the size of the game, we won't also have to change this code. We do the same thing to get a random row value, using Math.floor(Math.random() * (heightInBlocks - 2)) + 1.

Finally, at ❷ we create a new block object with our random column and row values and save this block in this.position. This means that the position of the apple will be updated to a new random location somewhere within the playing area.

You can test out the move method like this:

```
var apple = new Apple();
apple.move();
apple.draw();
```

PUTTING IT ALL TOGETHER

Our full code for the game contains almost 200 lines of JavaScript! After we assemble the whole thing, it looks like this.

```
// Set up canvas
❶ var canvas = document.getElementById("canvas");
var ctx = canvas.getContext("2d");

// Get the width and height from the canvas element
var width = canvas.width;
var height = canvas.height;

// Work out the width and height in blocks
var blockSize = 10;
var widthInBlocks = width / blockSize;
var heightInBlocks = height / blockSize;

// Set score to 0
var score = 0;

// Draw the border
❷ var drawBorder = function () {
  ctx.fillStyle = "Gray";
  ctx.fillRect(0, 0, width, blockSize);
  ctx.fillRect(0, height - blockSize, width, blockSize);
  ctx.fillRect(0, 0, blockSize, height);
  ctx.fillRect(width - blockSize, 0, blockSize, height);
};

// Draw the score in the top-left corner
var drawScore = function () {
  ctx.font = "20px Courier";
  ctx.fillStyle = "Black";
  ctx.textAlign = "left";
  ctx.textBaseline = "top";
  ctx.fillText("Score: " + score, blockSize, blockSize);
};
```

```javascript
// Clear the interval and display Game Over text
var gameOver = function () {
  clearInterval(intervalId);
  ctx.font = "60px Courier";
  ctx.fillStyle = "Black";
  ctx.textAlign = "center";
  ctx.textBaseline = "middle";
  ctx.fillText("Game Over", width / 2, height / 2);
};

// Draw a circle (using the function from Chapter 14)
var circle = function (x, y, radius, fillCircle) {
  ctx.beginPath();
  ctx.arc(x, y, radius, 0, Math.PI * 2, false);
  if (fillCircle) {
    ctx.fill();
  } else {
    ctx.stroke();
  }
};

// The Block constructor
❸ var Block = function (col, row) {
  this.col = col;
  this.row = row;
};

// Draw a square at the block's location
Block.prototype.drawSquare = function (color) {
  var x = this.col * blockSize;
  var y = this.row * blockSize;
  ctx.fillStyle = color;
  ctx.fillRect(x, y, blockSize, blockSize);
};

// Draw a circle at the block's location
Block.prototype.drawCircle = function (color) {
  var centerX = this.col * blockSize + blockSize / 2;
  var centerY = this.row * blockSize + blockSize / 2;
  ctx.fillStyle = color;
  circle(centerX, centerY, blockSize / 2, true);
};

// Check if this block is in the same location as another block
Block.prototype.equal = function (otherBlock) {
  return this.col === otherBlock.col && this.row === otherBlock.row;
};
```

```
   // The Snake constructor
❹ var Snake = function () {
     this.segments = [
       new Block(7, 5),
       new Block(6, 5),
       new Block(5, 5)
     ];

     this.direction = "right";
     this.nextDirection = "right";
   };

   // Draw a square for each segment of the snake's body
   Snake.prototype.draw = function () {
     for (var i = 0; i < this.segments.length; i++) {
       this.segments[i].drawSquare("Blue");
     }
   };

   // Create a new head and add it to the beginning of
   // the snake to move the snake in its current direction
   Snake.prototype.move = function () {
     var head = this.segments[0];
     var newHead;

     this.direction = this.nextDirection;

     if (this.direction === "right") {
       newHead = new Block(head.col + 1, head.row);
     } else if (this.direction === "down") {
       newHead = new Block(head.col, head.row + 1);
     } else if (this.direction === "left") {
       newHead = new Block(head.col - 1, head.row);
     } else if (this.direction === "up") {
       newHead = new Block(head.col, head.row - 1);
     }

     if (this.checkCollision(newHead)) {
       gameOver();
       return;
     }

     this.segments.unshift(newHead);

     if (newHead.equal(apple.position)) {
       score++;
       apple.move();
```

```
    } else {
      this.segments.pop();
    }
};

// Check if the snake's new head has collided with the wall or itself
Snake.prototype.checkCollision = function (head) {
  var leftCollision = (head.col === 0);
  var topCollision = (head.row === 0);
  var rightCollision = (head.col === widthInBlocks - 1);
  var bottomCollision = (head.row === heightInBlocks - 1);

  var wallCollision = leftCollision || topCollision || ↵
    rightCollision || bottomCollision;

  var selfCollision = false;

  for (var i = 0; i < this.segments.length; i++) {
    if (head.equal(this.segments[i])) {
      selfCollision = true;
    }
  }

  return wallCollision || selfCollision;
};

// Set the snake's next direction based on the keyboard
Snake.prototype.setDirection = function (newDirection) {
  if (this.direction === "up" && newDirection === "down") {
    return;
  } else if (this.direction === "right" && newDirection === "left") {
    return;
  } else if (this.direction === "down" && newDirection === "up") {
    return;
  } else if (this.direction === "left" && newDirection === "right") {
    return;
  }

  this.nextDirection = newDirection;
};

// The Apple constructor
❺ var Apple = function () {
    this.position = new Block(10, 10);
  };
```

```
// Draw a circle at the apple's location
Apple.prototype.draw = function () {
  this.position.drawCircle("LimeGreen");
};

// Move the apple to a new random location
Apple.prototype.move = function () {
  var randomCol = Math.floor(Math.random() * (widthInBlocks - 2)) + 1;
  var randomRow = Math.floor(Math.random() * (heightInBlocks - 2)) + 1;
  this.position = new Block(randomCol, randomRow);
};

// Create the snake and apple objects
❻ var snake = new Snake();
  var apple = new Apple();

// Pass an animation function to setInterval
var intervalId = setInterval(function () {
  ctx.clearRect(0, 0, width, height);
  drawScore();
  snake.move();
  snake.draw();
  apple.draw();
  drawBorder();
}, 100);

// Convert keycodes to directions
❼ var directions = {
  37: "left",
  38: "up",
  39: "right",
  40: "down"
};

// The keydown handler for handling direction key presses
$("body").keydown(function (event) {
  var newDirection = directions[event.keyCode];
  if (newDirection !== undefined) {
    snake.setDirection(newDirection);
  }
});
```

This code is made up of a number of sections. The first section, at ❶, is where all the variables for the game are set up,
including the canvas, context, width, and height (we looked at
these in Chapter 16). Next, at ❷, come all the individual functions: drawBorder, drawScore, gameOver, and circle.

At ❸ comes the code for the Block constructor, followed by its drawSquare, drawCircle, and equal methods. Then, at ❹, we have the Snake constructor and all of its methods. After that, at ❺, is the Apple constructor and its draw and move methods.

Finally, at ❻, you can see the code that starts the game and keeps it running. First we create the snake and apple objects. Then we use setInterval to get the game animation going. Notice that when we call setInterval, we save the interval ID in the variable intervalId so we can cancel it later in the gameOver function.

The function passed to setInterval is called for every step of the game. It is responsible for drawing everything on the canvas and for updating the state of the game. It clears the canvas and then draws the score, the snake, the apple, and the border. It also calls the move method on the snake, which, as you saw earlier, moves the snake one step in its current direction. After the call to setInterval, at ❼, we end with the code for listening to keyboard events and setting the snake's direction.

As always, you'll need to type all this code inside the script element in your HTML document. To play the game, just load *snake.html* in your browser and use the arrows to control the snake's direction. If the arrow keys don't work, you might need to click inside the browser window to make sure it can pick up the key events.

If the game doesn't work, there might be an error in your JavaScript. Any error will be output in the console, so look there for any helpful messages. If you can't determine why things aren't working, check each line carefully against the preceding listing.

Now that you have the game running, what do you think? How high a score can you get?

WHAT YOU LEARNED

In this chapter, we made a full game using the canvas element. This game combines many of the data types, concepts, and techniques you learned throughout this book: numbers, strings, Booleans, arrays, objects, control structures, functions, object-oriented programming, event handlers, setInterval, and drawing with canvas.

Now that you've programmed this Snake game, there are lots of other simple two-dimensional games that you could write using JavaScript. You could make your own version of classic games like Breakout, Asteroids, Space Invaders, or Tetris. Or you could make up your own game!

Of course, you can use JavaScript for programs besides games. Now that you've used JavaScript to do some complicated math, you could use it to help with your math homework. Or maybe you want to create a website to show off your programming skills to the world. The possibilities are endless!

PROGRAMMING CHALLENGES

Here are a few ways you could improve and add features to the game.

#1: MAKING THE GAME BIGGER

Change the size of the game to 500 pixels square. Where do you need to modify the code to make it work at 500 pixels?

#2: COLORING THE SNAKE

Our snake is a bit boring: every segment of the body is blue. It might look a bit more like a real snake if you alternated the colors to create stripes. For example, make the head green and then alternate between blue and yellow for the rest of the body, or choose your own colors.

(continued)

#3: MAKING THE GAME SPEED UP AS YOU PLAY

Modify the game so that every time the snake eats an apple, the game speeds up. To do this, you'll have to change the code to use setTimeout instead of setInterval, because setInterval keeps calling a function at a regular interval that cannot be changed. Instead, you can repeatedly call a function with setTimeout and change the timeout delay each time you call it:

```
var animationTime = 100;
var gameLoop = function () {
  // The code that draws and updates the game should go here
  setTimeout(gameLoop, animationTime);
};

gameLoop();
```

Instead of using setInterval to call a function repeatedly, the gameLoop function calls setTimeout(gameLoop, animationTime), which means "call gameLoop again after animationTime milliseconds." Like setInterval, this is a way to call a function over and over again, with a short pause between each function call. The difference is that you can easily modify the animation time from anywhere in your code by changing animationTime, and the program will use that value for subsequent calls to setTimeout.

(One other thing to bear in mind here is that you need to find a new way to stop the game from looping when the game is over. How would you do that?)

#4: FIXING THE APPLE.MOVE METHOD

Every time you move the apple, it moves to a new random location, but as written there's nothing to stop the apple from moving to a block that part of the snake is already occupying. To prevent this, modify the move method to take into account the current locations of the snake's segments. (Hint: Use a while loop to keep calling move until it picks a location that's not occupied by the snake.)

AFTERWORD
WHERE TO GO FROM HERE

Now that you've learned the basics of JavaScript, you're ready to venture out into a whole, wide world of programming. You could learn another programming language, or you could choose to build on your knowledge of JavaScript, taking your skills to the next level. Where you go next is entirely up to you, but here are some ideas.

MORE JAVASCRIPT

We've looked at a lot of JavaScript in this book, but there's much more you can learn about the language. Here are some books and websites that will help you learn more of the details of JavaScript:

- *JavaScript: The Good Parts* by Douglas Crockford (O'Reilly Media, 2008)
- *Eloquent JavaScript, 2nd Edition,* by Marijn Haverbeke (No Starch Press, 2014)
- *JavaScript: The Definitive Guide, 4th Edition,* by David Flanagan (O'Reilly Media, 2001)
- The Mozilla Developer Network's JavaScript resources: *https://developer.mozilla.org/en-US/docs/Web/JavaScript/*
- Codecademy JavaScript courses: *http://www.codecademy.com/en/tracks/javascript/*

WEB PROGRAMMING

To create websites, you need to use some HTML and CSS, along with JavaScript.

HTML

HTML is the markup language used for creating web pages. We learned some basic HTML in Chapter 5, but there's much more to learn. Here are some places you can learn more about HTML:

- The Mozilla Developer Network's Introduction to HTML: *https://developer.mozilla.org/en-US/docs/Web/Guide/HTML/Introduction/*
- Codecademy HTML & CSS course: *http://www.codecademy.com/tracks/web/*
- Mozilla Webmaker: *https://webmaker.org/*

CSS

CSS (short for *Cascading Style Sheets*) is the language used to control the appearance of web pages. Learn more about CSS here:

• The Mozilla Developer Network's Getting Started with CSS: *https://developer.mozilla.org/en-US/docs/Web/Guide/CSS/Getting_started/*

• Codecademy HTML & CSS course: *http://www.codecademy.com/tracks/web/*

SERVER-SIDE CODE WITH NODE.JS

Web pages live on *web servers*. A server stores all the HTML, CSS, and JavaScript for a web page, and it allows people to access the page from the Internet. You can also write programs for the server (called *server-side* code) to make the server generate new HTML files each time a web page is loaded. For example, when you visit *http://twitter.com/*, a program runs on a server that finds the latest tweets for your feed, generates an HTML file containing those tweets, and sends that file to your browser.

Node.js lets you write server-side code in JavaScript. Find out more about Node.js with these links:

• Node.js documentation: *http://nodejs.org/*

• The Node Beginner Book: *http://www.nodebeginner.org/*

GRAPHICAL PROGRAMMING

If you want to make interactive graphics in JavaScript, you have two main options: the canvas element and SVG.

CANVAS

We learned the basics of the canvas element in this book, but there's much more you can do with it. Here are some tutorials and games you can use to learn more:

• The Mozilla Developer Network's Canvas Tutorial: *https://developer.mozilla.org/en-US/docs/Web/API/Canvas_API/Tutorial/*

• Code Monster from Crunchzilla: *http://www.crunchzilla.com/code-monster/*

SVG USING RAPHAËL

SVG is an image format that lets you draw shapes and animate them without redrawing from scratch for each animation step. SVG programming can be difficult to get the hang of, but it's much easier if you use the JavaScript library called Raphaël. Here are some resources for learning Raphaël:

- Raphaël website: *http://raphaeljs.com/*
- An Introduction to the Raphaël JS Library: *http://code .tutsplus.com/tutorials/an-introduction-to-the-raphael-js- library--net-7186/*

3D PROGRAMMING

Remember how in Chapter 13 we told canvas we wanted to make a 2D drawing context by calling canvas.getContext("2d")? It's also possible to do 3D graphics using canvas. This is another one of those areas where it's easier to use a library, so I'd recommend using the library three.js. Here are some resources for learning three.js:

- three.js Manual: *http://threejs.org/docs/index.html#Manual*
- The Beginner's Guide to three.js: *http://blog.teamtreehouse. com/the-beginners-guide-to-three-js/*

PROGRAMMING ROBOTS

You can even control robots using JavaScript! For example, the Parrot AR.Drone is a small flying helicopter that you can control using Node.js. Or you can check out Johnny-Five, a JavaScript library that lets you use Node.js to control devices such as the Arduino (a popular microcontroller that's used in lots of homemade electronics and robotics projects). Here are some resources for learning how to control robots and other devices with JavaScript:

- node-ar-drone: *https://github.com/felixge/node-ar-drone/*
- NodeCopter: *http://nodecopter.com/*
- NodeBots: *http://nodebots.io/*
- Johnny-Five: *https://github.com/rwaldron/johnny-five/*

AUDIO PROGRAMMING

JavaScript also allows you to do advanced audio programming in web browsers using the Web Audio API (short for *application programming interface*). You can use the Web Audio API to make sound effects or even create your own music! Here are some resources for learning more about the Web Audio API:

- The Mozilla Developer Network's Web Audio API: *https://developer.mozilla.org/en-US/docs/Web/API/Web_Audio_API/*
- HTML5 Rocks: Getting Started with Web Audio API: *http://www.html5rocks.com/en/tutorials/webaudio/intro/*

GAME PROGRAMMING

If you want to do more game programming in JavaScript, you might want to try using a *game engine*. A game engine is a collection of code that handles a lot of the lower-level concerns of the game (like keyboard and mouse input), allowing you to concentrate on the parts that make your game different. Here are some resources you can check out to learn more about game programming and game engines:

- Crafty game engine: *http://craftyjs.com/*
- Pixi Renderer: *https://github.com/GoodBoyDigital/pixi.js*
- HTML5 Game Engines: *http://html5gameengine.com/*
- Udacity HTML5 Game Development: *https://www.udacity.com/course/cs255*
- *3D Game Programming for Kids* by Chris Strom (Pragmatic Programmers, 2013)

SHARING YOUR CODE USING JSFIDDLE

What if you want to share all the great JavaScript you've written with the world? There are many ways to do that. One of the easier ones is JSFiddle (*http://jsfiddle.net/*). Just type your JavaScript in the JavaScript box, add any HTML you want in the HTML box, and then click **Run** to run your program. To share it, click **Save**, which gives you a URL that you can then share with anyone.

GLOSSARY

The world of computer programming has all kinds of special terms and definitions that can take some time to get the hang of. In this glossary, you'll find definitions for many of the programming terms used in this book. As you're reading this book, if you come across a term that you don't quite understand, you can look here for a brief explanation.

argument   A value that can be passed into a function.

array   A list of JavaScript values. In an array, each value has an index, which is the numbered position of that value in the array. The first value is at index 0, the next value is at index 1, and so on.

attribute   A key-value pair in an HTML element. You can use HTML attributes to control certain aspects of an element, like where the element links to or the size of the element.

Boolean   A value that can be either true or false.

call   To execute or run a function. To call functions in JavaScript, you enter the function name followed by a pair of parentheses (with any arguments inside the parentheses).

camel case   A common way to name variables in which you capitalize the first letter of each word (except the first word) and then join all the words to make one long word, like so: myCamelCaseVariable.

comment   Text in a program that is not executed by the JavaScript interpreter—comments are just there to describe the program for the person reading the code.

conditional statement   A statement that executes code after checking a condition. If the condition is true, the statement will execute one bit of code; if the condition is false, it will execute a different bit of code or stop altogether. Examples include if statements and if...else statements.

constructor   A kind of function that's used to create multiple objects so that they share built-in properties.

control structure   A way to control when a piece of code is run and how often it's run. Examples include conditional statements (which control when code is run by checking a condition) and loops (which repeat a piece of code a certain number of times).

data   The information we store and manipulate in computer programs.

decrement   To decrease the value of a variable (usually by 1).

dialog   A small pop-up window. You can use JavaScript to open different kinds of dialogs in a browser, such as an alert (to display a message) or a prompt (to ask a question and receive input).

document object model (DOM)   The way that web browsers organize and keep track of HTML elements on a web page. These elements are organized in a treelike structure called the *DOM tree*. JavaScript and jQuery provide methods that work with the DOM to create and modify elements.

element   Part of an HTML page, such as a header, a paragraph, or the body. An element is marked by start and end tags (which determine what type of element it is) and includes everything in between. The DOM tree is made up of these elements.

event   An action that happens in the browser, such as a mouse click or a keyboard press by the user. We can detect and respond to these events with event handlers.

event handler   A function that is called whenever a certain event happens in a certain HTML element. For example, in Chapter 11's "Find the Buried Treasure!" game, we create an event handler function that is called whenever the user clicks on a map image.

execute   To run a piece of code, such as a program or function.

function   A piece of code that bundles multiple statements so that they are all executed together. A function makes it easy to repeat a certain action in different parts of a program. A function can take arguments as input, and it will output a return value.

increment   To increase the value of a variable (usually by 1).

index   A number that indicates the position of a value inside an array. The index can be used to access a specific value in an array.

infinite loop   A loop that never stops repeating (often causing the interpreter to crash). This error can occur if the conditions of a loop are set up incorrectly.

interpreter   A piece of software that reads and runs code. Web browsers contain a JavaScript interpreter, which we use to run our JavaScript throughout this book.

jQuery   A JavaScript library that provides many useful methods for modifying and working with DOM elements on a web page.

key-value pair   A pair made up of a string (called a *key*) that is matched up with a particular value (which can be any type of value). Key-value pairs go inside JavaScript objects, and they are used to define an object's properties and methods.

keyword   A word with a special meaning in JavaScript (for example, for, return, or function). Keywords can't be used as variable names.

library   A collection of JavaScript code that we can load into our web pages to provide additional functions and methods. In this book we use the jQuery library, which gives us functions and methods for working with the DOM more easily.

loop   A way to execute a piece of code multiple times.

method   A function that is a property of an object.

null   A special value that can be used to indicate that a variable is purposely left empty.

object   A set of key-value pairs. Each key is a string that can be paired with any JavaScript value. You can then use the key to retrieve whatever value it's paired with in the object.

object-oriented programming   A style of programming that takes advantage of objects and methods to organize the code and represent the most important features of the program.

programming language   A language that programmers can use to tell computers what to do. JavaScript is one programming language, but there are many others.

property   A name for a key-value pair in an object.

prototype   A property of a constructor. Any methods added to a constructor's prototype will be available to all objects created by that constructor.

return   The act of leaving a function and returning to the code that called the function. A function returns when it reaches the end of its body or when it reaches a return keyword (which can be used to leave a function early). When a function returns, it outputs a return value (if no particular return value is specified, it simply returns the empty value undefined).

selector string   A string that represents one or more HTML elements. We can pass this string to jQuery's $ function to select those elements.

string   A list of characters surrounded by quotes, used to represent text in computer programs.

syntax   How keywords, punctuation, and other characters are combined to make working JavaScript programs.

tag   A marker used to create HTML elements. All elements begin with a start tag, and most end with an end tag. These tags determine what type of element is created, and the start tag can include attributes for the element.

text editor   A computer program used to write and edit plaintext, without any special formatting like font style or color. A good text editor is helpful for writing programs, which are written in plaintext.

undefined   A value that JavaScript uses when something like a property or variable doesn't have any particular value assigned to it.

variable   A way of giving a JavaScript value a name. After you assign a value to a variable, you can use the variable name later to retrieve the value.

whitespace   Invisible characters like spaces, newlines, and tabs.

INDEX

SYMBOLS

&& (and), 30–31, 33
* (multiplication), 15–17
*= (multiply and assign), 23, 104
: (colon), 65
, (comma), 128
{} (curly brackets), 64, 67
$ (jQuery function), 149. *See also* jQuery
" (double quotation mark), 23–24, 65
= (assignment), 18
== (double equals), 36
=== (exactly equals), 35–36, 96
! (not), 3
/ (division), 15–16
/= (divide and assign), 23
> (greater than), 33–34
(id in selector strings), 149
- (subtraction), 15–16
-- (decrement), 21
-= (subtract and assign), 22
< (less than), 34
() (parentheses), 16–17, 27, 125
. (period). *See* dot notation
|| (or), 31–32, 33
+ (addition), 15–17
    with strings, 25, 61, 108
++ (increment), 21
+= (add and assign), 22, 73
; (semicolon), 14, 99
' (single quotation mark), 24
[] (square brackets)
    accessing a character
        from a string
        with, 26
    accessing elements from
        an array with,
        42–43, 45

accessing values in
    objects with, 66
adding elements to an
    array with, 43–44
creating an array with, 41

A

add and assign (+=) operator, 22, 73
addition, 15–17
    with strings, 25, 61, 108
alert method, 109–110
and (&&) operator, 30–31, 33
animation
    with canvas
        bouncing ball, 227–232
        changing size, 220–221
        moving horizontally, 218–221
        random bee, 221–226
    with setInterval, 159–161
append jQuery method, 150, 188
arc context method, 209–212
arguments, for functions, 126, 300
arrays, 39–40, 54–60, 300
    accessing, 42–43
    adding elements to, 47, 50
    combining multiple, 50–52
    combining with objects, 69–71
    converting to a string, 53
    creating, 41–42
    and data types, 45
    finding index of element in, 52–53
    finding length of, 46

looping through
    elements of,
    100–101
modifying, 43–44
vs. objects, 67–68
removing elements
    from, 48–50
assigning values, 18
attributes, HTML, 86–87, 300

B

beginPath context method, 206–210
block-level HTML elements, 81–82
body
    of a control structure, 92–95, 97, 99
    of a function, 124
body element, 84–85
Booleans, 14, 30–37, 300
    comparing numbers with, 33–37
    in conditional statements, 91–96
    logical operators, 30–33
    for yes-or-no answers, 108–109
brackets
    curly, 64, 67
    square. *See* square brackets
break keyword, 116

C

calling
    functions, 125, 126, 300
    methods, 47
camel case, 19, 300

canvas element, 199
  animating, 217–218
    bouncing ball, 227–232
    changing size, 220–221
    moving horizontally,
      218–221
    random bee, 221–226
  circles and arcs, 209–213
  clearing, 219
  colors, 203–204
  creating, 200
  lines and paths
    drawing, 206–207
    filling, 207–209
  rectangles and squares
    drawing, 201–203
    outlining, 205–206
  resources, 295
Cascading Style Sheets
  (CSS), 295
chaining if...else
  statements, 94–96
chaining jQuery
  animations, 152
Chrome, web browser and
  console, 7
clearInterval function,
  158–159
clearRect context method,
  218–219
clearTimeout function, 157
click events, 162
coercion, 108
collision detection, 229–231,
  278–280
colon (:), 65
comma (,), 128
comments, 10–11, 118, 300
concat method, 50–52
condition (of a control
  structure)
  in for loops, 99
  in if...else
    statements, 95
  in if statements, 92
  in while loops, 97

conditionals, 89, 300
  if...else statements, 91,
    93–96, 136–137
  if statements, 91–93
confirm function, 108
console, 7
  calling constructors
    in, 187
  exploring objects in,
    71–72
  finding errors with, 120
  logging values to, 91
  typing in, 42
  viewing output from
    keyboard events
    with, 237
console.log method, 91, 125
  vs. alert, 109–110
constructors, 185–186, 300
control structures, 90, 300.
    See also conditionals;
    loops
coordinates, browser, 163
CSS (Cascading Style
    Sheets), 295
css jQuery method, 188–189
curly brackets, 64, 67

D

data, 14, 300
decrementing, 21, 300
dialogs, 106–110, 300
divide and assign (/)
    operator, 23
division, 15–16
document object
    model (DOM),
    143–147, 301
document.getElementById
    DOM method,
    145–146, 200–201
DOM (document
    object model),
    143–147, 301
DOM tree, 144

dot notation, 66
  accessing object keys
    with, 69
  adding keys to objects
    with, 68
  adding methods to objects
    with, 182–183
  adding properties to
    objects with, 182
double equals (==)
  operator, 36
double quotation mark ("),
    23–24, 65
drawing context (for
    canvas), 201

E

elements, HTML, 80, 301
else keyword, 93, 95
em element, 82–83
end tags, HTML, 80, 303
equal to (===) operator,
    35–36, 96
errors, 120
event handlers, 162, 169,
    171, 301
event object, 162–163, 172
exactly equals (===)
    operator, 35–36, 96
execute, 8, 301

F

fadeIn jQuery method, 152
fadeOut jQuery method, 151
fadeTo jQuery method, 154
false (Boolean value),
    14, 30. See also
    Booleans
fill context method,
    207, 222
fillRect context method,
    200–205, 207,
    219–220, 258, 269
fillStyle context property,
    203, 223, 258,
    263–264, 269–270

fillText context method, 260, 262–264
Find the Buried Treasure! game, 167–169
  calculating distances, 172–174
  click handler, 171–172
  code for, 176–178
  creating web page, 169–170
  design, 168–169
  displaying hints, 175–176
  randomizing treasure location, 170–171
  win condition, 176
floor method, 57, 103
font context property, 262–264
for loops, 99–102
function keyword, 128. *See also* functions
functions, 123–124, 301
  arguments, 126–127, 128–129
  calling, 125, 126, 300
  vs. if...else statements, 136–137
  leaving early, 135
  returning values from, 125, 129–131, 302
  shorthand, 137
  simplifying code with, 132–134

G

games, programming, 6, 297. *See also* Find the Buried Treasure! game; Hangman game; Snake game
getContext canvas method, 200–201
getElementById, 145–146, 200–201

Google Chrome, web browser and console, 7
graphical programming, 4
greater than (>) operator, 33–34

H

h1 element, 80
Hangman game, 105–106
  choosing a random word, 113–114
  code for, 118–120
  creating with functions, 139–140
  design, 110–113
  displaying player's progress, 115
  drawing
    guesses, 266
    hangman, 215
  responding to player input, 115–116
  updating game state, 116–118
  win condition, 118
head element, 84–85
height attribute, 170, 200
hide jQuery method, 153
href attribute, 87
HTML, 77–88, 143–144, 294
  attributes, 86–87, 300
  elements, 80, 301
  hierarchy, 84–85
  nesting, 84–85
html element, 84, 164
hyperlinks, 78, 85–86

I

id attribute, 145, 149
if...else statements, 91, 93–96, 136–137
if statements, 91–93
img element, 169, 171, 188
incrementing, 21, 301

indexes, in arrays, 42–43, 301
  changing elements with, 43–44
  and data types, 45
  finding, 52–53
  with strings, 57–58
indexOf method, 52–53
infinite loops, 98–99, 301
inline HTML elements, 82–83
innerHTML property, 145–147
interactive programming, 155–166
interval ID, 159, 254, 264, 290

J

join method, 53–54, 61
jQuery, 143–144, 301
  $ function, 149
  animating elements with, 151–152
  creating new elements with, 150–151
  keyboard events, responding with, 236, 244
  loading on page, 148
  replacing page text with, 148–149

K

keyCode event property, 237, 281
keydown event, 236–238, 244, 281
keys (in objects), 63, 65, 182
  adding, 68
  and quotation marks, 65
key-value pairs (in objects), 63, 65, 182, 302
keywords, 17, 302

L

length property
  on arrays, 46, 60, 72
  on strings, 25–26
less than (<) operator, 34
libraries, 148, 302
lineTo context method, 206–208
lineWidth context property, 205–206, 223
links, 78, 85–86
literals, 64–65
logs, 91
loops, 89, 302
  for loops, 99–102
  while loops, 97–99

M

mathematical operators, 15–17
Math.floor, 57, 103
Math.PI, 210–212
Math.random, 57
Math.sqrt, 174
methods, 42, 302
  adding to objects, 182–183
  calling, 47
  sharing between objects, 183–185
  and this, 183
mousemove event, 164–165, 215
moveTo context method, 206–208
multiplication, 15–17
multiply and assign (*=) operator, 23, 104
music programming, 4, 297

N

new keyword, 185–187, 189
Node.js, 295
not (!) operator, 32
numbers, 14–23, 42, 66
null value, 37–38, 108, 302

O

Object.keys method, 67, 75
object-oriented programming, 181–196, 302
objects, 63, 72–75, 302
  accessing values in, 66–67
  adding keys to, 68
  adding methods to, 182–185
  adding values to, 67–68
  combining with arrays, 69–71
  creating, 64–65, 182
    with constructors, 185–186
  customizing with prototypes, 190–194
  exploring with the console, 71–72
offset jQuery method, 160–161, 164, 189
offsetX and offsetY event properties, 172
operators, 15–17
or (||) operator, 31–32, 33

P

pageX and pageY event properties, 162, 164–165
parentheses, (), 16–17, 27, 125
p element, 80–81
period (.). *See* dot notation
pi (π), 210–212
plaintext, 78
pop method, 48–49, 55
prompt method, 106–108, 146
properties, 46, 182, 302
__proto__ properties, 72
prototype property, 190, 228
prototypes, 72, 190–196, 228
pseudocode, 110–111, 253
push method, 47, 55
Pythagorean theorem, 173

Q

queue (data structure), 56
quotation marks, 23–24, 65

R

radians, 209–211
random number generation, with Math.random, 57
returning values from functions, 125, 129–131, 302
return keyword, 130, 132, 302

S

script element, 90, 148
selector strings, 149, 303
semicolons, 14, 99
setInterval function, 158–159
  bouncing ball, 231–232
  with canvas, 218–221
  with keyboard input, 245
  moving text, 159–161
  random bee, 225–226
  and Snake game, 254, 285–290
setTimeout function, 156–157
shift method, 50
show jQuery method, 153
single quotation mark, 24
slice method, 27
slideDown jQuery method, 152
slideUp jQuery method, 152
Snake game
  apple
    creating, 283–284
    moving, 284–285
  code for, 285–290
  collision detection, 272, 279–281
  design, 253–255
  displaying text, 260–264
  drawing
    circle, 270–271
    square, 269–270

ending the game,
264–265, 272
game grid
adding border, 258–260
creating Block, 268–269
setting up, 256–258
game play, 252
HTML code, 255–256
snake
creating, 273–275
moving, 275–277
setting direction of,
281–283
square brackets, [ ]
accessing a character
from a string
with, 26
accessing elements from
an array with,
42–43, 45
accessing values in
objects with, 66
adding elements to an
array with, 43–44
creating an array with, 41
square root, 174
src attribute, 148, 170
stack (data structure), 56
start tag, 80, 303
statements, 14
strings, 14, 23–24, 303
accessing single character
from, 26–27
changing case of, 28–30
finding length of, 25–26
joining, 25
looping through each
character of,
101, 116
as object keys, 63, 65, 66
slicing, 27–28
turning arrays into,
53–54

stroke context method,
206–210, 222
strokeRect context method,
205, 225, 231
strokeStyle context
property,
205–206, 223
strong element, 82–83
Sublime Text, 78–79
subtract and assign (-=)
operator, 22
subtraction, 15–16
SVG, 296
syntax, 10, 303
syntax highlighting, 79

T

tags, HTML, 80, 303
textAlign context property,
262–264
textBaseline context
property, 261,
263–264
text editors, 78–79, 303
text jQuery method, 176
this keyword, 183, 187,
191–192
timeout ID, 157
title attribute, 87–88
toLowerCase method, 28–29
toUpperCase method, 28–29
true (Boolean value), 14, 30.
See also Booleans

U

undefined value, 17–18,
37–38, 44, 125, 303
unshift method, 48–49

V

values (in objects), 63,
65, 182
accessing, 66–67
adding, 67–68
data type of, 65
variables, 17–23, 303
vs. arrays, 40
creating with math,
19–21
increasing and decreasing
values of, 21–23
naming, 19
undefined and null for,
37–38
var keyword, 17, 18, 19

W

web browsers, 6–7
while loops, 97–99
whitespace, 81, 82, 303
width attribute, 170, 200

UPDATES

Visit *http://www.nostarch.com/javascriptforkids* for updates, errata, and other information.

MORE SMART BOOKS FOR CURIOUS KIDS!

PYTHON FOR KIDS
A Playful Introduction to Programming
by JASON R. BRIGGS
DEC 2012, 344 PP., $34.95
ISBN 978-1-59327-407-8
full color

RUBY WIZARDRY
An Introduction to Programming for Kids
by ERIC WEINSTEIN
DEC 2014, 360 PP., $29.95
ISBN 978-1-59327-566-2
two color

LAUREN IPSUM
A Story About Computer Science and Other Improbable Things
by CARLOS BUENO
DEC 2014, 192 PP., $16.95
ISBN 978-1-59327-574-7
full color

SURVIVE! INSIDE THE HUMAN BODY, VOL. 1
The Digestive System
by GOMDORI CO. *and* HYUN-DONG HAN
OCT 2013, 184 PP., $17.95
ISBN 978-1-59327-471-9
full color

ELOQUENT JAVASCRIPT, 2ND EDITION
A Modern Introduction to Programming
by MARIJN HAVERBEKE
DEC 2014, 400 PP., $39.95
ISBN 978-1-59327-584-6

THE MANGA GUIDE TO DATABASES
by MANA TAKAHASHI, SHOKO AZUMA, *and* TREND-PRO CO., LTD.
JAN 2009, 224 PP., $19.95
ISBN 978-1-59327-190-9

800.420.7240 or 415.863.9900 | sales@nostarch.com | www.nostarch.com